OPTIMAL MOTHERHOOD AND OTHER LIES FACEBOOK TOLD US

OPTIMAL MOTHERHOOD AND OTHER LIES FACEBOOK TOLD US

**Assembling the Networked *Ethos*
of Contemporary Maternity Advice**

JESSICA CLEMENTS AND KARI NIXON

The MIT Press
Cambridge, Massachusetts
London, England

The MIT Press would like to thank the anonymous peer reviewers who provided comments on drafts of this book. The generous work of academic experts is essential for establishing the authority and quality of our publications. We acknowledge with gratitude the contributions of these otherwise uncredited readers.

This book was set in Adobe Garamond by Westchester Publishing Services. Printed and bound in the United States of America.

Library of Congress Cataloging-in-Publication Data

Names: Clements, Jessica, author. | Nixon, Kari, author.
Title: Optimal motherhood and other lies Facebook told us : assembling the networked
    ethos of contemporary maternity advice / Jessica Clements and Kari Nixon.
Description: Cambridge, Massachusetts : The MIT Press, [2022] | Includes
    bibliographical references and index.
Identifiers: LCCN 2021057604 | ISBN 9780262543620 (paperback)
Subjects: LCSH: Motherhood—Social aspects. | Mothers—Psychology. |
    Social media and society.
Classification: LCC HQ759 .C618 2022 | DDC 306.874/3—dc23/eng/20220207
LC record available at https://lccn.loc.gov/2021057604

10 9 8 7 6 5 4 3 2 1

Contents

Acknowledgments

We would like to thank our undergraduate student researchers for their valuable contributions to this book: Madison Binyon, Jamison Dover, Nina MacDonald, and Meredith VandeBunte. From data logging to social media ad analysis to health practitioner and mom interviews, this book would not be as rich without their work. Their participation was made possible through the Hugh Johnston Interdisciplinary Research Endowment Grant, awarded by Whitworth University in the summer of 2019.

INTRODUCTION

I think it began with food pouches. You know the ones—half-pint-sized vessels built from layers of laminated film. They contain mashed-up vegetables, laced with fruits to make kids eat it, and they have a convenient suck-spout to get it right down their gullets with minimal fuss or mess. Voila! Kid has their dose of veggies, and no one (mom or baby) has a meltdown.

I was standing in the aisle of the grocery store, holding two pouches in my hands, considering. On the one hand, the thought of getting something into this pipsqueak other than chicken nuggets felt like such an exhilarating win I could almost taste the success (apple-kale-mush-flavored success). On the other hand, shouldn't I be teaching her to eat food that looked like, well, food? Were there drawbacks to her not chewing or tactilely experiencing her food? What if she started demanding nothing but pouches (they seemed wildly popular with kids these days), and then she never learned to use a fork? What if I had a fork-challenged child going off to college one day? On the third hand (at this point in my life I had come to routinely wish I had three hands), she was presently screaming bloody murder at me for standing—the cart required constant movement to placate her, you see. There was no more time to think. I threw both pouches in the cart, grabbing a plastic spoon as an afterthought. *It'll be OK as long as I make her eat it with a spoon, right?*

Who knows, really. It could have been any of a million such moments that define modern motherhood, but I think that was the day I phoned my friend Jess, and we decided to write this book.

One thing has stuck with both of us since we became mothers: when you become a mother you enter a new world. That world involves a lot of baby care, of course, but here we also mean that the new mother enters a world in which she shares a subtle, vibrating electricity with every other mom she sees—the shared grasp of the tingling, raw, so-earnest-it-makes-your-eyes-sting, obsessive love for this tiny creature for whom you are suddenly responsible. The suffocating grip of that love is arresting—and suddenly, when you walk past a mother ruefully considering two slightly different flavors of pouched mush in the grocery store, what might have once seemed a laughably absurd first-world problem is suddenly a codex to your own world. You know pretty much everything she's standing there thinking. And because you know it, you know you are seen as well. Even if it goes unspoken, your struggles are seen and given space by some other mother who has been there. The planking eighteen-month-old refusing to get into the car seat is softened, here and there, by a knowing smile of a mother passing by with her four-year-old screaming something about Disney princesses. You don't have time to discuss it (because buckles are hard to navigate while under pressure, and Elsa *cannot* wait), but you both know you know, and somehow it helps you get through.

The next day, when Jess and I were in an all-faculty meeting and supposed to be listening to something or someone, we wrote. Surreptitiously, but insatiably—in tandem but in separate seats, linked only by a shared document—we wrote up the beginnings of what would become this book. Even as professors, supposedly hired to discourse—to teach and to write—we found no time to discuss in person the Elsas and the buckles and the pouches and the many, many other mandates of "good motherhood" that were weighing down our spirits. Our renegade discontent wouldn't be contained, though. So, silently, in protest of something much bigger than it all, we wrote our feelings.

As we continued writing our way into this book, detailing our thoughts in a stream-of-consciousness style, we circled around and around how much these worries stick with you. They grow as your child grows—from worrying about adequate nutrition to worrying if we've adequately helped our children develop character traits and habits that will equip them for success in the world. The worry sticks and grows. A persistent little mouse nibbling at the hem of your sleeve, gnawing away at your confidence. There's another little creature that sticks with you, though, knitting your sweater back up from the other side in bits and snatches: that community of mothers who *see* that persistent little mouse following you everywhere.

So what's up with the mommy wars, then?

If other mothers seem to be all we have to grasp at for solidarity in this equation, why is modern motherhood *also* marked by fights over the selfsame variables? Going back to the opening example: if another mother might be the only person who can really empathize with my agonizing decision between a vegetable-less life for my child and a possible future adult dependent on food pouches, why do I still think she might be judging me for not hand grinding my daughter's kale (which she obviously readily eats in this hypothetical Optimal Mother scenario)? In fact, why does the mother seem to fade away entirely from the maternal-fetal dyad?

As coauthors, we sat, a room apart, our simmering rage united only by interconnected screens, and our cursor suddenly slowed, pulsing interrogatively. Why, indeed.

WHY, INDEED

This book is our attempt to answer this question. From the beginning, we felt the internet and social media were a key piece of the puzzle. Perhaps our inspiration came from the fact that even while sitting in the same room with one another, we were communicating digitally, too busy to chat over a cup of coffee. Perhaps it's just a given that social media and smartphones infiltrate every aspect of our lives. Whatever the reason, we knew the internet as a source of parenting advice and as a host for parenting communities had to be a major part of our explorations. This kicked off a multiyear research plan where a large part of our time was spent joining a variety of mom groups on Facebook. What we saw, as a part of our formal observations, mirrored much of what we had informally observed in our (relatively) few years as mothers. On the internet, women are barraged with hosts of articles, memes, and infographics of what is "best," "healthiest," or "safest" for their children, with the implication that all good mothers would elect these things. This assumption (that all mothers would elect these things) seemed to create a perceived market demand for even more articles and infographics detailing even more things mothers should do to keep their children healthy and safe. The resulting cycle was a perpetual motion machine of demands for mothers. Social media interfaces, like Facebook, offered women what seemed like a safe haven; many Facebook groups offer membership to special interest groups, such as women who support breastfeeding older toddlers, or women who are committed to adhering to guidelines from the Centers for Disease Control and Prevention (CDC) for safe sleep. However, mothers joining such groups for solidarity and support from like-minded mothers still often discover these supposed safe havens to be rife with contention, aggression, and peer pressure to conform to groupthink rather than providing comforting support and discussion. The more detailed findings of this book track exactly how such discussions play out, and explore how groups meant to support and uplift mothers somehow tear them down and incite division. The next several chapters present our findings from these months of digital study, separated by the "mommy war"—or subject-specific debate—that they take up. The rest of the chapter at hand is devoted to explaining how we define Optimal Motherhood and how we think we could begin to build a better future for mothers.

THE ROOTS OF OPTIMAL MOTHERHOOD, PART 1: THE CULT OF TRUE WOMANHOOD

What exactly has created our belief that there is an Optimal Mother at all? How have we come to believe that there is a perfect answer to the food pouch dilemma—or any parenting question—to begin with? And when did these standards of perfection become attached to motherhood specifically? The meme in figure I.1 notes how parenting has changed over the years.

So, how did we get here? We believe the roots of this belief can be linked to the nineteenth-century concept of the Cult of True Womanhood. By the nineteenth century, housewives were seen as the moral force driving the entire household. It was thought that a woman's purity and dignity permeated her entire house. Before this period, childbearing was seen as an inevitable part of a married woman's life, something she had to endure as a descendant of a sinful Eve; by the Victorian era, however, a mother's child-*rearing* was seen

HOW TO BE A PARENT

IN 2019 VS IN 1982

Make sure your children's academic, emotional, psychological, mental, spiritual, physical, nutritional, and social needs are met while being careful not to overstimulate, understimulate, improperly medicate, helicopter, or neglect them in a screen-free, processed foods-free, GMO-free, negative energy-free, plastic-free, body-positive, socially conscious, egalitarian but also authoritative, nurturing but fostering of independence, gentle but not overly permissive, pesticide-free two-story, multilingual home preferably in a cul-de-sac with a backyard and 1.5 siblings spaced at least two years apart for proper development also don't forget the coconut oil.

Feed them sometimes.

JOSH SHIPP   Written by Bunmi Laditan

Figure I.1

Source: Xenia Tsolaki Metaxa Private Institute (2019).

as much more important than her child*bearing* (Freidenfelds 2020). This new emphasis on childrearing meant that maternal perfection was not only valued but demanded. Previously, women simply bore children. But now they were expected to have an impact on their upbringing in fundamental ways. For Victorians, maternal perfection was achieved through passivity: women were not to work, even in the domestic sphere, but rather to simply *be*, and in so doing, spread their purity to their families, strengthening and stabilizing them as strong family units. The standard wisdom of the day held that women had the power (and therefore the obligation) to stabilize the nation itself by creating strong, morally upright families.[1]

In the Victorian era, this concept applied to all aspects of women's lives as daughters, wives, *and* mothers (and for middle- and upper-class women, these were indeed most aspects of their lives, as such women were not employable in traditional jobs). The Cult of True Womanhood is still very much with us today, although it has adapted to the norms of our society.[2] Namely, we would argue that as women became more liberated over time, more able to leave the confines of the home, the demands for female perfection narrowed to focus *only* on motherhood, but with increased intensity. For instance, passivity was the name of the game for Victorian women's norms, whereas assertiveness and activity define Optimal Motherhood today. A Victorian mother was meant to demonstrate moral purity by example—her sheer presence could, in theory, purify her family and thereby the nation. In fact, some Victorian household guides advised women to outsource childcare so that they could better maintain an image of calmness and perfection for the short periods when they were in the presence of their children. A Victorian mother might, theoretically, have been able to simply demonstrate good and proper behavior to her children. Indeed, many Victorian motherhood guides make room for the possibility that mothers may not deeply *enjoy* child-rearing but may simply perform "goodness" while around their children to set behavioral examples (Nixon 2020).

Beginning in the 1900s, women were increasingly involved in the everyday care of their children as domestic servant labor became less common. Yet, linguistic patterns demonstrated that a woman's primary role was not purely defined by her identity as a mother. It wasn't until the 1970s that "parent" "gained popularity as a verb," speaking to this emphasis of "woman" as interchangeable with "mother," yes, but also suggesting that "mother" or "parent" was not her only or primary identifier (Senior 2014, 154). Consider how previous generations of mothers were apt to call themselves "housewives," whereas now most women in similar roles use the term "stay-at-home mom" (154). As Jennifer Senior notes, "The change in nomenclature reflects the shift in cultural emphasis: the pressures on women have gone from keeping an immaculate *house* to being an irreproachable *mom*" (154). Enter the Optimal Mother. Mothers now had to be not only present and proper (a Victorian notion) but excessively involved as well. And their involvement had to be perfect.

The Cult of True Womanhood and Optimal Motherhood Compared

In this book, we have set our sights on what we see as the mostly consistent trajectory of continuing the tradition of the Cult of True Womanhood, which we argue has subtly changed over time. We term this new transfiguration Optimal Motherhood. Optimal Motherhood involves all of the responsibility of the Cult of True Womanhood, with a couple of modifications: (1) as we've alluded to, it narrows its scope to involve only maternity issues; (2) it does so with a correlated increase in intensity of demanded perfection; and (3) it jettisons the collectivist values of shaping a nation for the more individualistic ideal of optimized personhood for which the mother is solely responsible (outside of community and state supports/assistance/relevance) and through which one reaps individual rewards relevant to only the individual nuclear family at hand.

It will be helpful to elaborate in some more detail the similarities and differences in these two feminine ideals. While cultural history is not within the scope of this book, at least a brief examination of the trajectory of the Cult of True Womanhood as it changed over the past 170 years will be helpful to the reader in conceptualizing Optimal Motherhood as it appears in the following chapters. One of the major differences is that Optimal Motherhood in the present day is highly individualistic *and* (and this bears saying *in addition*) stubbornly opposed to communitarian ethics. In fact, this difference is so vast that were it not for the shared imperative of female perfection between the two—their most important and overriding feature—it could nearly be said that Optimal Motherhood is entirely different from the Cult of True Womanhood. This is because, whereas the Cult of True Womanhood had everything to do with stabilizing national citizens through the combined efforts of individual women, Optimal Motherhood has only to do with personal improvement (extended to family improvement). It could be argued (and this will be elaborated on in the next section) that encouraging private citizens to better themselves is simply a way of outsourcing the labor of state improvement to individual citizens. Nevertheless, it remains important to our understanding of Optimal Motherhood that this selfsame means of private, personal improvement necessarily rejects *communal support* even while it contributes to a sense of nation-state moral superiority. As Senior notes,

"Today's parents are starting families at a time when their social networks in the real world appear to be shrinking and their communities ties, stretching thin. Without the vibrant presence of neighbors, without life in the cul-de-sacs and the streets, the pressure reverts back to the nuclear family" (66). And since maternal caregiving can constitute as much as 74 percent of *total* caregiving, Senior's statement should be revised to indicate that the pressure reverts back to the mother (Hays 1996).

Thus, Optimal Motherhood is more individualistic than the Cult of True Womanhood was—but only insofar as it deprives mothers of their ability to *receive* support—and it is therefore much more insidious than the Cult of True Womanhood was. As problematic as nationalism itself is, one must at least admit that the Victorians were more direct in their motivations, and in exchange for female perfection, women were granted some sense of contributing to a higher (if problematic) cause. These women believed they were receiving something in exchange for their perfection. In Optimal Motherhood, women contribute to neoliberal aims of constructing a perfect country through individually contributed, individually perfected private families, but they are unaware that what was promoted ideologically as "being their personal best" or "ensuring a healthy family" was in fact a nationalistic act. They are thus paying the price—doing the work—without receiving anything in return. In this manner, mothers are both cut off from any awareness (a.k.a. psychological validation) of contributing to communal goals and (more importantly) taught to shun community *contributions* or aid. The Optimal Mother must perfect her family, and she must do so in a vacuum, because perfect women shouldn't need help.

Another important difference (outlined in the previous section) is that the Cult of True Womanhood dealt with *all* aspects of a woman's life: her role as a daughter, as a wife, as a hostess, and as a mother. Of course, in the Victorian era, the only women to whom the Cult's mandates truly applied (middle- and upper-class women for whom employment outside the home would have been disreputable) did not work. It made sense in this context that the "entire scope" of women's lives, as addressed by the Cult of True Womanhood, dealt only with their domestic relationships with others.

Optimal Motherhood has maintained the Cult's focus on women's roles in the home. However, since women's roles in the home have changed so vastly, its actual scope tends to deal only with maternity issues. There is a description for such relationships: they are called chiastic.

As the scope of women's freedoms increased (solid line), the scope of the Cult of True Womanhood (dashed line) *narrowed* or decreased, to include only those activities that were necessarily domestic: in this case, motherhood seems to be the last stronghold of the Cult of True Womanhood (see figure I.2). There it has stayed embedded and, we believe, has intensified, as all of its ideological heft is packed into one realm of a woman's life. Senior notes that "history certainly suggests as much": "In the past, at just the moments women had gained some measure of education or independence, the pendulum often took a wild swing backward, with the culture suddenly churning out the unambiguous message that women ought to be seated back at the hearth" (2014, 151). Indeed, Sharon Hays explains that, ironically, many of the policies are aimed at social justice, such as "child labor laws and compulsory schooling . . . coupled with powerful efforts to solidify the family-wage (male-breadwinner) system. At the same time an increasing number of protective labor laws excluded women from certain kinds of work and cut back their hours so that their employment would not interfere with their mothering role. These combined actions seemed to have gradually resulted in the assimilation of the form of the cult of domesticity among working-class women" (1996, 43).

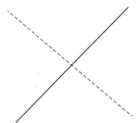

Figure I.2
Women's freedoms versus the Cult of True Womanhood.
Source: Nixon (2020).

THE ROOTS OF OPTIMAL MOTHERHOOD, PART 2: NEOLIBERALISM EXPLAINED

If the Cult of True Womanhood is the scaffolding upon which Optimal Motherhood was built, neoliberalism is its building materials, the brick and mortar that allows Optimal Motherhood to affect so many women—even those who would like to believe they are above such Pinterest Mom aspirations. "Neoliberalism" describes the way norms in modern, developed nations are enforced not by literal state force but more subtly through adding a moral value to the behavior. In other words, we no longer put citizens in debtors' prison, but we have talking heads like Dave Ramsey to drive home the message that if people were just disciplined enough, then they could avoid coming up short at the end of the month. The neoliberal message in this example is too general to be useful to specific families' situations, yet it also simultaneously puts the burden on the individual family who should have tried harder to succeed. Such logic neatly sidesteps the responsibility of other organizations or groups to contribute to local success. Affordable health care, for instance, provided by the state, would be an equally valid hypothetical solution to such a family's financial strain. Whether one agrees with universal health care or not, this example nevertheless illustrates the fundamental logic of neoliberal culture (which we argue defines our present moment in all spheres): deflect public recognition away from systemic or infrastructural gaps and failings and instead redirect focus on how the individual should have helped optimize their own life. As the zeitgeist of our era, the examples are endless. Body cameras are not the answer to police brutality against Blacks—combating systemic racism is. Teen pregnancy isn't the crisis we should be addressing—it's pragmatic sex education and contraceptive accessibility. Insisting on the importance of mammograms isn't the answer to breast cancer—affordable health care is. Neoliberalism is especially noticeable in the realm of health care, and therefore in the realm of choices mothers are told they must make to ensure their children's physical and emotional well-being. Particularly by "the 1980s and 1990s, [public health efforts] increasingly sought to leverage individuals' choices to improve health on a population scale, emphasizing personal responsibility rather than communal solutions such as political action to clean up health hazards in the environment" (Freidenfelds 2020, 105). For Optimal Mothers, this means a "good" mother "seek[s] information on children's needs, . . . attempt[s] to meet those needs through their child rearing practices, . . . [and] they regularly reflect on their own childhoods, attempting to repeat what they felt was right and to avoid the mistakes their parents . . . made in raising them" (Hays 1996, 155).

The Victorian roots of the Cult of True Womanhood mixed with the particular flavor of 2000s-era neoliberalism has resulted in the strange alchemical mess that we are calling Optimal Motherhood. Optimal Motherhood is the imperative expressed by the meme in figure 0.1, that a woman is responsible for manifesting and perfecting every aspect of her child's being: physical, spiritual, emotional, psychological, cognitive, and behavioral. It is simultaneously—and equally as important—the notion that "good mothers" will strive to do these things and do them properly, and "bad mothers" will fail or not try hard enough to do so (or, per attachment theory, not enjoy doing these things well). Reader, it is the mouse nibbling at your sleeve. It is every dilemma of how much screen time to allow, which direction to face a car seat, what clothes are currently least flammable, when to potty train, how to discipline, when to start kindergarten, and, yes, even which damn flavor of kale pouch to get.

But it is also the shadow crisis that follows each mouse nibble: Too much screen time results in poor social development, but what if my kid is the only one who enters elementary school with no digital literacy? Rear-facing is safer, but when are they too big for it? Might they suffer from not seeing our faces enough? Will a mirror make me a less safe driver? Haven't those fire-retardant chemicals been linked to thyroid cancer? Potty training too early is supposed to be bad, but how else can I get them into the preschool I've handpicked and that I'm certain provides the best education for my child? Time-outs are useless, but how do I teach my child that hitting is unacceptable? Early literacy is important, but haven't new studies shown that we start our children in curricular education too early, thereby stifling creativity?

It's exhausting.

Class and Ideologies

Of course, it will be obvious that in the Victorian era the leisure to simply "be" was one open only to middle- and upper-class women, and the same goes for outsourcing childcare. Accordingly, one undercurrent of this book will be to demonstrate how so many of the requirements of Optimal Motherhood today are class dependent as well. Meeting the World Health Organization (WHO) recommendation of two years of nursing, for instance, requires that one have the luxury of working from home or in a job flexible enough to allow constant disrobing and feeding, or that one have a partner with a job that pays well enough so that the nursing mother need not work. Sleep training may very well not seem to be a "choice" but, rather, a necessity for a single mother working two jobs who *must* rest or risk being unable to keep the lights on, so to speak.

It is imperative, then, that we acknowledge the demographic from which we drew our analytical observations for this book: native English speakers from the United States and Canada. More specifically, those who populate the online social media mothering groups we analyzed primarily fall into the categories of white and middle class. We are acutely aware that gender, race, and class are intersecting variables that affect all aspects of life, especially the circumstances that lead to choice—or lack thereof—in parenting decisions. While we attempt to acknowledge the limitations of our observations in this regard throughout this book, we know that focusing on white culture and privilege provides only one piece of the very complex puzzle that makes up modern mothering discourse. We hope scholars will heed our concluding call to extend and elevate the conversation surrounding online parenting debates and their role in constructing contemporary Optimal Motherhood by exploring the discourse practices of heterogeneous mothering communities.

The Roots of Optimal Motherhood, Part 3: Risk Aversion and the Modern Western World

To stay with our previous building metaphor, where the historical Cult of True Womanhood is the framework on which Optimal Motherhood is built, and neoliberal ideals are the pleasant-looking and necessary-seeming brick and mortar that enables it to work so well, risk aversion is the electricity in the building—it is what keeps the whole thing running, like a perpetual motion machine. At its core, Optimal Motherhood is the product of a risk-averse modernity, which is itself the result of a privileged, Western, first-world context.

As Nixon (2020) has argued, beginning with the development of germ theory and bacteriology in the 1880s, Western society increasingly believed that if risks could be identified (Nixon discusses such risk in the form of bacteria), they could by definition be avoided. The formula was deceptively simple for a society still rocked by post-Darwinian secularism and on the lookout for new modes of understanding and thriving in an often chaotic world. Although the Victorians of the 1880s did not yet have antibiotics or other effective cures for infectious disease, product advertisements in periodicals, often promoting a variety of antiseptic panaceas, spoke to the instantaneous development of a *fantasy* of a risk-free life (Nixon 2020). This fantasy (for it remains and will always be a fantasy) was only emboldened by ever-evolving Western medicine, which, as the century rolled over, began to develop cures only imagined in the 1880s.

Of course, all of these medical innovations as well as the beliefs surrounding them occurred amid a host of other modern-day developments. However, for our purposes, the development of twentieth-century medicine is a useful and clear example by which to make our point about risk aversion and its contribution to Optimal Motherhood today. As the theoretical availability of a risk-free life seemed increasingly possible (in this example, the hope of cures for disease *seemed* just around the corner), a funny thing happened: society became generally more paranoid about risk *because* they felt it was avoidable. To put it another way, the more that perfect safety and health seemed within Western society's grasp, the more people began to feel a pressure to maintain vigilance and *avoid* these risks. If disease were theoretically avoidable, it also seemed that everyone ought to do everything they could to avoid it. Thus, the moment disease was no longer seen as an inevitability, neoliberalism swooped in to make it seem like good, responsible people would obviously find ways to successfully avoid such risks.

Hypervigilance itself became nonnegotiable as well. Good, responsible people were always on guard against risk—always watching, always aware—and their careful vigil, like that of an ever-wakeful night watchperson, would ensure that no harm would come. If it did, then it must be the victim's own fault. To keep with the disease and hygiene examples, as early as 1910, if a child died, a woman might be blamed for neglecting to keep a house clean enough to keep a child safe from disease (Leavitt 1996). Today, your downfall might be your choice of food for your baby or the way your baby sleeps. If something happens to your baby—catastrophic death, or something less serious, like a milestone delay or a tendency toward tantrums—a complex cocktail of historical demands on women, neoliberalism, and Western risk aversion point the accusing finger straight at the mother. She should have tried harder, remained more vigilant, cared more, and enjoyed parenting more.

Such risk aversion has had direct consequences for mothering beliefs and advice in our present era. Angela Garbes characterizes risk aversion in the United States as follows:

> Perhaps the darkest side of pregnancy is being routinely infantalized by people who offer their advice and opinions on how to be the best possible host/incubator for your baby. . . . Eat nutritiously but not too much. No soft cheeses, deli meat, or raw fish. . . . Beware of coffee. Exercise, but don't elevate your heart rate too much. . . . Individuals arrive at pregnancy with habits, weaknesses, familial triggers, illnesses, predilections—the human baggage we are born with can accumulate over the course of a lifetime. Would-be mothers are no more or less virtuous than any other person, but our expectations for them immediately shift when pregnancy enters the picture. (38)

We would extend this to all of motherhood praxis, not simply to pregnancy. If neoliberalism inspires the belief that one should rely on oneself (instead of a community) to achieve success, and if the Cult of True Womanhood insisted that women were the core of family success, then this risk aversion added to the mix the idea that for mothers to fulfill their role as managers of their family's success, they had to be constantly on the lookout for risks of all kinds—and to work hard to avoid them. From the pregnant "good mother in waiting" to the "risk-conscious" good mother ad infinitum—who would "never 'choose' to place the 'innocent' child at risk" (Hookway, Elmer, and Frandsen 252, emphasis added)—the ideal citizen mother must choose (yes, must, from the moment a woman begins thinking about the act of procreation) to fulfill the duty of child-centered, risk-aware, blame-ready incubator.

"WE DROVE IN A BODY TO SCIENCE": RISK
AS SCIENTIFICALLY DETERMINED

The quote "We drove in a body to science" is from George Meredith's 1879 novel *The Egoist*. The full quote reads as follows: "We have the malady, whatever may be the cure or the cause. We drove in a body to Science the other day for an antidote" (4). Writing around the same time as the shifting attitudes toward medicine just mentioned, Meredith refers to the consequences of such cultural tendencies. Germ theory's prevalence is, of course, just one example of the ways in which modern, Western science produced the tendencies toward risk aversion just described. Such behaviors were obviously not limited to the realm of germ theory and infectious disease. One could just as easily have used the example of Darwinian evolution instantly inspiring society with a sense of alarm lest they *de*volve. And, indeed, much of the Cult of True Womanhood was related to pervasive social anxieties that, without careful maintenance of the moral fiber of Britain's children, British society might evolutionarily degenerate.

We use germ theory, then, as just one example of the overarching fact that, beginning in the late nineteenth century, regardless of the moral, physical, or existential dilemma, society turned to science for answers and a sense of stability (via a perceived ability to control outcomes through risk management). In a society increasingly less under the pervasive influence of the church, science seemed to be the new system of guidance in an uncertain world. What people knew was that they had "the malady" (that is, uncertainty), "whatever the cure or the cause," and they needed to believe someone had "the antidote" (a means of certainty and control). In the 1880s, through to today, this was science.

It is no accident that Meredith capitalizes the word; this was not a conventional grammatical choice at the time. In doing so, he insists—and we would agree—that "Science" came to represent the new primary source of truth and certainty from the late nineteenth century onward. The problem with this, of course (as any laboratory scientist can attest), is that science is *messy*. Data is *messy*. Data science and quantitative research design are specialty fields, demonstrating the continued need for evaluating how we understand science to begin with. There are rarely simple, perfectly generalizable recommendations without caveats and qualifications.

And yet, a subcomponent of modern risk aversion is a desire for and perhaps even belief in scientific results as unilateral conclusions that belie the messy data beneath them. A ubiquitous term we noted in our observations was "woo"—a pejorative term used to describe anything a speaker deems "unscientific" or bespeaking poor understanding of quantitative practices (we would note the rhetorical vagary of this term itself as bespeaking poor qualitative communicative praxis). As we will show, mothers' scientific literacy itself is not generally lacking in parenting debates; in fact, the opposite tends to be true. Nevertheless, we believe that a pervasive cultural attitude that treats science as a single entity without individualized actors contributes to a tendency to problematically think about and invoke science in ways convenient to the user at a given time. This nostalgic longing for a singular (modernistic) authority to guide contemporary maternal decision-making poses a problem in the reality of complex life situations. In a society that believes risk awareness is equal to perfect risk avoidance, and one where women bear the brunt of the moral burden to attain such perfection, public health science itself then becomes an agent of guilt-ridden enforcement of Optimal Motherhood: "New knowledge and new technologies seem to hold out the guarantee of safety and happiness for our children, if only parents apply them meticulously enough. And, as with early pregnancy, parents feel anxious and guilty when they inevitably fall short of perfection" (Freidenfelds 2020, 198). Indeed, because of neoliberalism's role in this tripartite mixture of maternal burden and risk aversion, the imperfect mother is necessarily instantly portrayed as an unloving mother, and public health recommendations picked up on the persuasive heft of this sensibility. Sharon Hays, among others, has recognized the socially constructed nature of what has come to be portrayed as a given fact: the conflation of good parenting with the extent of parental love. The depths of our love are measured by how well we do by proxy of our children. "Without question," Hays confirms, "mothers experience their own child-rearing beliefs and practices as a measure of love for their children" (155).

The Complexity of the (Mother's) Postmodern Condition

We offer, by way of our critique, several challenges to the logic of Optimal Motherhood, which we hope will inspire readers to begin to dismantle it, by questioning its authority and its logics. Postmodern thinking offers one of these inroads, and it is a way of considering the world that we will invoke throughout this book.

First, postmodernism itself has worked to disrupt the idea of universal authority. A postmodern approach to science might first advise mothers of the very fact (just mentioned above) that science *is* messy, and it rarely offers particularly clear suggestions for perfect behavior outside the laboratory. Second, postmodern thinking offers ways to reconfigure how we discuss knowledge creation and circulation. "Authors," "geniuses," and "truth" have also come to be seen as things that are created incrementally, over time, as ideas are discussed and mulled over by society. Thomas Kuhn most famously suggested, for instance, that there are no sudden "discoveries," but that communities and societies slowly adapt their ways of thinking about and viewing the world, and thus society itself creates the supposed "discovery" or "genius" and their "sudden epiphany." There are in fact no "eureka moments" where a superior genius suddenly achieves inspiration. Instead, there are many individual, subtle shifts that allow a thinker to slowly adapt and then reflect findings *back* to the society that in fact collectively shaped the thinker and their thoughts. It is then also society that diffuses a thinker's findings among their peer groups, and so become as important (according to postmodern thought) as the thinker themselves in publicizing and circulating findings.

Postmodern views would argue that there is not even one single "author" or that knowledge itself can even exist independently of the whole collective activity of society. Gone are the solitary geniuses who emerged out of nowhere, simply to bestow their greatness on us. Instead, postmodernist understandings of the world ushered in a cultural view—pervasive for most of us today—that each thinker is simply one node in a nexus of interactions, each of us affecting some part of the other, like ripples in a pond. Even if I am no great physicist like Einstein, for instance, my discussion of Einstein with a friend may vastly change the way they think about space and time, and so *I* have become an Einsteinian actor myself—an agent of his theories through my casual conversation with a friend. Taking this a step further back in time, Einstein was not simply a "great physicist" who emerged out of nowhere but was influenced by the artists and scientists of his time to consider space and time differently.

Third and finally, there is the postmodern viewpoint of "the death of the author," developed by philosopher Roland Barthes. By this, Barthes means not only that, say, Fitzgerald was created *by* society as much as he created art *for* society (the first point above) and that readers' actions in circulating information about Fitzgerald and *The Great Gatsby* are as important as Fitzgerald's own (the second point above)—although Barthes does indicate these things. He also means something much more vast: that any reader of *The Great Gatsby* has their own interpretation and their own contribution to discussions and discourse about the novel, and that these discussions—which circulate via word of mouth (a network now expanded via social media)—create their own conglomerate meaning that is bigger and more expansive than *The Great Gatsby* itself or any intentions Fitzgerald had about it. Rather, *The Great Gatsby* is the sum of what people think, say, and believe about it, and act on because of it.

Of course, this all applies to more than actual literary authors. Consider the Einstein example above, or any recent argument you've had with a friend on Facebook. These discussions function as actors in their own right, spreading discourse (about conservative politics, about Black Lives Matter, or any topic) farther than the reach of the individual, farther, of course, than the reach of the actual author themselves, and often possibly using such discourse in ways the author themselves wouldn't have imagined. If you've ever witnessed people on social media flinging Bible verses back and forth at each other, each arguing for opposite points using the same tome, you've seen firsthand how we are each authors of meaning and knowledge—both for ourselves and for those with whom we have contact.

"Author," says the influential postmodernist philosopher Michel Foucault, is no longer about attributing discourse to an individual but involves a complex interaction of "the operations that we force texts to undergo, the connections that we make, the traits that we establish as pertinent, the continuities that we recognize, or the exclusions that we practice" (1984, 110;

among other things). Postmodern discourse—including and especially that which is born, grown, and circulated within and outside of social media mothering groups—is inherently influenced by many actants and actors, and these actors and actants act as nodes in a network that affect what we consider normal or expected in our lives.

One of our main claims in this book is that in the realm of parenting advice, this collective creation of knowledge has too often been erased, and parenting recommendations are treated instead like sacred, preexisting facts created by lone scientific geniuses in isolation. In addition to re-creating this much older view of unilateral authority handed down by individual geniuses, mothers further entrench themselves in actions and conversations that resist these postmodern notions of collective knowledge creation. Instead of coming together to mull over and make meaning of findings and data together, mothers in social media mothering groups fling data back and forth at one another like weapons, engaging in team-based polarizing discourse. This seems to be an inevitable outcome when data is treated as sacred, neat, and authoritative and handed down from on high. Therefore, we would suggest that the postmodern views of data, authority, authors, and knowledge creation offer a way out of—possibly the only way to begin to escape—these mommy wars.

Philosopher Donna Haraway (1990), too, urges readers to accept that there is no such thing as an autonomous, unmediated subject (that is, there is no person who isn't influenced by hundreds of thousands of tiny other things—people, places, ideas, events—over time). She also worries about a lack of collective awareness about our networked knowledge. This aligns with our sense that twenty-first-century mothers should not give in to the temptation to stake loyalties exclusively to one team or the other in any given maternal decision-making discussion—doing so assumes that beliefs and opinions can exist in vacuums. Haraway says, "Feminist embodiment resists fixation and is insatiably curious about the webs of differential positioning . . . linking the cacophonous vision and visionary voices that characterize the knowledges of the subjugated" (196). In our view, Haraway is imploring us to make space for a nuanced continuum of mothering decisions in social media mothering groups—to *acknowledge* that no one lives in isolation, even from the opposing view or practice (as Optimal Motherhood would beg us to believe). We are all shaped by an infinite number of forces around us, and acknowledging that with self-awareness could very well be an important step toward relocating ourselves on realistic continuums within communities that also exist on these continuums, rather than deluding ourselves with the belief that we can in fact exist in pure, isolated opposition to any person or group of people around us. These very same people, after all, are actively shaping our perceptions of and beliefs about the world as we know it, including what prejudices and privileges we might un/consciously carry regarding the intersections of gender, race, and class.

Perhaps the most novel argument that postmodern scholars make room for comes from sociologist Bruno Latour and his emphasis on acknowledging the actions of objects in our networks. For Latour, not only people and discourse but also *things and objects* have lived lives through their impact on our own. Think of this as the philosopher's version of the butterfly effect. For Latour, and for our own thinking in this book, memes affect thinking as much as Facebook arguments do—especially because the latter is so often interspersed with the former. Google's algorithms, which influence what results an individual mom—whose data has been gathered and mined—is presented with when she googles "baby feeding," are therefore also an actor. A mother's birth plan, presented to her doctor or midwife, has an impact on those people as well as their moods and assumptions about the mother, and, therefore, becomes a third-party actor. Technological encounters like cycle trackers, baby message boards, and phone-pinging milestone alerts have *all* become a part of this nexus. These apps have "mandate[d] heightened attention, early emotional investment, and round-the-clock concern" for mothers and pregnant women (Freidenfeld 2020, 113). Consequently, we argue that in women's maternity choices, these technologies are as influential as, if not *more* influential than, other humans she encounters face to face. Latour states that "*any thing* that does modify a state of affairs by making a difference is an actor—or, if it has no figuration yet, an actant" (2005, 71). For the purposes of consistency, we will call nonhuman actors "actants" in this book. Both other moms (actors) and the memes and data they use to support their claims (actants) affect the web of knowledge mothers find themselves navigating as they struggle to determine exactly how to be an Optimal Mother.

Assembling Everything You Ever Wanted to Know about *Ethos*

One cannot discuss maternal decision-making without analyzing the *ethos*, or appeal to credibility and authority, in the hashing out of parenting advice. Most modern-day definitions and usage of the term "*ethos*" can be traced back to the rhetorician Aristotle. Aristotle (2007) refers to *ethos* in *On Rhetoric* when he reminds us that persuasive discourse (such as maternal decision-making—though we doubt this, specifically, was on Aristotle's mind) is built on more than just content; the "kind of person" the speaker is can have as much influence, or more, over the audience as the form and content of a given speech (112). George A. Kennedy, translator of Aristotle's *On Rhetoric*, suggests that Aristotle's *ethos* was intimately tied to moral character (148). In short, Aristotle's ethical appeal is about securing the audience's trust by conveying a trustworthy character through a speech (38). Significantly, Aristotelian *ethos* is based on an *embodied* act of persuasion, one in which the audience sees and experiences the speaker speaking in order to be persuaded. The audience is persuaded based on the performance of the speaker's past and present personality and actions and how they convey a sense of a trustworthy identity (or lack thereof) mid-speech. There is no room to doubt the significance of *ethos* to Aristotle and to persuasive discourse when he says, "character is almost, so to speak, the *most authoritative form of persuasion*" (39; emphasis added). With the invention and popularization of writing, however, one can (and should) argue that the rhetorical significance of *ethos* began to change.

When a face and name could no longer be scrutinized in the dynamic act of text making, *ethos*, and knowledge creation writ large, became dependent on what was written into and passed along via a static work. A fairly dynamic and flexible oral medium was exchanged for a fixed and predominantly inflexible print one. This transformation was solidified in the nineteenth century. *Ethos*, or, more specifically, Aristotelian *ethos*, did not have a place in nineteenth-century rhetorical theory, then, as the enlightened individual need only appeal to the authority of scientific Truth (with a capital "T") rather than defer to their own moral uprightness or to the experience and reputation of others; the only "*ethos*" available to the modern writer was to report in error-free standard Academic English what science had already invented for them. It is here that we see traces of the intractable loyalty to one side of a data-driven debate that contemporary mothers feel pressured to perform in social media mothering groups. In a world where "we drove in a body to Science," there is a tension between what postmodern thought has suggested (that we all actively interpret and shape data and information *as* we receive it and converse about it) and the presumption that *ethos* must be maintained by a rigidly inflexible set of scientific Truths gleaned from data and studies. Here, we can see how Haraway's call for women to acknowledge that we all exist in networks (communities) that shape us would alleviate some of this tension. Such subjectively discerned knowledge is likely to be scorned with cries of "woo," however, as we noted earlier. And so, women are urged to uphold the *ethos* of their beliefs by parading around the studies they've found that validate them. What to do, then, when a mother from the opposing side of the debate parades around data for her cause too?

Here is one major dynamic we seek to explore in this book. This is Optimal Motherhood under pressure. The Optimal Mother must prove that she is Optimal. And she has been taught to do this on the virtue of scientific Truth claims as her proof of *ethos*, and to deny differing interpretations of data, or, rather, the actants and agents that affect how any of us accesses or perceives such data. When she meets her own match (that is, another other also touting data, but in the service of an opposing view), the Mommy Wars erupt. Everyone's identity as a good mother is at stake, after all, and if both mothers seem to have been playing the Optimal Motherhood game "correctly," all that's left to do is duke it out—digitally, anyway.

The problem, as we see it, is that social media mothering group discourse precludes the continuum of real-world parenting practices; though it has the potential to do so much good, the *ethos* work being done there is harming more than helping new mothers.[3] *Assembling the Networked Ethos of Contemporary Maternity Advice* serves as the subtitle of our book because part and parcel of advocating for dismantling the Mommy Wars is a conscious act of making visible *what* actors and actants are actually participating in these discourses and how they make claims to *ethos*. We believe that digital technologies, specifically search engine algorithms, memes, and social media interfaces, have become an actor in and of themselves in human reproduction, influencing not only procreative decision-making but also health outcomes affecting contemporary citizenship, thus shaping society itself from conception through birth—even (and especially) family nutritional and caretaking choices.

Even more radically, we conceptualize this techno-agent as one that is in many respects personified through the representative avatars of "people" encountered digitally in social media spaces. The "pings" and voices of social media activity are hard to escape when our smart devices confront us at every turn—in our pockets, on our desks, mounted on our dashboards, and all synced with one another. And yet, it hardly needs stating that such digital connections function quite differently, socially speaking, than direct interpersonal contact. As social media specialist Sherry Turkle has noted, our society has mastered being alone together (2012, 155).

Our aim in this book, then, is to shed light on a complex network of technology, social connectivity, and immediate information circulation as it has affected modern motherhood in a digital age.[4] In a Western world where digital interfaces have ironically allowed for more isolation than ever, message boards have usurped the *ethos* of midwives, and fetal threats and shouts of "bad mother!" are publicized at the click of a button. Such digital networks often serve as the only community-based resource for mothers in a neoliberal world that has isolated women from communities of help, but they necessarily lack the nuance and critical discernment that face-to-face support systems provide to individual mothers. The female support communities that do form online are formed around polarities (e.g., formula vs. breastfeeding groups, co-sleeping vs. safe sleeping groups) rather than unifying factors. Even this grouping factor tends to suggest to mothers that polarized party lines exist and must be towed by aggressive and systematic meme sharing and message-board vigilantism. Within this web of party-line advocacy, digital interfaces, and personal-but-impersonal social media connections, modern motherhood is made, and Optimal Motherhood has metastasized.

CRITICAL DIGITAL HEALTH METHODOLOGY

More specifically, this book operates on the premise that conception, pregnancy, childbirth, and the experience of maternity are increasingly not simple biological processes but complex social constructs produced at the intersection of biological fact, technological interpretation, and the consequent synthesis of subjective experience. As scholars of feminist discourse and digital, scientific, and technological realms, we've organized this project topically: each chapter addresses a different, generally contentious, issue along the spectrum of pregnancy, childbirth, and postpartum child-rearing. Each of these issues involves binary choices, or those that necessitate an either-or decision, on the part of the mother. Additionally, we have selected choices that must be made in the void of clear scientific consensus, enabling us to focus on individually determined decision-making tactics that occur at the intersection of risk assessment, outcome determiners, and information gathering. Ironically, these individual decisions often occur in digital social spaces, as mothers crowdsource, technologically supplement, and otherwise attempt to navigate choices that do not have clear answers but that have outspoken data-mongers supporting either side of the debate. Beyond this, we have generally organized the book according to biochronicity so that we track women's decision-making processes across the reproductive spectrum, through pregnancy and childbirth, and into early childcare decisions.

Methods

In conjunction with the mandate of Internet Research Ethical Guidelines 3.0 (IRE 3.0) that "pluralistic approaches . . . foreground the role of judgment and the possibility of multiple, ethically legitimate judgment calls—in contrast, that is, with more rule-bound, 'one size fits all ethical and legal requirements'" (franzke et al. 2019)—we met with our institutional review board (IRB) on multiple occasions to ethically plan, discuss, and revise our approach to this study.[5] A key area of contention in our study is articulated by IRE 3.0 as follows: "One notorious problem was that especially younger people were sharing more and more information online in what amounted to public or quasi-public fora (the latter protected, e.g., by passwords, registered profile requirements, etc.). But they often nonetheless expected that these exchanges were somehow private—either individually private or in some form of group privacy. Even though these expectations were not warranted by the technical realities of a given forum or SNS [social networking site], especially deontological ethics calls for respecting these expectations" (franzke et al. 2019, 7). That is, while we were deeply convinced that observing, documenting, and reporting on direct quotations from social media mothering group discourse would afford the most powerful insight into the phenomenon being studied, we knew, ethically, we would be compromising the understanding of anonymity, confidentiality, and *privacy* these group members believed they had signed up for. Garnering explicit consent from group administrators, let alone from the thousands upon thousands of members within each group, would prove tedious and ultimately counterintuitive (believe us, we tried; see chapter 5, "Precious Little Sleep ™: Total Risk Aversion, Neonate Sleep, and the Erasure of Maternal Needs)—the subject that is aware of being observed and assessed cannot be assumed to be performing as if those conditions were not affecting their behavioral decision-making.

We chose to focus on Facebook because our key demographic (contemporary mothers in Western society—or, more specifically, white, middle-class, native English speakers of the United States and Canada) does a lot of discoursing on that platform. According to the Pew Research Center, 75 percent of Facebook's users are female, and the majority of users fall in the age range of eighteen to forty-nine (with a particularly high number of twenty-five- to thirty-year-olds using the platform) (quoted in Chen 2020). We investigated a sample of generalized and specialized (by binary-bound parenting decisions, including feeding and sleeping) new parent groups on Facebook. We used a random date generator to identify a more specific focus within a time span of four years (2016–2019, given that covering the entirety of maternal decision-making discourse in these groups would be quantitatively impossible). Within these randomly generated dates, we recorded the name of the group, the date and time of the original posts, and the attendant dates and times of comments and coded each response as PD (pregnancy decision), DRN (delivery room narrative), PDD (postpartum disorder discussion), PBF (pro breastfeeding), ABF (anti-breastfeeding), PFF (pro formula feeding), AFF (anti–formula feeding), MFP (moderate feeding position), PSS (pro safe sleep), ASS (anti–safe sleep), PCS (pro co-sleep), ACS (anti–co-sleep), MSP (moderate sleeping position), Other, or Unsure. Confidentiality was ensured, as usernames were removed and data was stored under password protection.

While our IRB did not allow us to use exact quotations and conversations from mothers in this book out of concern for women's privacy, this nonparticipatory ethnographic approach allowed us to gather data and survey conversations to build the representative samples (thick descriptions of people's subjective understanding and responses in the form of composites and vignettes) that speak to the rhetorical pathways of these debates. Ethnography is a well-established research method common to anthropology in which researchers simply observe groups without interacting. It allowed us to ethically observe mothers' interactions online without invading individual privacy or needing to report specific quotations—instead, ethnography often relies on general rules, patterns, and findings.

We report on commonly used linguistic signifiers and discourse themes rather than on direct quotations in the identified groups. The direct quotations that do appear in this book were taken from *public* forums and media platforms, such as Instagram, and are documented anonymously whenever possible to protect users' privacy; we offer these public conversations as both relevant to and representative of similar debates that take place in the privately built maternal discourse villages on Facebook.

In the interest of exploring the lived experiences of those making and affecting maternal health care and parenting decisions, we also interviewed a convenience sample of mothers and health-care practitioners regarding their thoughts on postpartum depression, infant feeding, infant sleeping, and social media mommy groups. Facilitation and examination of these interviews, rooted in interpretative phenomenological analysis, allowed us to gather a richer and more detailed description of actors and actants in the networked *ethos* of contemporary maternity advice. The interviewed moms became new moms between 1996 and 2018 at the ages of seventeen through thirty, mirroring the demographics of those discoursing on the social media platforms we studied.

Because both face-to-face and online human communication are necessarily supplemented by techno-agents and digital data-human assemblages, we further label our approach as a "multispecies ethnography" (Kirksey and Hemlmreich quoted in Lupton 2016, 4). A multispecies ethnography attempts "to research the entanglements of humans and their digital companion species, by investigating the nature of co-humanity and the co-evolution of these species, their symbiotic interminglings and becomings and their 'mutual ecologies and coproduced niches'" (quoted in Lupton 2016, 4). In essence, we pay attention to things like the influence of memes, birth plans, labels on formula cans, and Facebook marketing (to name a few actants) in maternal decision-making because they have critical agency in and of themselves irrespective of and in addition to the human actors in social media discourse. Any study of contemporary motherhood that willingly ignores these actants necessarily misses a key node in assembling the networked *ethos* of contemporary maternity advice.

CHAPTER REVEAL

Chapter 1: It Was Never about the Coffee: CDC Recommendations, Fetal Alcohol Fears, and Figuring the Collective Body of Woman in Digital Public Health Campaigns

Chapter 1 discusses the CDC's role in shaping discourses about fetal alcohol syndrome in digital public health campaigns in the United States. In February 2016, the CDC released a recommendation situated clearly on one side of a yes-no binary: *no* amount of alcohol was considered safe during pregnancy, and *no* woman of childbearing age should drink unless she was on birth control. Women were advised to carefully regulate their reproductive abilities, given the unpredictable and unruly nature of the process and given that any fertile woman's body should be ready to host a fetus product at any given time. Women blustered over the CDC publications and yet simultaneously felt their pervasive cultural heft.

In this chapter, we conduct a visual rhetorical analysis of images in the official CDC campaign, women's responses to the images on Facebook, and parodies of the original images to explore the impact of this campaign on middle-class women with internet access (those identified in studies as the most likely to engage in moderate wine drinking during pregnancy).

Chapter 2: Take Back the Delivery Room: Narrative Control, Traumatic Discourse, and the #MeToo Labor Movement

In chapter 2, we analyze women's attempts at exerting discursive and experiential control over their labor and delivery experiences. We include the history of birth intervention practices predominating in the United States in the wake of germ theory through the 1980s, when women sought to take back control of desired birth experiences in the form of birth plans. Birth plans are often digitally circulated and crowdsourced in social media groups but not always directly with care providers, creating a problematic battleground where women "lose" when delivery processes don't go according to plan. Even more specifically, we consider the lack of voice given to mothers whose birth experiences are labeled "traumatic."

In this chapter, then, we explore the raw and gritty gap in maternal social media discourse and the ways women are seeking to bring to light what actually goes on in the delivery room, drawing dark and disturbing but purposeful and powerful connections to the contemporary #MeToo movement and how women circulate postbirth birth stories to further empower larger communities of women in decision-making related to labor and the delivery room.

Chapter 3: We Have Never Been Normal: Postmodern Postpartum Experiences and Their Discontents

In chapter 3, we discuss the social space in which medical diagnoses are constructed. In the postpartum period, *all women* experience hormonal changes that are unlike the hormonal baselines experienced in nonpregnant states. Thus, women often experience uncertainty whether their feelings are normal or abnormal and question when they should seek help; they also experience fear regarding the repercussions of seeking help knowing that the "normalness" of their state is assessed and observed by another who is, usually, a medical professional outside the woman's immediate, local community.

This chapter has three parts. In initial foundations, we tackle the slippery issue of diagnostic binaries in and of themselves. Then, we address women's self-perception and needs as weighted against the labels of "ab/normal." Finally, we explore the structural design of support groups developed for a variety of postpartum conditions (such as postpartum depression), considering the structural integrity of those groups designed *for* versus those groups designed *by* the communities of women themselves.

Chapter 4: Breast/Fed Is Best: Whose Algorithm Is Feeding My Baby?

Perhaps no parenting-choice debate has been as highly publicized as that of feeding methods. The very term "mommy wars" was usurped to explain binary online debates about infant feeding choices. Interestingly, however, breastfeeding advocates claim that formula companies marketed the phrase to further encourage a sense of marginalization on the part of both groups: online debate would intensify, usage of the term "formula" would increase, and smart-ad algorithms would proliferate—complicating the issue even further.

In chapter 4, the history of infant feeding methods foregrounds our analysis of current social media discussion forums built around breastfeeding *or* formula feeding. After highlighting the rhetorical means by which *both* groups of women label themselves a marginalized and shamed population, we then analyze how algorithms influence women on such social media platforms. We conclude by comparing how commonly "breast is best" versus "fed is best" slogans surface and evaluating WHO code limitations for bottle-imagery prevalence, for example.

Chapter 5: Precious Little Sleep™: Total Risk Aversion, Neonate Sleep, and the Erasure of Maternal Needs

Among new mothers, perhaps the only issue as divisive as feeding methods is the agonizing process of getting an infant to sleep. There are equal cohorts of women vehemently protesting the permanent brain damage that is certain to result from the cry-it-out methods and those claiming that co-sleeping is a primary cause of preventable infant death. Mothers on both sides of the debate, then, are left in a high-stakes game of (1) validating their sense of personal efficacy and concern as caregivers and (2) owning their role, by proxy, as culprit in infant death or brain damage—no matter the choice they make.

In chapter 5, we review trends in scientific and "scientific" data regarding infant sleep needs and infant sleep training methods. We follow by analyzing social media interfaces that binarily embrace different sides of the infant sleep training debate. We note how discourse patterns from both groups tend to be offensive rather than defensive, castigating the opposed group rather than defending their own choices, and that mothers debate scientific data in this regard astutely but self-interestedly.

Chapter 6: "Can I Get a Tweak?": Toward a Politics of Female Biolinguistic Agency in the Age of New Media

We end, ironically, at the beginning. Using specialized apps and filters, members of "tweaking" forums alter the contrast and color saturation of photographed home pregnancy tests, attempting to discern a "pregnant" line at the earliest possible date. Experienced "tweakers" act as organized service providers, and users line up in digital queues requesting their tests be "tweaked" next. Yet these tweaking groups offer so much more than photoshopping skills.

Chapter 6 ethnographically considers women's grassroots movements in new media spaces created for and by women actively trying to conceive. With their own language, unique and complicated menstrual cycle charting methods, and pregnancy test tweaking processes, these groups build community around reproduction and structure it according to evolving crowdsourced vocabulary that changes according to group-identified needs. Our analysis explores the ways in which these new media spaces offer novel avenues for collective female empowerment in health contexts, and we conclude with a discussion of how this could provide the beginning foundations for a women's community ethics that first operates within digital spaces and then has the potential to expand outward into physical spaces, such as in lived communities and within clinics and doctors' offices.

A VERY COVID CONCLUSION

Instead of "sanctimoms" and "mom bullies" wreaking havoc with "anecdata" in "shame groups," we hope this book will inspire social media mothering

Although the popularly desired outcome is 'healthy baby,' I think there is room in that equation for happy, non-traumatized, empowered and elated mother and baby.

—Midwifery Today

Figure I.3
Source: Puget Sound Birth Center (2018).

group discourse grounded in a sense of communal empathy and predicated on normalizing the real (but currently concealed) continuum of diverse mothering experiences (see figure I.3). Our "Very COVID Conclusion" outlines action steps so that rather than binaristic teams of mothers shouting at one another through the void of Web 3.0, our collective raised awareness can inspire productive changes. Let's reinvent everything we thought we knew about the practices of maternal care and develop new sociocultural and political frameworks that can make that care and support more accessible to all. The first step toward doing this, we think, is debunking the myth that Optimal Motherhood is good, possible, or even exists at all. To that goal we have devoted this entire book. May mothers not be judged against the impossible standard of Optimal Motherhood—but reborn, empowered.

1 IT WAS NEVER ABOUT THE COFFEE: CDC RECOMMENDATIONS, FETAL ALCOHOL FEARS, AND FIGURING THE COLLECTIVE BODY OF WOMAN IN DIGITAL PUBLIC HEALTH CAMPAIGNS

No coffee. No seafood. No bicycles. No deli meat. No alcohol. Almost as soon as she sees the telling double lines, the pregnant woman in modern America is bombarded with new regulations for her body. The dynamic, ever-changing nature of pregnancy seems to induce a state of risk aversion that demonstrates our key argument in this book quite well: in spaces where scientific evidence is incomplete or unclear, the default is to subject women to more—not fewer—restrictions. As stated in our introduction, this dynamic is the result of a complex braid of US risk aversion, the legacy of the Victorian Cult of True Womanhood (what we term Optimal Motherhood in this book), and a neoliberal culture that reveres a reductive version of science that does not make room for complex, nuanced answers. Like the Cult of True Womanhood and Optimal Motherhood, these restrictions have a history. Technological developments, for instance, played a major role in *awareness* of fetal risks. As Freidenfelds notes, developments in "obstetric care and educational materials advocating self-care during pregnancy made women newly self-conscious about their pregnancies and encouraged them to feel responsible for their pregnancy outcomes" (2020, 8). As outlined in the introduction, it seems to have been the *mere awareness* of risk that led to an increased hypervigilance about risk *factors*, followed by a belief that such risk factors could be perfectly controlled. The mere possibility of being aware of risks to the fetus, aided by technological advancement, "further fed the expectation that careful planning and loving care ought to produce perfect pregnancies, an expectation belied by the miscarriages that were often confirmed in heartbreaking ways by these same technologies" (Freidenfelds 2020, 8).

While the demands on maternal health-care decisions for the neonate demonstrate this quite well, we have observed that the transitional state of pregnancy itself elucidates, perhaps better than anything, the aversive reactions to the "unknown" in our culture, in which science is used more to undergird a fear response rather than to encourage women to "proceed with caution." Freidenfelds notes in her book on the history of miscarriage and pregnancy in the United States that by "the 1980s, concern about prenatal exposures and uterine environment soared. Pregnant women came to be seen increasingly in terms of the threat they posed to their expected children's well-being" (2020, 105). In fact, we would argue that the body, once pregnant, suddenly becomes a stand-in for risk itself. We suggest this is because the pregnant body is the ultimate unknown: (1) it is corporeally veiled—showing and yet hiding the fetal body within; (2) it is constantly changing by the second, and, therefore, its risk status is always ineffable, always just beyond the graspable present; and, finally, (3) in a culture obsessed with evidence-based medicine, we have very little "good" data about fetal risks.

"GOOD" DATA AND MICROWAVED BOLOGNA

We say very little "good" data because double-blind studies with control groups are impossible, ethically, to conduct on pregnant women. This sort of randomized study is the gold standard for being able to—as closely as we really ever can—make claims of *causation*. A simple example will make this clear. Say we want to know whether a given food promotes positive mood during the premenstrual period. Researchers will then conduct a study in which two randomly selected groups of women are randomly assigned to two groups: "food in question" (the one researchers are concerned about) and some "control" food (one that is known not to have any relationship with mood). A research assistant or intern, rather than the researchers themselves, assigns the women to these groups; this is known as blinding the study so that the researchers are not biased in their observations of the women's resultant moods. The study can also be double-blind, meaning the research participants also do not know which group they are assigned to—for example, all the women receive identical-looking supplements. The researchers would need to protect against the participants mistakenly believing they have an improved mood due to suggestion or a placebo. Additionally, in assessing the participants for signs of improved mood, the researchers need to be free from unconscious bias; and for this reason, double-blind setups are used.

For the purposes of studying fetal risk during pregnancy, the largest issue is less about blinding and more about control groups. It is simply unethical—a researcher would never dare to propose such a thing—to randomly assign a group of pregnant women to eat lead paint daily and another group of pregnant women *not* to do so and then observe the results. While the impact of ingesting lead paint during pregnancy may seem obvious, this sort of randomized, control-based study would in fact be the only way to claim true causal relationships between lead-paint consumption and fetal risk. An issue like lead paint ingestion, which is known to be harmful to all creatures, may seem like a relatively easy one to develop recommendations about (i.e., probably best avoided entirely, and certainly to be avoided during pregnancy), but pregnancy risk assessments become much murkier in regard to substances that are not necessarily harmful to nonpregnant people. For this reason, most of the known world exists in an odd, "somewhat risky" limbo in regard to pregnancy.

With a few exceptions, all the data we have is correlational, and this can take us only so far, because correlational data is much more subject to what are called confounders. Confounders are variables that could inadvertently be responsible for the observed dynamic. Emily Oster (2013), in *Expecting Better*, provides a good example of what this could look like regarding coffee. Currently, pregnant women are advised to limit caffeine intake because of correlational data showing a relationship between caffeine consumption and miscarriage. Oster points out that morning sickness could be a potential confounder here. Greater intensity of nausea in early pregnancy, for instance, is associated with lower miscarriage rates. It seems to be that more intense nausea may indicate higher levels of pregnancy hormones and, therefore, the lower chance of pregnancy loss. Perhaps, Oster suggests, women who are less nauseated are simply more inclined to find coffee palatable (whereas a nauseated woman might develop an aversion to coffee). In this scenario, coffee itself would not be responsible for *causing* pregnancy loss but, instead, is linked to extant chemistry in the woman's body that *already indicates* a pregnancy is not going well. This, of course, is speculative, and it is but one example—but it demonstrates the case well. Virtually all pregnancy risks exist because of correlational data and, therefore, are subject to sets of confounding variables that could change the meaning of the data entirely.

Pregnancy decisions are complex decisions, and we live in an increasingly fast-paced society. Little wonder, then, that most women opt to err on the side of caution and adhere to the culture of restriction they find themselves in while pregnant. I, myself, with a background in quantitative research design and now a professor whose research focuses on the social construction of fact and risk, remember scowling each day when I microwaved my deli meat. I was frustrated that I was succumbing to acting on what I knew was a minute risk of *listeria* in the meat, but I knew I'd never forgive myself if something happened to my baby because I was too self-centered to microwave my bologna (which, to be clear, is disgusting). I felt overly equipped with my unique educational background—pairing critical analysis of study design *and* risk aversion in modern society—to think for myself about these issues. And yet here I was, microwaving meat anyway, because I had fifteen minutes to get to work, I had to eat something, and I was tired from another uncomfortable night's sleep while very pregnant. It was easiest to microwave the damn bologna. Many mothers, regardless of background, waddle tiredly through this pathway as well, finding it easier to err on the side of safety than to resist, when resistance is loaded with such high stakes—both physical and existential. How important is that cup of coffee anyway? As we've said, by the 1980s, the list of possible risks during pregnancy seemed to grow, less out of clear scientific causal evidence, and more out of a belief in a risk-averse society that for the very reason that scientific evidence *was* unclear, it was better to be safe than sorry—about everything. As Freidenfelds notes (2020, 106),

> The concern about the uterine environment extended far beyond avoiding specific dangerous substances and taking a prenatal vitamin. Women were increasingly urged to do their best to perfect the uterine environment, not just to avoid a few specific dangers and follow their doctors' advice. . . . The list of specific hazards grew longer, and the bad outcomes they might cause were increasingly rare. Don't change the kitty litter, don't eat unpasteurized cheese,

avoid sushi, heat your lunchmeat until it is steaming. In 1984 *What to Expect When You're Expecting* introduced the "Best Odds Diet," with the principle that "you've got only nine months of meals and snacks with which to give your baby the best possible start in life. Make every one of them count. Before you close your mouth on a forkful of food, consider, 'Is this the best I can give my baby?'" (94). The standard of good prenatal mothering was perfection.

This chapter takes as its case study the 2016 CDC campaign regarding fetal alcohol syndrome. As in many other cases, the data is mixed and often imperfect regarding alcohol consumption during pregnancy; however, the United States' puritanical roots make the risk assessment of this substance and its use during pregnancy even more fraught. If I, a data-fluent scholar of the biases in science, can hate myself while I microwave lunch meat because the implicit message of "what kind of mother values mesquite-smoked turkey over her baby?" was too strong for me, what, then, of alcohol? Deli meat at least serves a nutritive purpose, and yet even bologna manages to cue the strange amalgam of guilt and careful bodily regimenting that pregnancy incites. Alcohol is decidedly *un*necessary to human health and, particularly in the United States, is often negatively associated with partying and nightlife. Alcohol is itself typically construed along a binary of complete abstinence or flagrant excesses, and it therefore certainly flies in the face of the Cult of True Womanhood, which mothers are still judged against. Thus, alcohol, as imperfectly studied as any other potential pregnancy risk and burdened with moral judgment, intensifies the risk aversion we noted in the introduction, which we will continue to address throughout this book. If the pregnant body seems symbolically converted into pure risk in modern society, then alcohol casts this fact in even higher relief.

DRINKING AND ITS DISCONTENTS

In the 1970s, correlations were noticed between children with developmental delays and mothers who had drunk alcohol during pregnancy; the observed condition was called fetal alcohol syndrome (FAS) (Jones and Streissguth 2010). The principal investigator on this study, David Smith, conducted his research on a sample size of eleven children, each born to an alcoholic mother; of these initial eleven, he was able to longitudinally study the development of eight of them, four of whom exhibited delays (Jones and Streissguth 2010). After these findings were released, "drinking during pregnancy quickly became taboo" (Moskin 2006). Eventually, however, a confounding variable became publicized: class-based dietary factors coinciding with binge drinking may have played a large role in the development of FAS (May et al. 2014). That is, it was quite possible that *poor nutrition combined with high levels of alcohol use* was to blame for the resultant condition. Subsequently, for many years, most claims about alcohol use during pregnancy (particularly in the United States) followed the predictable pattern of acknowledging scientific uncertainty about safe levels of alcohol consumption during pregnancy and *then* advised women to err on the side of caution. While such stances still take the position of policing the female body through the medical gaze and risk surveillance, they do so by informing women about risk uncertainty and *then* rendering stringent admonitions. Thus, while "fetal alcohol syndrome was not well understood . . . the consensus was that it was better to be safe than sorry: the public health message was that no amount of alcohol was known to be safe during pregnancy and therefore not a single drop should be swallowed. Women worried themselves sick over a few drinks imbibed before they got positive pregnancy test results" (Freidenfelds, 2020, 106)

In the early 2010s, however, new studies emerged, some of the first to study *moderate* use of alcohol in pregnant mothers. These studies revealed no differences between groups longitudinally (Kelly et al. 2012; Mamluk et al. 2016, and one study, in fact, suggested moderate *positive* impacts on the children whose mothers had imbibed in moderation during pregnancy (Humphriss et al. 2013). It should be noted that these studies still fall victim to the same shortcomings that all pregnancy risk research does—namely, that there are still potential confounders here. For instance, the greatest proportion of "moderate" drinkers are women in the upper-middle class, and it could be that the correlation here has more to do with class than with alcohol, as with the earlier studies. Regardless, a casual Google search from 2014 about the risks of drinking during pregnancy brought up the most liberal results that had been seen in decades, advising mothers that some of the best studies currently available suggested a little wine was acceptable (we return to the specific choice of wine directly). By 2016, however, the pendulum had swung back the other direction, and doctors and medical groups were taking great pains to warn the public *against* using these studies to justify drinking even a little during pregnancy. Most of these articles went back to the old mantra "We don't know how much is too much; so imbibe not at all." One *New York Times* article, written by ob-gyn Jen Gunter (2019), demonstrates this rather well:

> So my opinion, especially as someone who believes strongly in a woman's right to make decisions about her own body, may come as a surprise: It's medically best not to drink alcohol in pregnancy. Not even a little. The source of that viewpoint? My training and practice as an OB-GYN.
>
> Some attribute this abstinence approach to the patriarchy: Clearly we doctors know that moderate alcohol is safe (we don't!), and we just don't trust women with that knowledge. According to this theory, we think a woman who hears that an occasional drink is O.K. will blithely go on a bender. (We don't think that.)

While performing her simultaneous awareness and dismissal of women's- and gender-studies-minded texts like the one you're reading, the author in fact demonstrates the precise dynamic we describe here: "We don't. . . . know that moderate alcohol is safe"; therefore, "it's medically best not to drink alcohol in pregnancy. Not even a little." On the one hand, the author acknowledges (but disdains) the importance of feminist-informed understandings of health decision-making; on the other hand, she doubles down on the supposed certainty of uncertain knowledge.

WHY WINE?

It is perhaps easy to gloss over the insistence on wine in these discussions. Anyone scouring the internet for these conversations is, after all, interested in the issue of alcohol in general, and so the repeated and almost exclusive use of "wine" in these discussions as a synecdoche for "alcohol" could seem insignificant enough. In a world of Optimal Motherhood, however, we suggest every recommendation is a loaded one. Therefore, we think it bears asking: Why wine?

A 2017 CNN article (Howard 2017) notes the examination of the impact of "two pints of beer or two glasses of wine," for instance, while an interview with economist Emily Oster argues that "the value of a few glasses of wine during a pregnancy is not that the mom-to-be gets to relax, or even that she enjoys the taste of wine—although these are nice side benefits" (Pappas 2017).

In the United States, wine is certainly not ubiquitous enough as a drink of choice to warrant its excessive use as a stand-in for alcohol in these debates. Exchanging the word "wine" for the word "vodka" is a revealing exercise. We would suggest that wine has a greater feeling of refinement, culturally, owing to its French and Italian roots—which, for Americans, feels exotic and taste-ful. Moreover, as both France and Italy are known for their culinary cultures and histories, wine is more easily seen as part of a dining experience rather than enjoyed for its own sake, which we believe serves to make it seem more innocent in articles that promote the safety of wine in moderation during pregnancy. It is apparently too egregious to suggest that a pregnant woman might simply want a glass of wine for its own sake. Even when sipped alone, outside of mealtimes, wine is more frequently appreciated for its "notes" and flavors, much like cuisine. Although the same is becoming true of beer following the craft beer boom of the past ten years, beer, nevertheless, lacks the long cultural legacy of such tastefulness.

Indeed, in nineteenth-century Britain, beer was more akin to water, a quotidian drink of hydration—neutral at best and pedestrian at worst. Cocktails, too, lack the cultural clout of refinement, and liquors in general are much more often colloquially invoked to indicate substance abuse or dependence, generally with moralizing tones. Consider a few representative examples of contemporary "mommy wine culture" memes. Substituting the word "vodka" for "wine" in any of these memes would certainly have a quite different tone. Doing so highlights the role of memes as techno-agents or (borrowing Latour's language referenced in our introduction) actants; such memes are positioned as influencers in contemporary maternal decision-making—functioning as filters of cultural attitudes through which mothers make health-care choices.

Figure 1.1 offers the lighthearted image of a well-kempt mother gazing bemusedly at the giggling infant in her arms. The text reads, "And you're why Mommy drinks wine. Yes you are; oh yes you are." We collectively employ an affectionate baby voice as we read: the high pitch, the vocal fry (the rumbling of our lowest natural register), and uptalk (ending the sentence with a rising-pitch intonation as if asking a question) of "Yes you are; oh yes you are." We grin because it's an amusing incantation and visually heartwarming representation of our everyday existence. When we replace "wine" with "vodka," however ("And you're why Mommy drinks vodka"), we find ourselves inherently implored to repunctuate: "Yes you are. Oh yes, you are." A carefree meme suddenly connotes a dark and desperate reality in which a mother self-medicates to survive the tortured existence with her offspring.

Consider figure 1.2. The image reveals a woman with her face buried in an armchair, her book open on the floor in front of her. We might be tempted to read the image as the woman burying a face full of tears, though the text suggests a less grave reading: "MOTHERHOOD: Powered by love. Fueled

Figure 1.1
Source: Sobe (n.d.).

MOTHERHOOD

Powered by love.
Fueled by coffee.
Sustained by
wine.

someecards
user card

Figure 1.2
Source: Colleen (n.d.).

by coffee. Sustained by wine." We are asked to see wine on a level playing field with and as equal in importance to coffee and love. The woman is not weeping in grief; she is *tired* from a day of tending her children. Replace "wine" with "vodka," however, and we (again, because of the cultural rhetoric attached to vodka that we insert from outside the bounds of the image itself) perhaps read the mother as passed out from negligently overimbibing.

As illustrated in figure 1.3, eight glasses of wine in one meal sounds, arguably, funny. Eight glasses of vodka sounds dangerous. Yet, both have the same alcohol content, when using standard serving sizes. The difference is not in *kind* but in *cultural attitudes*. And, while "mommy wine culture" has been widely taken to task in recent years for normalizing a host of problematic discourses, the very fact that it flew under the radar for so long, being simply accepted as innocent humor, bespeaks precisely wine's status as a "safe" alcohol.

We also cannot neglect to note—in a book dedicated to dismantling the binaries of maternal decision-making discourse—that "mommy wine club," if you will, is one of the most inclusive "teams" in modern-day mothering

It's strange how 8 glasses of water a day seems impossible but 8 glasses of wine can be done in one meal.

som**ee**cards
user card

Figure 1.3
Eight glasses of water vs. eight glasses of wine.
Source: Justin (n.d.).

group collectivism. That is, while one cannot (in social media representation, at least) be on team formula feeding *and* team breastfeeding or on team co-sleeping *and* team safe sleep, one can identify with team "mommy wine culture" from a variety of vantage points: "The parameters for what constitutes a wine mom are very forgiving. You can be in your 20s and have zero kids, but if you are sprawled on a couch wearing sweatpants and drinking a crisp chardonnay after a long day of hard work and taxing emotional labor, you are well within your rights to call yourself a wine mom. Conversely, you can be a tired mom whose wine rack has been empty since 2015 and still identify as a wine mom" (Gorter 2018).

Thus, we find it noteworthy that even in articles allowing for moderate alcohol consumption during pregnancy, the most frequently mentioned form of alcohol is wine. Here we note a decided rhetorical concession to broad cultural judgments against women and mothers: it seems that these authors have decided that if they are going to go so far as to proclaim pregnant women may drink alcohol, such affordances must be cloaked in (very much classed) cultural refinement and gastronomy. Even these allowances for culturally acceptable, class-prescribed drinks were shored up, however, when the CDC released its new FAS campaign in 2016.

NOT A DROP TO DRINK

In February 2016, the CDC released a media campaign warning women of the effects of FAS, a broad-spectrum disorder that has some correlative ties to alcohol consumption during pregnancy. The interaction between alcohol intake and development of FAS is poorly understood—a fact readily admitted by most physicians, research scientists, and if one reads carefully enough, even health campaigns that promote teetotalism. While it *is* clear that alcohol consumption has led to the syndrome set now known as FAS, studies have been largely indeterminate about the specific amount of alcohol required to catalyze it (Hendry 1999). For this reason, most neoliberal governments sternly warn women that there is no known safe amount of alcohol and stress that the only recourse is total abstinence. Recall that neoliberalism, particularly in the realm of health policy, works by transferring state and national risk aversions (that is, avoiding anything that might result in less than perfect citizens) onto individuals, who are urged through moralistic arguments to uphold certain norms. Thus, the medical establishment's concerns about the prevalence of FAS are translated into moralizing lectures about responsible pregnancy and motherhood; the subtext here is very important: mothers who are not "responsible" do not love their children enough to protect them in utero. Such wording can be seen in almost any ad campaign or article on the topic, or indeed the images themselves (see figure 1.4).

That is, most US recommendations about alcohol and pregnancy advise women not to take any risks—a neoliberal ideology that is, in fact, nearly impossible in most realms of life (such as driving while pregnant or potentially consuming spoiled food while pregnant); however, many argue that alcohol consumption *is* an avoidable risk and, therefore, should be undertaken as a controllable variable by the mother.

There are clear parallels to smoking as an avoidable risk for the pregnant mother. Hookway, Elmer, and Frandsen's (2017) "Risk, Morality,

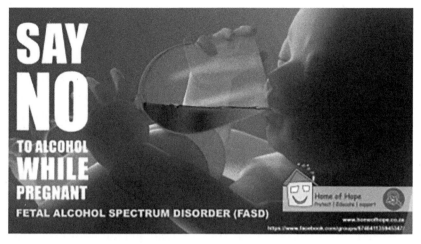

Figure 1.4
Home of Hope campaign to create awareness about Fetal Alcohol Spectrum Disorder.
Source: Home of Hope (2014).

and Emotion: Social Media Responses to Pregnant Women Who Smoke"
explores commenters' moral outrage attached to viewing media articles about
a research study with an incentive for pregnant women to quit smoking.
Researchers found that posters' comments largely centered on emotional dis-
gust and repulsion for what they deemed "deviant and harmful" behavior on
the part of the pregnant mother (who was taking part in the research study *to
quit smoking, for her unborn baby*). Irrelevant of the sociocultural and physi-
ological challenges inherent in quitting smoking (251, commenters chose to
condemn the women for subverting their duty as "risk-averse reproductive
citizens who actively screen and avoid risks" (252). The commenters clearly
thought the unborn baby's health should be privileged over the mother's
(248), as a "'good mother' . . . would never 'choose' to place the 'innocent'
child at risk by smoking while pregnant" (252).

Hookway, Elmer, and Frandsen (2017) highlight the morally righteous
judgment that tends to dominate such public health discourse. Victim blam-
ing, stigmatization, and marginalization (256–257) permeate this discourse
because "the ideal citizen is someone who is actively and rationally engaged
in rigorous management and assessment of future risks and their avoidance,"
especially when that citizen is pregnant. Pregnancy, in fact, has been labeled

a "risk event" (Andy Alaszewski, quoted in Hookway, Elmer, and Frandsen 2017, 2). And it is not just an individual risk event but "a source of personal and collective anxiety requiring close management by the informed risk consumer and medical experts" (247). Even if unintentionally so, digital media shared about alcohol use during pregnancy often mirror public health recommendations as trusted sources of fact, and thereby function as an actant in this dynamic, effectively policing women's behavior during pregnancy through guilt and shaming. While they are possibly often unaware that they are doing so, the community nevertheless polices the pregnant woman anytime they click the "share" button on a meme or infographic like this (see figure 1.5), and such policing—intentionally or not—tries to ensure that the mother is being a responsible reproductive citizen, both risk aware and risk averse (247–248).

Our point, again, is not to debate the relative good or ill of choices such as smoking or drinking during pregnancy. Our point is to demonstrate the binary responses that such debates perpetuate. For one, there are few studies on *moderate* drinking during pregnancy, perpetuating the fact that pregnant women who drink are likely to be seen as binge drinkers if they are not the polar opposite, teetotalers. Second, women in these positions are inherently demonized irrespective of both social context (in the case of smoking) and solid scientific evidence (in the case of drinking). Finally, there is no room for moral care and concern for the mother, only an assessment of how well (or, let's face it, how *not* well) she measures up to the standards of Optimal Motherhood. Defining and managing risk has become the hallmark of public health (at the cost of erasure of the parturient mother), and this framework is not likely to disappear any time soon. Rather, "as medical dominance combined with new surveillance and technologies results in more sophisticated methods and techniques for calculating and responding to health risks" (Andy Alaszewski, quoted in Hookway, Elmer, and Frandsen 2017, 247), the Optimal Motherhood–bound risk culture is more likely to intensify. For that reason, it's important that we look at how one technological actant, a 2016 CDC infographic, uses problematic appeals to credibility and authority to persuade pregnant mothers to take a no-holds-barred position on pregnancy and alcohol consumption.

Drinking too much can have many risks for women.

For any pregnant woman and baby

miscarriage
stillbirth
prematurity
fetal alcohol spectrum disorders (FASDs)
sudden infant death syndrome (SIDS)

For any woman

injuries/violence
heart disease
cancer
sexually transmitted diseases
fertility problems
unintended pregnancy

Drinking too much for women includes...

PREGNANT

any alcohol use
by women who are **pregnant**
or might be pregnant

NON-PREGNANT

8 or more drinks
per week (more than 1 drink
on average per day)

binge drinking
(4 or more drinks within
2-3 hours)

any alcohol use
by those under age 21

Doctors, nurses, or other health professionals should screen* every adult patient, including pregnant women, and counsel those who drink too much. Providers can help women avoid drinking too much, including avoiding alcohol during pregnancy, in 5 steps.

1 Assess a woman's drinking.
- Use a validated screener (e.g., AUDIT (US)*).
- Take 6-15 minutes to explain results and provide counseling to women who are drinking too much.
- Advise her not to drink at all if she is pregnant or might be pregnant.
- Come up with a plan together.

2 Recommend birth control if a woman is having sex (if appropriate), not planning to get pregnant, and is drinking alcohol.
- Review risk for pregnancy and importance of birth control use.
- Discuss full range of methods available.
- Encourage her to always use condoms to reduce risk of sexually transmitted diseases.

"The best advice is to stop drinking alcohol when you start trying to get pregnant."

3 Advise a woman to stop drinking if she is trying to get pregnant or not using birth control with sex.
- Discuss the reasons to stop alcohol use before the woman realizes she is pregnant.

4 Refer for additional services if a woman cannot stop drinking on her own.
- Provide information on local programs or go to SAMHSA treatment locator. www.findtreatment.samhsa.gov
- Consider referral to treatment or recommend Alcoholics Anonymous. www.aa.org

5 Follow up yearly or more often, as needed.
- Set a time for return appointment.
- Continue support at follow-up.

*Learn how to do alcohol screening and counseling at www.cdc.gov/ncbddd/fasd/alcohol-screening.html.

SOURCE: Adapted from American College of Obstetricians and Gynecologists. www.acog.org/alcohol

Figure 1.5
Centers for Disease Control and Prevention's "Drinking Too Much Can Have Many Risks for Women" infographic.
Source: Centers for Disease Control and Prevention (2016).

The 2016 CDC campaign goes beyond the timeworn debate regarding drinking during pregnancy, however. In a soothingly muted color palette, bedecked with calm, happy looking (albeit faceless) women, the ad campaign gently but firmly warns that "drinking too much can have many risks for women" (figure 1.6).

Deftly setting aside the rather obvious fact that drinking too much can have many effects for men, too, the infographic then visually and figuratively bifurcates pregnant from nonpregnant women with two illustrations of women who are featureless other than their demurely bowed heads, complacent smiles, and, in one case, a noticeably pregnant abdomen. Below the image of the pregnant woman, the infographic goes on to confidently state that "drinking too much for [pregnant] women" involves any drinking whatsoever. Importantly, this belies the openly acknowledged fact that studies vastly disagree about whether moderate drinking might be safe during pregnancies.

The CDC's 2016 suggestions for pregnant women beg for discursive analysis and will be returned to shortly; here, however, we want to discuss the issue of this infographic that stuck most in the collective craw of American women: the other side of the bifurcated page representing *non*pregnant women.

While the infographic rehashes long-debated concerns about drinking during pregnancy, the February 2016 CDC campaign goes on to insist that, in fact, overindulging is a problem for *all* women (perhaps better emphasized as all *women*), particularly regarding their reproductive health (or, again, perhaps more aptly, because of their reproductive abilities). The image notes that women who drink too much risk contracting sexually transmitted diseases or unwanted pregnancies and even risk developing eventual fertility problems while under the influence, and advises that no woman of childbearing age

Drinking too much can have many risks for women.

Figure 1.6
An infographic header for Centers for Disease Control and Prevention's "Drinking Too Much Can Have Many Risks for Women."
Source: Centers for Disease Control and Prevention (2016).

should drink unless she is using birth control. This was not the first time that US-based risk aversion—writ large during pregnancy—dialed its risk aversion so far backward that it addressed even the *pre*-pregnant body. In the late 1990s, the March of Dimes assessed that folic acid could reduce birth defects by 70 percent (Freidenfelds 2020). It instantly extended its supplement recommendations to *all* women, just in case they became pregnant: "In 1999–2001, the organization ran a comprehensive publicity campaign to teach women and their doctors that every woman of childbearing age, regardless of whether she was planning a pregnancy, should take a daily folic acid supplement" (Freidenfelds 2020, 106).

The CDC's infographic thus simply continued a longer tradition of extending maternal risk factors to the pregnant body, and then even further to the maybe-someday pregnant body. The top portion of the 2016 CDC infographic, then, visually bifurcated between pregnant and nonpregnant women, sets up an ideological binary for all women (figure 1.7). If pregnant,

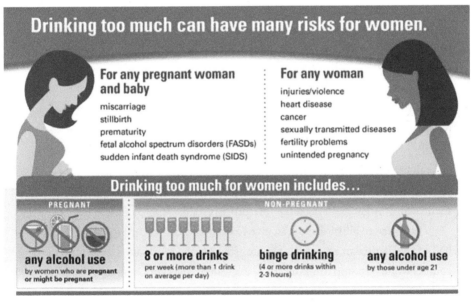

Figure 1.7
The top half of the "Drinking Too Much Can Have Many Risks for Women."
Source: Centers for Disease Control and Prevention (2016).

the ad indicates, a woman risks the health of her baby (read: quality of production of able bodies for the neoliberal state). Even if she is not pregnant, however, the graphic indicates that a woman remains a threat to society when she drinks by rendering the space of her already threateningly productive uterus (a threat that seems tolerable only when under the control of neoliberal mandates) potentially even more out of control. The potential impact of *both* "fertility problems" and "unintended pregnancy" makes this abundantly clear. The already threatening productive potential of the uterus will either over- or underproduce if the female does not carefully surveil and regulate it. Thus, even nonpregnant women must fear pregnancy risks. Female alcohol consumption presents the risk, according to this campaign, of either producing new citizens from less-than-perfect bodies or biochemically "deforming" a woman's body such that it can no longer produce new, healthy citizens.

Neoliberal theory aside, the message to women here is clear: if you drink, you might become pregnant when you don't want to or risk being unable to become pregnant when you do want to. On the most basic level, one very possible—even likely—reading of this infographic within the context of a neoliberal, risk-averse society that desires maternal perfection and purity is to read the women depicted and described in it as always already potentially pregnant bodies—and little else. While such a portrayal may or may not have been intentional on the part of the CDC, it represents an important artifact of how women are constructed and seen in our present day. Whether pregnancy is construed as threatening ("unwanted") or dangerously desirable (fertility "problems"), the faceless women in this advertisement are in fact a productive visual representation of the infographic's ideological work—presenting women as human-producing machines with no subjectivity of their own. Margaret Atwood fans are probably shivering by now.

Pathos-laden allusions to speculative fiction aside, we turn to the bottom half of the campaign ad, which features suggestions for doctors as to how to counsel women to stop drinking "in 5" easy "steps" over the course of the oddly specific "6–15 minutes" of an appointment (figure 1.8).

The neoliberal mandates scream loud and clear in this campaign through this provisioning of physician time, down to the minute, in a climate where doctors are ever more taxed with patient loads and appointment time limits

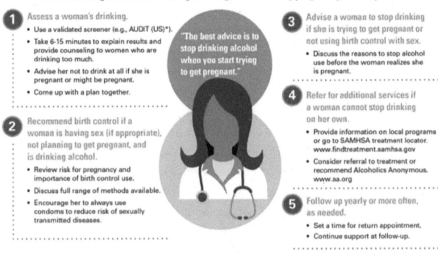

Doctors, nurses, or other health professionals should screen* every adult patient, including pregnant women, and counsel those who drink too much. Providers can help women avoid drinking too much, including avoiding alcohol during pregnancy, in 5 steps.

1 Assess a woman's drinking.
- Use a validated screener (e.g., AUDIT (US)*).
- Take 6-15 minutes to explain results and provide counseling to women who are drinking too much.
- Advise her not to drink at all if she is pregnant or might be pregnant.
- Come up with a plan together.

2 Recommend birth control if a woman is having sex (if appropriate), not planning to get pregnant, and is drinking alcohol.
- Review risk for pregnancy and importance of birth control use.
- Discuss full range of methods available.
- Encourage her to always use condoms to reduce risk of sexually transmitted diseases.

"The best advice is to stop drinking alcohol when you start trying to get pregnant."

3 Advise a woman to stop drinking if she is trying to get pregnant or not using birth control with sex.
- Discuss the reasons to stop alcohol use before the woman realizes she is pregnant.

4 Refer for additional services if a woman cannot stop drinking on her own.
- Provide information on local programs or go to SAMHSA treatment locator. www.findtreatment.samhsa.gov
- Consider referral to treatment or recommend Alcoholics Anonymous. www.aa.org

5 Follow up yearly or more often, as needed.
- Set a time for return appointment.
- Continue support at follow-up.

*Learn how to do alcohol screening and counseling at www.cdc.gov/ncbddd/fasd/alcohol-screening.html.

SOURCE: Adapted from American College of Obstetricians and Gynecologists. www.acog.org/alcohol.

Figure 1.8
The lower half of the "Drinking Too Much" infographic
Source: Centers for Disease Control and Prevention (2016).

in the increasingly privatized, corporatized, US health-care system. (But that is a topic for another book.) These suggestions for physicians take the subtle implications of women-as-faceless-uteruses even further, for doctors are counseled to "advise a woman to stop drinking if she is . . . not using birth control with sex." Here, any women between menarche and menopause are posited clearly as potential mothers for whom imbibement should be disavowed unless their uteruses are properly controlled. We would note that such a sentiment only seems possible within the culture of Optimal Motherhood, in which risk is unacceptable, management of risk is an individual's personal responsibility, and—this is perhaps most significant for the case at hand—mothers in particular are seen through a lens of purity. It is notable that the physician pictured is gendered female, as if to sidestep concerns of paternalistic authority on the part of the physician. In the culture of Optimal Motherhood, we'd argue, however, the judgment of another woman, possibly another mother, is no better.

The odd notion that not just pregnant women or women attempting to become pregnant, but *all* women between the ages of thirteen and fifty-five or so should fear alcohol as a potential risk to as-yet nonexistent pregnancies did not go unnoticed. Even if the undertones of neoliberal production of new working citizens are perhaps subtle unless highlighted with complex biopolitical theory, the clear-cut message of women as helpless owners of risky uteruses rang loud and clear to women who read this infographic. Parodies from numerous fronts soon followed. One such parody invites the reader to consider why the CDC singled out women for being at risk of things like violence when drinking, when the reverse situation could be said of men (figure 1.9). The same parody also points out that men, too, could create unintended pregnancies while drinking. In the bottom left-hand corner, in the admonition to abstain from all alcohol use, the infographic replaces "women who are pregnant or might be pregnant" with "men who are violent or might be violent," a cutting response to the CDC's hypergendered campaign.

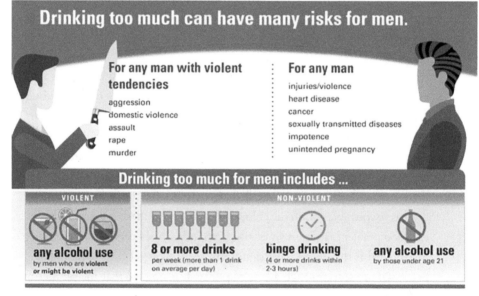

Figure 1.9
Chris Giganti's parody infographic.
Source: Chris Giganti (2016).

The CDC has since removed this portion of the infographic from its website (although the lower portion, showing a faceless female doctor and advising said doctor on how to counsel women who drink too much, remains [CDC 2016]).[1]

Titles of editorial responses struck similar chords across the board. "The CDC Has Some Insulting Advice for Women Who Drink" (Zielinski 2016) was the title of one article, while another resonated similarly with its title "CDC's New Infographic Blames Women's STDs on Their Drinking Habits" (Filloon 2016). The subheading of the latter article reads, "Warning: This will enrage you." A *Washington Post* editorial by Alexandra Petri sardonically begins, "Who knew that drinking alcohol could give 'any woman' a sexually transmitted disease? That's the last time I drink merlot alone in my apartment. I don't want herpes" (Petri 2016). The article continues, "Furthermore, I had no idea that drinking eight beverages a week could result in a baby. I always thought, somehow, that there were other activities involved. But the CDC knows best" (Petri 2016).

The editorial titles in and of themselves compose an intriguing critique of the CDC's *ethos*. The CDC (trademarked "Saving Lives, Protecting People") self-identifies "as the nation's health protection agency" that "saves lives and protects people from health threats. To accomplish our mission, CDC conducts critical science and provides health information that protects our nation against expensive and dangerous health threats, and responds when these arise" (CDC 2020).

Considering a trademarked motto to focus on the fight against "expensive" health threats, we cannot ignore the neoliberal undertones here, but, more importantly, the CDC's well-credentialed organizational leadership has "enjoyed a reputation as one of the leading public health organisations in the world, having played a key role in mitigating previous global outbreaks such as Zika, Ebola and Sars" (Stacey and Kuchler 2020). The CDC, in name and deed, is generally a trusted (credible, authoritative) source in such medical matters, yet the editorial titles purposefully tie the CDC—by name—to the disparaging effects of the multimodal message in its 2016 say-no-to-pregnancy-drinking infographic. One hardly needs to dig into the editorials themselves to understand the persuasive force and viral impact of the visual techno-actants within the infographic itself.

Lest it seem that the visual and linguistic elements of the CDC's infographic have been stretched too far by such sardonic interpretations, it is important to note the widespread, serious impact this campaign had. Among major news outlets, this infographic was taken as a "new" finding, and the risks of drinking during pregnancy acquired a renewed tone of urgency in the media. An article in *USA Today*, titled "CDC: Young Women Should Avoid Alcohol Unless Using Birth Control," opened with the even more specific sentence, "Women of *childbearing age* should avoid alcohol unless they're using contraception, federal officials said Tuesday" (Szabo 2016; emphasis added). The message of this infographic, while perhaps merely implicit, nevertheless was interpreted quite clearly and uniformly by media recipients. Thus, the menarche-to-menopause risk message was clearly heard across the board, by opponents as well as proponents, and by serious as well as parodic sources recounting the information.

Many respondents quickly keyed into the campaign's victim-blaming tendencies, as the first "risk" of alcohol noted by the infographic was "injuries/violence." An article by Whitney Filloon (2016) castigates the campaign:

> It's possible that intoxicated women may be at a greater risk of those things [named in the infographic]—but it's disturbingly irresponsible for the CDC to frame them in this way, a way that very strongly suggests that the burden of avoiding violence, unwanted pregnancy, and STDs falls to women, and that the route to avoiding them is to drink less. The idea that daring to have a cocktail may make women the target of violence (and, on the flipside, that a woman who is aware of this risk and chooses to have a cocktail *anyway* is arguably inviting that outcome) is an example of victim-blaming so flagrant and extreme that it's almost hard to believe it's real. (It seems unlikely that the CDC will distribute a comparable infographic to warn men that drinking too many Jager-bombs can lead to herpes, or swinging a punch, or getting a woman pregnant.)

Another article, with the subtitle "As if pregnant women who dare to pick up a glass of Champagne aren't policed enough, the CDC is now telling all fertile women who aren't on birth control to stay away from alcohol," sums up the infographic with its title, "*Non-Pregnant* Women Now Guilted for

Fetal Alcohol Syndrome" (Zadrozny 2017; emphasis added). The article itself quotes Professor Lisa Wade as expounding that the guidelines "suggest . . . that we are willing to compromise a woman's autonomy and quality of life on the tiny sliver of a possibility that she might get pregnant and have a child that is diagnosed with FAS."

WHEN TO PUMP AND DUMP (OR NOT)

The levying of shame and guilt attached to maternal decision-making and alcohol consumption is also well illustrated in social media "pump and dump" debates. The question is whether a breastfeeding mother needs to express ("pump") and discard ("dump") her milk as opposed to delivering it to her nursing baby when (if) the mother chooses to consume alcohol. Evidentiary information regarding maternal blood-alcohol levels and transmission to breast milk is lacking, and the "risks" of consuming alcohol while breastfeeding are considered even less clearly defined than those of consuming alcohol while pregnant (Burbidge 2019). Enter Shawn Johnson, 2008 gold medalist on the US Olympic balance beam team, who was captured in an Instagram video that incited just such fraught discourse.

Enjoying a night out together, Johnson's husband posted a video of his tipsy wife, wine glass in hand. The caption read, "9 months no drinking = lightweight @shawnjohnson. Are you more of a wine, beer, or soda person? #wine #lightweight #marriage" (East 2019). The post garnered over half a million views as well as some scathing discourse exchange (figure 1.10).

One commenter's reply aptly captured the incendiary nature of responses:

> Chill people, she is allowed to have a glass or 2 of wine. It's not like she was slamming a bottle of Jack. Let her be. I'm pretty dang sure she knows all about alcohol and breast milk and probably like most 1st time moms talked to her doctor before having it. She read anything and everything about being pregnant. Give her some credit for knowing what to do postpartum. 💔[2]

The commenter not only harks back to the wine versus liquor paradox discussed earlier in this chapter but also invokes the good-mother-in-waiting (Lupton quoted in Hookway, Elmer, and Frandsen 2017, 247) neoliberal

Figure 1.10

Andrew East's Instagram post from November 14, 2019, teasing wife Shawn Johnson about her diminished alcohol tolerance post baby delivery

Source: East (2019).

mandate, insisting that all first-time moms know they must bow to the credibility and authority of their doctors before making any potentially risky pregnancy decisions (risky to the growing fetus, that is). The commenter, furthermore, doubles down on their assurance of Johnson's child-centered, risk-aware approach to mothering by insisting "she read anything and everything about being pregnant." Even her defenders could only defend her by portraying her as an Optimal Mother, thus upholding the very binary that had caused the debate to begin with.

Some commenters seized the opportunity to wage other binary-bound maternal decision-making battles, such as the following defensive stance on formula feeding:[3] "Formula is just as healthy. . . . Please don't say otherwise because there are lots of women who can't breastfeed, and this hurts them even more!" Other commenters found this particular situation (of a tipsy sports-celebrity mom being lambasted on the internet for drinking while momming) as well as contemporary maternal decision-making writ large to be overly fraught with overanalytic opinion: "All the judging and nursing advice. Remember your moms probably drank while pregnant and nursing. It's called moderation. Everyone will live and be safe. 😭" Still others wanted to give Johnson kudos, rather than shame or guilt, for her chosen methods of surviving contemporary motherhood—but not before giving an extensive explication of why she was deserving of that kudos in light of communal public health risk surveillance. The following comment is worth reproducing at length:

> Preach! Like she doesn't have access to all of the same info! She can call her own pediatrician or specialist if she has a question. I understand most are trying to be helpful, but, in the same sense, leave her alone, and let her enjoy a glass of wine 🍷. It would be different if she has posted, "Hey, guys, what do I do if I drank some wine," but, guess what guys, they are simply sharing their dinner post. Let her mom. We have all seen how much research they both have done, so I'm sure this topic is no different, and she has researched the hell out of it! Good job, momma! Enjoy your wine!

Here the commenter casually invokes issues of sociocultural class and (in the case of this celebrity mom, unlimited or easy) access to mothering knowledge, admonishes the wave of *other* "well-meaning" commenters who (in the view of this particular commenter) *thought* they were being helpful, and proceeds to mention that more basic questions ("What do I do if I drank some wine?") would be—clearly—far more absurd and significantly more concerning. Johnson's knowledge of risk factors already demonstrates her Optimal Motherhood, whereas, this commenter suggests, if she had been less certain about her risks of drinking, she would be more worthy of criticism for asking information-gathering questions. The commenter then *immediately* juxtaposes an imperative "Let her mom" with a petition for community corralling of the mother's body: "We have *all* seen how much research they both have done" (emphasis added). In the view of this officer of public health risk aversion, Johnson has done her due diligence and proved to the community that she has earned the right to, you know, just (wine) "mom."

While the ethical appeals of celebrity social media discourse are worth studying in and of themselves,[4] it is not Johnson, the celebrity, with whom we are most concerned here. Johnson is the stand-in—scapegoat, even—for contemporary mothers in the hypervigilant public health context of Western society (i.e., white, middle-class, native English speakers of the United States and Canada). What we think is most worth our attention is the nodal community that assembles and exerts ethical force on a mother who has made the "risky" decision to consume alcohol while momming. The commenters mentioned above cry foul at the attempts of the social media community to layer shame and guilt on Johnson. Yet (and this is an important "yet"), they layer their own judgment on Johnson, offering their assessments of the rigor of her risk research and the Optimalness of her Mothering. The discourse operates as if Johnson needs the community's blessing to bring confidence to this—and perhaps future—maternal decision-making. But from where, or what, is the community drawing *their ethos*: community lore or communally constructed knowledge? "good data" from the CDC's "critical science"? viral mommy memes?

CONCLUSION

Thus far we have considered *ethos* in maternal decision-making for human actors in relationship to, for example, "good" data and the CDC's "critical science" or the social media mothering group community's insistence on what constitutes enough "research." We've also begun to broach the topic of techno-agents or nonhuman, object-oriented actants that become a persuasive force in parental discourse encounters, such as viral mommy wine culture memes or the visual rhetoric of a just-say-no-to-pregnancy-and-alcohol infographic. There's a ripe metaphor from Annemarie Mol that drives home the importance of considering the influence of such actants.

Mol talks about eating apples. Once one swallows the apple, the human actor loses direct control over what happens to that apple (that object actant). The body responds; digestion takes place: "The eating subject is able to choose what food she decides to eat, but after this point, her body decides how to deal with the components of the food, selecting certain elements and discarding others" (quoted in Lupton 2016, 3). A comparison between the ingestion of apples and the consumption of alcohol is begging to be made here, but, more importantly, we want the reader to note how this metaphor speaks to the ingestion of data, or techno-actants, and what agency, force, or influence they hold in and of themselves outside of human intervention: "So too, the digital data-human assemblages that are configured by human users' interactions with digital technologies are different versions of people's identities and bodies that have material effects on their ways of living and conceptualising themselves" (Lupton 2016, 3).

What we produce, consume, and circulate on social media creates and defines our identities and bodies—our parental identities and maternal bodies, in this case. It is an incredibly complex discourse context in which a host of social, cultural, political, historical, and *textual* nodes assemble and reassemble (at a remarkably fast pace) maternal decision-making meaning. It is our charge to explore and explicate these nodes to create perhaps radical, but inarguably necessary, change: render the fading visage of the mother visible, begin dismantling the myth of the Optimal Mother, and make room for normalized continuum decision-making experiences in the otherwise binary-bound narrative of contemporary motherhood in which good, but imperfect, mothers can exist.

Chapter 2, "Take Back the Delivery Room: Narrative Control, Traumatic Discourse, and the #MeToo Labor Movement," takes up another important node in this charge: querying the rhetorical force of birth plans and what's *not* being said in and around the delivery room.

2 TAKE BACK THE DELIVERY ROOM: NARRATIVE CONTROL, TRAUMATIC DISCOURSE, AND THE #METOO LABOR MOVEMENT

Twinkly lights. Peppermint oil. "Circle of Life," by Elton John.[1] What do these things have in common? They are all options on your extensive, easy-to-customize, downloadable birth plan.

The purveyors of such birth plans have good intentions: "Not only can a good birth plan deliver a *better birth experience*, it can also head off *unrealistic expectations, minimize disappointment,* and *eliminate major conflict and miscommunication* between a birth mom and her birth attendants. It's also a springboard for dialog between patient and practitioner" (What to Expect Editors 2019; emphasis added). Birth plans were created with the intention of offering pregnant women an optimal birth experience; in reality, birth plans seem to have accomplished just the opposite.

BUT, I HAD A PLAN . . .

A January 24, 2020, Google search for "birth plan template" brought up "about" 66,700,000 results in just over half a second. Birth plans, then, are readily available and (one would assume) relatively common in contemporary women's labor and birth preparation processes. But you wouldn't know it based on how often they are discussed on social media. "Birth plan" showed up less than an average of two times per month as a specific term in one group we searched. Given that the group has more than 50,000 members who communicate through two to three dozen original posts (not including comments) per day, and the prevalence of the term on Google, we found this absence surprising. When the term did arise, it was often from an original poster asking for good birth plan templates, or more often from an original poster inquiring about the efficacy of a particular approach to laboring or birthing (such as the pros and cons of induction or whether to use an epidural). In either case, group members resoundingly responded with words of caution. We felt that observing and documenting common themes would be revealing—and it was.

A common theme of caution was voiced about the unpredictability of laboring and birthing. Group members invoked passive-voice metaphors, suggesting the likelihood of birth plans being "thrown out the window." The use of passive voice is revealing because this form of sentence structure removes a subject (or actor) from the sentence. There is a difference between your supervisor saying "You have been tardy to work for many days in a row" and "There has been a problem of tardiness in the office." By using the passive voice, mothers posting their advice about birth plans to mothers-to-be rarely pointed fingers at themselves or at their medical practitioners; instead, they implied that labor and delivery evolves, and it will evolve with no particular actor or actant to champion or blame. When group members mentioned actors, mothers invoked "baby" and "body" as responsible for deviation from the birth plan. Consensus surrounded the idea that baby and body were in control of the labor and birth process, which would often *not be what* the laboring mother had written in her birth plan. In fact, baby and body (often mentioned together as a maternal-fetal dyad) were labeled as the actors responsible for making the birth plan null and void. We deliberately use legalistic rhetoric here because, indeed, some mothers mentioned such stringent commitment to their birth plans that they had them notarized well in advance of their due dates.

"Better Birth Experience"

Posters often related that they had a printed plan that represented their desires for the laboring and birthing process, but that reality intervened and they often ended up with the exact opposite of what they had written they wanted. Another common theme was mothers who had birthed two or more babies indicating that they had changed their approach for the second baby and had fared far "better." A complementary theme included mothers who had birthed (presumably) only one child who, after reflection, wished they had approached the context of using birth plans differently. For example, one poster invoked the desired "birth plan" versus the opposing "birth experience" binary in a telling way. The poster related having written a birth plan in preparation for laboring and birthing her first child. The process did not go as planned and, in fact, was the "total opposite" of what had been planned. In birthing her subsequent child, she opted *not* to create a birth plan. She labeled this experience not just better but "perfect," just what she had "wanted." Some labeled the experience of birthing sans birth plan as simply "fine," but, overall, the choice to "go with the flow" was commonly cited as resulting in a preferable birthing experience. There seems, then, fascinating moments of awareness in which mothers realize that by rejecting a "plan," they reject the possibility of any contingency being "opposed" to the plan—that is, by avoiding a plan they avoid the possibility that a birth will not go according to plan—and thereby circumvent the construction of their labor and delivery on a binary altogether. Yet, the predominance of birth plans remains, insisting, through its tantalizing illusion of control, on this binary.

"Unrealistic Expectations"

There's something to be said about veteran mom recommendations and the medium in which a birth plan is composed. That is, a birth plan, traditionally, is a word-based, print-based genre meant to help women regain control in the labor and birthing process—the word made flesh, if you will. This gives agency to a piece of paper, a scary thought if only because the genre doesn't add up to actionable outcomes, since, as moms note, the baby and the maternal body are in control of the birth process and are outside the mother's willpower (see "Analysis of a Birth Plan" later in this chapter). This assertion is supported by the veteran moms who posted about preferable second and subsequent birthing processes when they chose not to put their plans in writing. Posters either abdicated all control and "went with the flow" or chose to work cooperatively with medical practitioners by *orally* communicating their wants as the laboring process evolved. There are plenty of variables in individual birth experiences that might negate the effectiveness of oral communication of plans, wants, and other factors. The point here isn't to exalt one type of communication over another; the point is to suggest that pigeonholing our options for communicating birth plan desires into a preformed written document is, in fact, *setting up* unrealistic expectations rather than heading them off. As so many posters mentioned, their laboring and birthing processes did *not* go as their plans suggested they would.

"Minimize Disappointment"

Along with the overarching theme of birth plans setting up unrealistic expectations given the *un*predictability of birth, some specific descriptive keywords commonly surfaced in social media mommy group discussion of birth plans. Posters associated birth plans, and their execution (or lack thereof) in the delivery suite, with a new mom who is "upset," "depressed," and "stressed." These terms capture the complex emotions associated with the often-ironic outcomes of birth plans. That is, the drafting of a birth plan incubates the hope of a specific future bodily state; yet birth plans confound their own efforts, creating a sense of loss in a postpartum body that would know no such loss without having birthed such desires via the plan in the first place. Havi Carel, Ian James Kidd, and Richard Pettigrew (2016) addressed this phenomenon in the context of chronic illness or do-not-resuscitate plans, arguing that transformative bodily states themselves—because they transform us at the moment they occur—prevent us from actually knowing what we would want in that moment. Thus, they argue that it may well be considered unethical for doctors to encourage patients to predict what they might feel in a life-or-death scenario, which might—in its very occurrence—change the patient fundamentally and in ways unpredictable before this event. As they state,

> So, how does this change our view of informed consent, risk assessment, advance directives, and other decision-making junctures in a patient's health-care journey? How do you discuss possible future outcomes for a current patient, knowing full well that she may be quite a different person by the time these outcomes unfold? How can we ask a patient to choose a course of action in the present when we know that the future patient will be transformed by their illness experience in unanticipated ways? (1153)

While their article focuses more on diagnoses of chronic and life-threatening illnesses, Carel, Kidd, and Pettigrew in fact open their article with a thought experiment about the decision to become a parent, arguing that the unknowns of this identity transformation are similar. Beginning in the nineteenth century, obstetrics began to classify childbirth as inherently pathological (instead of natural) and imbued with risk that women could not handle without a physician. Since the idea of "taking back the birth room" through birth plans, among other things, developed out of this recognition, we would argue that the authors' discussion of physical illness is in fact hyper relevant. Ironically, in attempting to take back the birth room and recode parturition as a nonpathological state, birth plans have, in fact, fought against a binary by insisting on the other half of the binary. Unfortunately, this has only allowed the pathological coding of "failure" and the unattainable goal of Optimal Motherhood (even and especially through labor and delivery) to persist. As Audre Lorde (1983, 27) famously said, "The master's tools will never dismantle the master's house. They may allow us temporarily to beat him at his own game, but they will never enable us to bring about genuine change. And this fact is only threatening to those women who still define the master's house as their only source of support." As human beings, we get upset, depressed, and stressed when even trivial daily activities don't go as planned. Out of your favorite coffee creamer? Upset! Heavy traffic and worried you won't make it to the post office in time? Stressed! Imagine spending nine (or more) months envisioning bringing life into this world naturally and then being told you have no choice but to move forward with a fully medicated surgical birth. It's almost laughable. Laughable?

Strangely, or not so strangely, the idea that expecting your labor and delivery process to go "as planned" was marked by posters as "laughable." "LOL" often appeared in social media mommy group postings discussing birth plans, almost always next to the expression of the un/likelihood that birth plans would result in the mother's desired laboring and birthing experience. "LOL" was sprinkled into birth plan discussions, perhaps as a way to suggest that expectant mothers shouldn't take themselves and their birth plans too seriously, and at least one poster put her birth plan online explicitly for humorous spectacle. She began her post by suggesting that what the reader was about to engage with would, certainly, make them laugh and proceeded to display a visual image of her two-year-old birth plan. One might wonder whether this is an example of dark, cryptic humor or humor with a didactic purpose. The complementary phrasing of "mom lessons" used in the post would suggest the latter. That is, even when posters invoked "LOL" or other humor-laden verbiage, they often paired it with discourse suggesting that the experience, though laughable, carried an important lesson for soon-to-deliver moms: "You can't control everything." Interestingly, posters couched this challenge to moms-to-be as the *first* lesson of motherhood.

Birth plans, for these posters, set up the inherent expectation that a mom could maintain complete agency in her laboring and birthing process. Composing a birth plan falsely ensures that everything will go "right." While these posters helpfully pointed out that birth plans can construct a harmful "right/wrong" birthing binary, they created yet another harmful binary in the process: that embracing the idea of complete lack of agency, complete lack of control in one's motherhood journey, is the *only* way to succeed as mother, starting with delivery. Once again, commenters attempted to fight against a binary with another binary: women were depicted as either believing they had complete control in the birth room (via a birth plan) or accepting that they had *none*. Very rarely did we see discussions that, as with all things, there are some things one can control and some things one cannot. In the discussions we observed, no birth plan = no expectations = no stress = you understand the *first* lesson you need to learn as a mom, these posters seem to say. But we don't think oversimplifying in that direction is entirely prudent either. Consider the complexity inherent in the emojis (another form of text-becomes-flesh) commonly used in birth-plan-related threads in social media mommy groups: 😭 😂 😑.

Studies in neurology and communication have identified the primary use of an emoji as an attitude/emotional signifier or an emotional intensity enhancer, but, importantly, in ways that do not simply mirror in-person nonverbal cues but rather clarify text-based message intentionality, "compensating for the absence of nonverbal cues in written communication" (Li and Yang 2018, 1–2). We are particularly interested in the laughing-til-crying emoji and what we will term the "unamused" emoji (the one with the straight-line mouth and closed eyes). If these are the emojis primarily used in response to women's discussion of their birth plans, what might they be doing in *adding to* but not *mirroring* what a face-to-face interaction might look like? Certainly, the adage that people are more willing to be unkind in internet interactions likely influences these emoji choices—one is rarely met with mocking laughter in daily life, much less when discussing one's health plans with another. Of course, one has self-selected one's in-person friends much more intentionally than the acquaintances one encounters in a Facebook group that could be populated by thousands of members. Oddly, the humble emoji, then, seems to reveal the often-unhelpful group dynamics masquerading as supportive community that occur in social media mothering groups. As Luke Stark and Kate Crawford (2015, 1) put it, emojis can be seen as figures that "both embody and represent the tension between affect as human potential, and as a productive force that capital continually seeks to harness through the management of everyday biopolitics. Emoji are instances of a contest between the creative power of affective labor and its limits within a digital realm in the thrall of market logic."

As this chapter will outline, birth plans, often presented through proprietary templates from websites like The Bump, are imbricated in corporate branding and promotional practices. The communication of mommy-group judgment via emoji seems to reveal this tension through the unfortunate vehicle of mockery. Such mockery presumably demonstrates women's frustrations with a corporatized model of birth that is out of sync with biological realities; however, the narrow range of emotion afforded by emojis restricts the ways in which women might more effectively resist what they seem to see as already restricting, corporately provided birth plans. Stark and Crawford say it best when they explain that "emoji, like th[e] original smiley, are prophylactic—they help people in digital environments cope emotionally with the experience of building and maintaining social ties within hierarchical technological platforms and unjust economic systems that operate far outside of their control" (2015, 8). A woman's "unamused" emoji might depict—as much as a corporately developed schema of facial expressions can—her frustration with The Bump and other companies' offerings for women's supposed freedom of choice in their birth plans. It's easy to imagine a seasoned mom's growing annoyance upon realizing the "choice" offered by websites catering to expectant moms, in fact, hems in their birth experience by the very act of *urging them to choose* from a limited series of options. Yet, her very expression of "unamusement" is itself limited by these same corporate structures (the Emoji or even Bitmoji platforms), as well as the inability of the emoji itself to effect any real, productive discourse. For this reason, the emoji perhaps represents women's frustrating paradox of options-that-limit better than almost anything else. Not only can an "unamused" emoji do absolutely nothing to stand in the way of big data's representation of pregnancy choices, but it also—via the sheer ambiguousness and vagaries of emojis themselves—shuts down conversation as it opens the floodgates for assumptions of meaning or emoji-based retorts that further muddy the waters instead of allowing for productive conversation. As Ngai (2015) has noted, the problem with the emoji is that it masquerades as "sociability itself," when it is in fact simply another form of commodity production (quoted in Stark and Crawford 2015, 2). Thus, what may appear as a gentle means of expressing uncertainty (unamused face emoji) and also a means of resisting the strictures of birth plans is in fact a form of expression that caves even further to structures that limit women's language and ability to envision mechanisms outside of such structures. So much is lost through mere text-based messaging, the standard wisdom goes. And, while emojis might seem to add clarity where there once was obscurity, we would argue they only further obscure messages and, worse, shut down conversations. Thus, emojis in maternal health-care choice discussions leave by the wayside a space in which women might instead come *together* in rejection of what we will argue is merely a new mechanized binary of women's bodies. these tiny faces "'emit desire and identification with the affective ties of collegiality' even as the logic of capitalism constantly undercuts those social bonds" (Lauren Berlant, quoted in Stark and Crawford 2015, 8). Indeed, "emoji offer us more than just a cute way of 'humanizing' the platforms we inhabit: they also remind us of how informational capital continually seeks to instrumentalize, analyze, monetize, and standardize affect" (Stark and Crawford 2015, 8). To this end, in addition to discussing how birth plans themselves operate as corporate materials, we will also discuss how the birth room itself developed out of market concerns in the Jacksonian era. The solution, then, toward shirking all of these binaristic modalities will be more complex than merely reversing them.

"Eliminate Major Conflict and Miscommunication"

While a few posters seemed blessed to have had to change their plans only "a little" throughout the labor and delivery process, the most difficult posts to read were those referring to the significant intervention of a key node in the communication network of contemporary birth plans: medical practitioners. We say "difficult to read" because, in the context of birth plan discourse, medical practitioners were often not mentioned in these social media mommy groups. But when they were, they were not portrayed in a flattering light. One poster wrote that her practitioner consistently referred to her birth plan as a "wish list"; the poster went on to conclude that the practitioner was "right" because nothing went as planned. This example accords with contemporary medical rhetoric research. Amy Michelle DeBaets, for example, found that "staff members sometimes feel *hostile* toward women who have birth plans," "'patients' birth plans usually provoked some degree of annoyance,'" and, in one extreme case, a popular obstetrician blogger labeled the development of birth plans as "women . . . having 'tantrums' filled with 'ultimatums' given 'to defy authority'" (2016, 31; emphasis added). With such lack of trust—on both sides—it is no wonder that birth plans have not done much to "eliminate major conflict and miscommunication" or to serve as a "springboard for dialog" (What to Expect Editors 2019).

An interesting, if problematic, corollary came in the form of suggestions from members of social media mommy groups that even stories from veteran moms might not be particularly helpful. Oversharing is the way of the internet, and, therefore, posters cautioned moms-to-be that engaging with veteran moms' birth stories might *seem* "comforting" and "informational" but that doing so is not advisable since each birthing experience is unique. We are not to trust birth plans, we are not to trust doctors, and we are not to trust each other. So, who can we trust? After a brief history of how birth plans came to be, we will examine some good reasons why even the scary stuff (see "The First Rule of Birth Club Is Don't Talk about Birth Club" later in this chapter) is worth reckoning with if we are to better understand the complex communication network that informs the circulation of contemporary maternity advice.

HOW BIRTH PLANS CAME TO BE

Throughout history, the process of laboring and birthing (or "management" of labor and delivery) has shifted from female-dominated contexts to medically dominated hospital contexts (Hausman 2005, 33). This was particularly true in the United States, beginning as early as the 1850s, when the oversaturated physician pool required market expansion (Nixon 2017). This was in fact the impetus for the development of the field of obstetrics, the first-ever medical specialization (Nixon 2017). In order to gain control of this market, however, doctors had to force female midwives out of the birthing market, and they did so largely through promoting the idea that birthing was inherently pathological and required medical intervention (to this end, doctors brought tools such as forceps and various medicines to the table [Leavitt 1986; Nixon 2017; Wertz and Wertz 1989]). Doctors also embarked on very specific campaigns to discredit midwives as antiscientific and therefore unsafe (Leavitt 1986; Nixon 2017; Wertz and Wertz 1989). By the 1860s, no fashionable woman would have given birth without an obstetrician. Ironically, as obstetricians were increasingly prevalent in birthing rooms, so, too, was a fatal form of streptococcal infection (colloquially referred to as childbed fever). Data collected and informally observed by physicians, most famously Ignaz Semmelweis, suggested that doctors' unwashed hands were responsible for these deaths, but a great many doctors were outraged by the very suggestion that male authority was responsible for female death (Brodsky 2008; Bynum 1994; Wertz and Wertz 1989). The debates over this etiology were highly publicized and incredibly intense—in fact, they ultimately helped prove the accuracy of germ theory, and Semmelweis's name is to this day memorized by medical students the world over. In the 1860s, however, he was fired for the implications of his claims, demonstrating the heated nature of medical authority in the labor and delivery room from the very moment of its inception (Nixon 2017). In spite of Semmelweis's claims ultimately seeming to prove (at least by the 1900s) that doctors themselves were responsible for maternal mortality, the initial marketing campaign of obstetricians maintained its hold on the public's sense of risk, and pregnancy and childbirth nevertheless remained coded as inherently pathological, risky, and, most ironically, needful of physician-based authority to guarantee maternal safety.

Maternal and infant mortality, therefore, remained of great concern, and in the 1920s and 1930s, middle-class women started choosing hospitals over house calls more and more for a perceived "safe," science- and technology-supported laboring and birthing process (again, this in spite of the fact that "such claims were not well founded" [Hausman 2005, 34]). The 1940s and 1950s *did* see a slight decrease in maternal mortality with more prevalent interventions such as antibiotics, blood transfusions, and prenatal care (as well as a general tightening of regulations for obstetric practice within hospitals); however, that tightening resulted in an obsession with medical risk management throughout pregnancy and birth: "The represented risks of fetal injury or harm, however, continue to drive the medical management of pregnancy and childbirth *as well as to insure women's complicity with its norms*; the risk of doing damage to their babies (as well as fears of giving birth to babies already 'damaged') propels many women to demand highly technological and interventionist management of pregnancy and childbirth" (34). There is an important gender dynamic to note here given that males have long dominated the medical field; current statistics (as of March 2019) suggest that, of actively practicing physicians, 36 percent are female, and 64 percent are male (Kaiser Family Foundation 2019). Men were doing the management, and continue to do so, while women are being acted upon.[2]

The 1980s, and second-wave feminism, produced the genre of birth plans "as a response to pregnant women's sense of loss of agency in the birth process" (DeBaets 2016, 31). Focusing on issues of equality and discrimination, women tried to take back control in the delivery room (Drucker 2018). Because natural childbirth advocates were largely responsible for pushing birth plans into the public spotlight, medical practitioners tended to respond to the movement by couching it as "antiscientific" given its antagonism toward medical intervention (the discursive similarity here to 1860s-style antimidwifery campaigns is striking). The desired goal was to facilitate constructive communication between patients and practitioners, and the desired outcome was to avoid unnecessary interventions and help patients exercise informed consent, *but* historical birth plans tended to engender distrust on both sides of the patient-practitioner dynamic, as do contemporary birth plans today. Practitioners point out that birth plans tend to come in the form of checklists, with little to no guidance regarding "why one would choose to have or avoid [interventions]" and "how to have their values reflected in their care choices" (DeBaets 2016, 31). Practitioners also point out that such template-based forms tend to have "trivial" and "outdated" choices. The binary, then, comes in medical practitioners believing that time constraints in laboring and birthing necessitate an implicit reliance on the medical personnel's *ethos* ("time constraints warranted making decisions *for* women instead of going 'through the lengthy process of dialogue and negotiation to find a way to respect the women's wishes'") versus women who, through birth plans, "are seeking to exercise the same right to informed consent regarding medical interventions that all competent adult patients have" (31). Women are attempting to navigate the time-sensitive nature of labor and delivery decisions by writing out their wishes in advance, but the birth plan, as a genre and *as an actant*, undermines that potentially empowering move by paradoxically reinforcing the same binaries and power struggles that women have seen since the beginning of obstetrics.

ANALYSIS OF A BIRTH PLAN

Medical practitioners term the internet template birth plan a "patient-initiated birth plan" (Anderson et al. 2017). This is because the patient searches (most likely, the internet) for an extensive, easy-to-customize, and downloadable plan, template, or example from which to compose their desires for the laboring and birthing process. Whether one enters "birth plan," "birth plan template," "birth plan generator," "birth plan examples," or even "visual birth plan" into Dr. Google, the top result is a question from ViaCord: "Creating Your Birth Plan? | ViaCord Cord Blood Banking." One might expect no less in our neoliberal society that defines citizens as consumers, but two observations are worth mentioning before continuing the analysis of a typical patient-initiated birth plan: (1) if umbilical cord blood banking—an exorbitant procedure with few replicable, aggregable, and data-driven studies asserting its utility—wasn't previously on a pregnant woman's radar, it probably is now; (2) she may or may not realize that Google's algorithm is largely responsible for the presentation of her search results, and, therefore, her un/willingness to dive deeply into the search results says something of the *ethos* she affords it as a technological actor in her maternal decision-making process. That is, Google will present results (in this case, answers to women's medical questions) as *Google* prioritizes it—informed by a search algorithm designed to filter for "relevance" and "usefulness." These two words prioritize neoliberal efficiency but don't necessarily accord with the "credibility" and "authority" of a licensed medical practitioner or experienced parturient participant, two actors we assume would rise to the top of the list of likely credible sources of maternity advice.

But let's be practical. For the sake of said expediency (and the likelihood that the sleep-deprived pregnant woman does not have the energy or time to scroll through and deeply analyze the more than one billion results that surface upon googling "birth plan"), consider the first result *after* the ViaCord plan: "Writing a Birth Plan? There's a Tool for That," from The Bump editors. They suggest that there is "a lot to consider" and that their tool "breaks down all the key questions" and will "help you *get started*." We emphasize "get started" because the downloadable PDF is, notably, six pages long (The Bump, n.d.). The "easy fill-in-the-blank" birth plan is labeled as useful for delivery preparation and communication of wants and needs. A space for demographic details is followed by a small box for critical medical information (such as group B strep status, Rh in/compatibility, and gestational diabetes). Critical medical information is juxtaposed against a global desires box, a checkbox list if you will, that reads: "My delivery is planned as

☐ Vaginal
☐ C-section
☐ Water birth
☐ VBAC"

Prioritizing crucial medical information by placing it near the top of the birth plan accords with productive document design: make the most important information easily accessible by locating it near the top left of the draft, where a Western audience (inherently trained to read documents left to right, top to bottom) will look first. It might seem that placing global desires in this same relative position also makes sense for that reason, yet this move might undermine good intentions by playing to readers' preconceived notions of what a "vaginal," "C-section," "water birth," or "VBAC [vaginal birth after cesarean]" labor and delivery could and *should* look like rather than encouraging the reader to look more carefully at the individual items that follow. Digital natives and time-pressed professionals alike are accustomed to scanning documents in an "F" pattern: starting at the top left, taking in headlines across to the top right, moving back to the left and down until another headline or "important bit" of information catches their eye, and scanning briefly across again to the right. Scanners then tend to, time permitting, skim the rest of the page for information predetermined as important—or stop the reading task altogether (Moyers 2017).

Given that medical practitioners share digital natives' concern with time and the confirmation bias inherent in all human beings, it is not a stretch to suggest that after reaching box 4 in figure 2.1, they will begin making decisions regarding the actualization of the pregnant woman's birth plan—decisions that privilege their prior medical knowledge,[3] especially after assessing the medical authority and credibility (or lack thereof) of (1) The Bump (from the Knot), (2) clip art in a "professional" document, (3) the curtailing of medical history, and (4) the invisible best practices associated with the listed large-scale frameworks for birthing.

In concert, we need to examine the diction of the individual itemized choices that follow. Remaining boxes are largely dominated by language of "I would *like*":

"During labor I'd like . . . □ Music played (I will provide)"
"For pain relief, I'd like to use: . . . □ Distraction";
"I'd like my partner: □ To have unlimited visiting"

Presumably, "like" is a means to demurely acquiesce to the medical practitioner's expertise; these are merely the laboring woman's requests rather than her demands. The connotation of the word "like" in conjunction with the

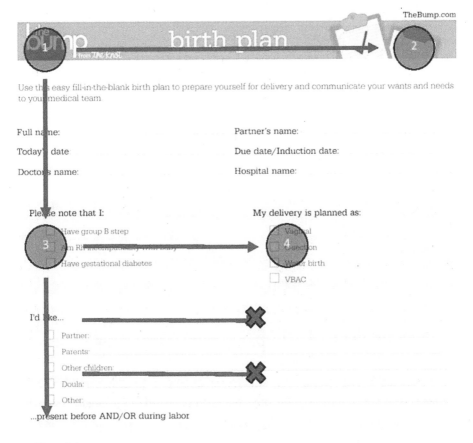

Figure 2.1
Birth plan.
Source: Modified from The Bump (n.d.).

sheer number of things "I'd like" presented in this birth plan, however, tends to negate the rhetorical goals of those individual requests and, consequently, the ultimate outcome of laboring women taking back control of (or at least exerting due agency in) the delivery room. Figure 2.2, for example, outlines seventeen options for pain relief. Putting ourselves in the shoes of the medical practitioner, the actor who is most directly responsible for actualizing the birth plan document, we find we are not likely to debate the merits of the seventeen options and that the chance of the birth plan acting in the woman's favor is undeniably attached to the practitioner's preconceived understanding

For pain relief I'd like to use:

- [ ] Acupressure
- [ ] Acupuncture
- [ ] Breating techniques
- [ ] Cold therapy
- [ ] Demerol
- [ ] Distraction
- [ ] Hot therapy
- [ ] Hypnosis
- [ ] Massage

- [ ] Meditation
- [ ] Reflexology
- [ ] Standard epidural
- [ ] TENS
- [ ] Walking epidural
- [ ] Nothing
- [ ] Only what I request at the time
- [ ] Whatever is suggested at the time

Figure 2.2
Birth plan: box 5, page 2.
Source: Modified from The Bump (n.d.).

of best practices in delivery care. Even the less passively phrased requests are still laced with ruthlessly polite language: "Please don't give baby" and "As needed post-delivery, please give me."

Besides being a lengthy document and literally putting women's choices into "polite" boxes, this sample birth plan contains some additionally revealing rhetorical choices worth examining. Presence of supporting personnel is presented as an "and/or" choice for prelabor and active labor rather than separated out as postlabor permitted guest decisions are. This is another example where the care of the infant seems to be privileged over that of the mother given that crowd control is broken down in a nuanced way according to time and place of baby's arrival (e.g., "immediately after delivery," "only in the nursery") but articulated as an "and/or" for the mother's time of preparation and pushing.

Figure 2.3 shows that music and lighting choices are lumped together in the same checkbox as things such as "As few vaginal exams as possible." This seems problematic given the physical invasiveness of vaginal exams versus the possible impact of pleasing environmental choices like music or lighting. While we might argue that music and lighting absolutely can and do affect the well-being of the mother in the act of labor and delivery, we

During labor I'd like...

- ☐ Music played (I will provide)
- ☐ The lights dimmed
- ☐ The room as quiet as possible
- ☐ As few interruptions as possible
- ☐ As few vaginal exams as possible
- ☐ Hospital staff limited to my own doctor and nurses (no students, residents or interns present

- ☐ To wear my own clothes
- ☐ To wear my contact lens the entire time
- ☐ My partner to film AND/OR take pictures
- ☐ My partner to be present the entire time
- ☐ To stay hydrated with clear liquids & ice chips
- ☐ To eat and drink as approved by my doctor

Page 1 of 6

Figure 2.3
Birth plan: box 4, page 1.
Source: Modified from The Bump (n.d.).

must recognize the seriously vulnerable position of the woman in labor, who must trust her medical practitioner to not put her in a physically precarious position that could lead to sexual abuse and/or a traumatic birth experience. In yet another example of problematic organizational choices, outdated labor and delivery interventions, such as "an enema" and "shaving of my pubic area," receive, design-wise, prime placement in the upper-right corner of the second page of the birth plan template. Both of these examples leave the woman placing her hope in the birth plan's unrealistic portrayal regarding what her imminent birthing experience *could* look like.

The sample birth plan document is rife with such confusing conjecture. The presence of the "I will bring . . ." box suggests that birthing institutions typically do not offer access to birthing stools, birthing chairs, squatting bars, and birthing tubs. In fact, the availability of particular tools, which speaks to the un/willingness of particular institutions and/or practitioners to work with the mother-to-be for an individualized birthing experience, varies widely. For a template birth plan to suggest that a woman *must* bring a particular birthing tool of choice sets up inevitable confrontation: the woman brings the tool and is told she cannot use it, or the woman brings the tool and is chastised for bringing unnecessary equipment / not trusting her doctor, or the woman is persuaded (by the birth plan document) *not* to broach the subject of bringing such tools in order to avoid confrontation altogether.

In figure 2.4, the section titled "As the baby is delivered" offers choices such as "Use whatever methods my doctor deems necessary" and "Let my partner catch the baby." This example of total acquiescence to the medical practitioner versus a firm desire for prime participation by the parenting bodies is repeated throughout the document. The problem is largely that there is little nuance in the continuum of such choices, and when two extremes are juxtaposed in proximity, it is more likely to cause confusion than it is to result in the outcomes favored by the birth plan author (mother-to-be) or the birth plan actualizer (the medical practitioner). Similarly, there is redundancy in large-scale choices. There are boxes for both "I would like to breastfeed" and "I'd like to feed baby" (figure 2.5). The choices are *not* identical in these boxes, and it is possible that a mother-to-be may inadvertently check off conflicting or otherwise competing desired choices.

As the baby is delivered, I would like to:

- [ ] Push spontaneously
- [ ] Push as directed
- [ ] Push without time limits, as long as the baby and I are not at risk
- [ ] Use a mirror to see the baby crown
- [ ] Touch the head as it crowns
- [ ] Let the epidural wear off while pushing
- [ ] Have a full dose of epidural
- [ ] Avoid forceps usage
- [ ] Avoid vacuum extraction
- [ ] Use whatever methods my doctor deems necessary
- [ ] Help catch the baby
- [ ] Let my partner catch the baby
- [ ] Let my partner suction the baby

I would like an episiotomy:

- [ ] Used only after perineal massage, warm compresses and positioning
- [ ] Rather than risk a tear
- [ ] Not performed, even if it means risking a tear
- [ ] Performed only as a last resort
- [ ] Performed as my doctor deems necessary
- [ ] Performed with local anesthesia
- [ ] Performed by pressure, without local anesthesia
- [ ] Followed by local anesthesia for the repair

Page 3 of 6

Figure 2.4
Birth plan: boxes 3 and 4, page 3.
Source: Modified from The Bump (n.d.).

Perhaps it is obvious, then, why some practitioners criticize patient-initiated birth plans: "(a) Parents sometimes become inflexible and difficult when changes, no matter how small, to their plan are necessary or (b) birth plans often contain outdated, useless, or defensive-sounding information" (Kaufman 2007, 47). If birth plans are not helping parents maintain a usefully flexible and contemporarily well-informed agency in the labor and delivery process, then where do we go from here?

BREAKING DOWN THE BIRTH PLAN BINARY

We've outlined a binary that pits pregnant women and internet-*ethos*-laden birth plans against practitioners with medical expertise but little patience for engaging individualized birthing experiences. We've tracked how birth plans are often digitally circulated and crowdsourced in social media interfaces but not always directly with care providers. We've detailed history that shows that even though birth plans were created as a tool for negotiating birth decisions with a pregnant woman's immediate care team, larger networked actants in the creation of birth plan discourse can transform the delivery room into a problematic battleground where women "lose" when delivery processes don't go according to plan. This doesn't mean, however, that birth plans should be dismissed as a potentially empowering actant in the negotiation of *ethos* in contemporary maternity decision-making. Research at the crossroads of medicine and rhetoric points promisingly to "standardized birth plans," "discussion birth plan—hospital birth plan" continuums, and "birth partnerships."

Standardized Birth Plans

According to Anderson et al. (2017, 305) "standardized birth plans" are "designed by health care providers to present women with a standard series of questions that allow them to delineate their wishes for labor and delivery." This puts primary authorship in the hands of those most directly responsible for actualizing the plan, ensuring that included options are available at the pregnant woman's facility of choice and affording a platform for discussion that is more likely to result in connection rather than tension. It also

birth plan

Immediately after delivery, I would like:

- ☐ My partner to cut the umbilical cord
- ☐ The umbilical cord to be cut only after it stops pulsating
- ☐ To bank the cord blood
- ☐ To donate the cord blood

- ☐ To deliver the placenta spontaneously and without assistance
- ☐ To see the placenta before it is discarded
- ☐ Not to be given Pitocin/oxytocin

If a C-section is necessary, I would like:

- ☐ A second opinion
- ☐ To make sure all other options have been exhausted
- ☐ To stay conscious
- ☐ My partner to remain with me the entire time
- ☐ The screen lowered so I can watch baby come out

- ☐ My hands left free so I can touch the baby
- ☐ The surgery explained as it happens
- ☐ An epidural for anesthesia
- ☐ My partner to hold the baby as soon as possible
- ☐ To breastfeed in the recovery room

I would like to hold baby:

- ☐ Immediately after delivery
- ☐ After suctioning
- ☐ After weighing
- ☐ After being wiped clean and swaddled
- ☐ Before eye drops/ointment are given

I would like to breastfeed:

- ☐ As soon as possible after delivery
- ☐ Before eye drops/ointment are given
- ☐ Later
- ☐ Never

I would like my family members:
(names:)

- ☐ To join me and baby immediately after delivery
- ☐ To join me and baby in the room later

- ☐ Only to see baby in the nursery
- ☐ To have unlimited visiting after birth

Page 4 of 6

Figure 2.5
Birth plan: pages 4 and 5.
Source: Modified from The Bump (n.d.).

birth plan

I would like baby's medical exam & procedures:

- [ ] Given in my presence
- [ ] Given only after we've bonded
- [ ] Given in my partner's presence
- [ ] To include a heel stick for screening tests beyond the PKU
- [ ] To include a hearing screening test
- [ ] To include a hepatitis B vaccine

Please don't give baby:

- [ ] Vitamin K
- [ ] Antibiotic eye treatment
- [ ] Sugar water
- [ ] Formula
- [ ] A pacifier

I'd like baby's first bath given:

- [ ] In my presence
- [ ] In my partner's presence
- [ ] By me
- [ ] By my partner

I'd like to feed baby:

- [ ] Only with breastmilk
- [ ] Only with formula
- [ ] On demand
- [ ] On schedule
- [ ] With the help of a lactation specialist

I'd like baby to stay in my room:

- [ ] All the time
- [ ] During the day
- [ ] Only when I'm awake
- [ ] Only for feeding
- [ ] Only when I request

I'd like my partner:

- [ ] To have unlimited visiting
- [ ] To sleep in my room

If we have a boy, a circumcision should:

- [ ] Be performed
- [ ] Not be performed
- [ ] Be performed later

- [ ] Be performed with anesthesia
- [ ] Be performed in the presence of me AND/OR my partner

Figure 2.5

(continued)

produces textual evidence a priori of physician buy-in to a birth plan, as it is the health-care provider who presents a list of options to the woman. We suggest that beginning from a position of physical evidence of health-care provider buy-in may also lead to *maternal* buy-in in trusting her physician, who has made the first move in bridging the communication-practice gap. A birth plan that is two pages in length (and can be completed in less than ten minutes) and that avoids annoyance-inducing phrases such as "unless absolutely or medically necessary"[4] creates a communicative context that is more universally applicable—accommodating for those new to the birthing process and useful for those with years of experience at either end of the pushing/catching delivery continuum. Anderson et al. suggest that additional study is needed but that they "found statistically significant increases in scores for satisfaction, communication, and trust after delivery" in a test of the standardized birth plan with educationally and culturally diverse women presenting for obstetric care in Honolulu, Hawaii (305, 307). While the standardized birth plan may be read as constraining in its developmental and temporal confines, we would argue that the choices presented are at least more straightforward in that they are realistically possible at the given birthing facility, which has already signed on to the document. Conversely, the corporately constructed birth plan may lead a woman to believe she has choices that will not, in fact, be honored by an independent set of health-care providers. To further engage the standardized birth plan as a potential for increased maternal satisfaction, Kaufman (2007) encourages stakeholders to consider birth plans a "live" document.

Discussion Birth Plans—Hospital Birth Plans

Kaufman (2007) re-visions birth plans not as static, binary documents that either succeed or fail when measured against birth experiences and delivery outcomes but as a living continuum: discussion birth plans working in concert with hospital birth plans. Birth plans will accomplish what birth plans are supposed to accomplish, Kaufman argues, if we think of them "as an evolving document that requires information gathering, reflection on beliefs about birth, and ongoing discussion" (47). This accords with Carel, Kidd, and Pettigrew's (2016) theories of epistemic transformation through life-changing experiences and makes room for such change, if it occurs.

The "discussion birth plan" is a "communication tool" that encourages expectant parents to explore health-care choices and resources and to discuss questions with practitioners in a timely manner and, more importantly, in a way that practitioners will listen. Kaufman (2007) suggests that a child-birth educator is particularly well equipped to assist expectant parents in developing appropriate research and communication skills that will produce a "birth philosophy" (48) likely to be taken seriously by the care provider. This includes not only investigating a comprehensive list of interventions and options as a starting point for expectant parents' research efforts (49), but also enhancing expectant parents' respect and self-confidence so that they can realistically determine "whether their beliefs, values, and view-points . . . match their care provider's approach. . . . Parents have the time to determine whether they can adjust their desires, whether the care provider can adjust his/her practice, or whether they need to consider finding another care provider" (50). Although there are few specific details regarding what the communicative coaching looks like, it is a key node in contemporary maternity decision-making, one bolstered by childbirth educator *ethos* and one that is not inherently in force in the typical internet-harvested birth plan. Indeed, since it is a new form of eschewing binaristic control of women's bodies—one that upends 160 years of birthing history—we might expect it to be inchoate as of yet. What's more, its vaguely formed notions, as we have shown, may very well be the key to its success at circumventing binaries.

Kaufman's (2007) "hospital birth plan" looks and feels much like a pre-cursor to Anderson et al.'s (2017) "standardized birth plan." It is, intuitively enough, "the document presented to the health-care staff upon admission to the hospital" (Kaufman 2007, 50). The hospital birth plan is a synthesis of the discussion birth plan, a one-page, bulleted-list version of that discussion birth plan, because "a shorter, more concise birth plan for the nursing staff is more likely to be read and remembered" (50). The bulleted-list format forces expectant parents to prioritize what is most important—avoiding redundancy while clarifying the intersection of their beliefs, best evidence, and available options (52). While a bulleted list might seem to pin down and otherwise limit flexibility, our research has demonstrated that its simplicity paradoxically allows for more conceptual flexibility and avoids potential constructions of if-then failure-success binaries (either you are making decisions in accordance with the illusive Optimal Motherhood or you are not). The discussion birth plan to hospital birth plan communication-informed continuum ensures that the potentially contentious work is done before the birth (51) and that expectant parents are well equipped to function as educated, assertive, and respectful patients. Of most importance to this book, we emphasize Kaufman's assertion that "birth plans may not influence immediate change in care practices; however, over time, they may help increase women's real choices" (52). The delivery room is a complex communicative context where literal life-altering decisions are made, and the birth plan *can* be a productive actant for the life bearers involved, circumventing its binary trap by acknowledging the dynamic variables involved. DeBaets (2016) captures those dynamic variables in her discussion of "birth partnerships."

Birth Partnerships

DeBaets (2016, 31) criticizes traditional (checklist, sans decision-making guidance) birth plans as unidirectional. A "birth partnership," on the other hand, "can build trust and facilitate constructive 2-way communication and shared decision-making between patient and obstetric care provider" (32). DeBaets outlines five key ways that birth partnerships differ from traditional birth plans:

1. Birth partnerships privilege *ongoing* conversation, both before and during the birth process.[5]
2. Birth partnerships hold practitioners accountable to proactively provide patients with "high-quality, evidence-based sources."
3. Birth partnerships also hold practitioners accountable to do "conversation work" that engenders trust, and to generally be trustworthy and respectful in all encounters with patients.
4. Birth partnerships ensure that care providers are up-to-date on current interventions and work as a team to offer interventions as necessary rather than as a convenience.
5. Birth partnerships ask patients and providers to work together on "a short list of key preferences and exceptions" that may be quickly shared with all team members in the event unfamiliar providers enter into a woman's birthing experience. (32–33)

DeBaets consistently calls on medical practitioners to take ownership of the failure of traditional birth plans and their part in reinscribing the damaging narrative of Optimal Motherhood as crowning maternal achievement: "Obstetric care providers who are willing to talk with their patients, to educate them on what options are available and consistent with each other, and to take the time to listen to the patient's values and concerns can practice effective prevention of many of the conflicts that arise" (33). As refreshing as this may seem to the parturient woman who doesn't feel listened to, we must return our attention to what is arguably the more prevalent locus of day-to-day mommy-to-be talk and the circulation of birth plan/discourse: social media.

What we can take from all of this is that research, information sharing, and general communication in a woman's preparation for birth is a good thing, but when and how we communicate about these things, and from whom we take advice, absolutely matter. Most importantly, we cannot and should not erase the potential power held by social media mommy groups and their discourse on birth experiences. When expectant mothers feel they have lost control over their impending birthing experience, a loss that is often exacerbated by internet communities' input of perhaps irrational or at least unrealistically "perfect birth" plan components, it can negatively affect a mother's confidence in her future parenting choices. In fact, women are already starting to recognize the repressive effects of *not* talking about the difficult, dirty, or downright traumatizing aspects of laboring and birthing.

FIRST RULE OF BIRTH CLUB IS DON'T TALK ABOUT BIRTH CLUB

Amanda Bacon's July 6, 2016, "Motherhood uncensored" Facebook post was positively viral, with 602,000 "likes," 181,000 "comments," and 184,000 "shares." In the photo's foreground, a new father (Bacon's husband) smiles proudly, cradling his sleeping newborn and offering a thumbs-up. Bacon stands in the background facing the window, in front of a tray of hospital food. Most noticeably, she is sans shirt but fully decked out in hospital-grade postpartum mesh panties and a mom diaper. The caption reads as follows:

> I'm sharing this picture because it's real. This is motherhood; it's raw, stunning, messy, and freaking hilarious all rolled into one. Having a baby is a beautiful experience, and the realities of postpartum life aren't spoken enough about. And definitely not photographed enough. Some people probably find this uncomfortable, but why? I seriously don't get it! It's probably because this part isn't talked about. We all should try and educate, empower and embrace every aspect of childbirth, including moments like this. And do it while having a sense of humor. Nothing says welcome to motherhood like an adorable squishy baby, and a giant mom diaper. 😊
>
> Edit. I posted this picture. Not my husband.
>
> http://www.facebook.com/bitsobaconblog

In photographic terms, the rule of thirds demands we give our viewing attention to the, as Bacon calls it, "giant mom diaper." But we don't have to embrace photographic frameworks to know why Bacon's post held our cultural attention: the less flattering realities of the birthing experience are *not* typical media fodder (or typical fodder for face-to-face mom-friend conversations, for that matter). This is further demonstrated by the 2020 media buzz regarding ABC's decision not to air Frida Mom's postpartum recovery ad during the Oscars. The ad featured a new mom who struggles to use the bathroom in the middle of the night but is aided by products meant to help in this precarious time of postpartum need (including mesh underwear that are invisible to the media but pervasive in the birthing experience). In response to the banning, a chorus of women began using social media platforms to call for the normalization of women's bodily experiences in media (Carter 2020). Like viral sensation Amanda Bacon—who implores "We all should try and educate, empower, and embrace every aspect of childbirth, including moments like this"—celebrity Busy Phillips, among others, suggests that the uncomfortable aspects of childbirth deserve attention and involve choices that an expectant mother should be educated about. By not acknowledging the uncomfortable aspects, we further entrench the unrealistic binary that there is a right (pleasant—perfect, even) and a wrong (ugly and uncomfortable) birthing experience. The unpleasant moments need to be communicated in this complex continuum if we are ever to reach the empowerment goals that anchored the birth plan movement.

THE #METOO LABOR MOVEMENT

Above and beyond imagery of mesh diapers and padsicles, women are discouraged from sharing traumatic birth stories—especially stories that involve abuse or assault at the hands of care providers who have actively chosen to ignore a patient's birth plan or who otherwise acted in the moment of labor and delivery upon the mother's body without the mother's consent. These women are quietly but adamantly silenced by social media first-time mommy group administrators who condemn the posting of anything "disturbing" or "controversial." In fact, while many social media mommy groups ban both "judgment" and "controversy" in their ground rules (to which you must agree to remain in the group), it seems only "controversy" is universally silenced.

Consider, however, what we learn about the empowering potential of circulating "controversial" parturient narratives from Evelyn Yang, who revealed she was sexually assaulted by her ob-gyn while pregnant (Bash et al. 2020). Yang detailed a troubling practitioner-patient relationship in which her ob-gyn began asking her unnecessarily sexualized questions, followed by longer, more frequent, and seemingly irrelevant medical examinations. It culminated with a last-minute, ungloved examination that she could not deny was sexual assault. Despite the potential trauma inherent in revisiting one's experience of sexual assault, Yang felt it was important to speak up: "'Everyone has their own MeToo story. It's far too prevalent,' Yang added. 'But not everyone can tell their story. Not everyone has the audience or platform to tell their story, and I actually feel like I'm in this very privileged position to be able to do that.'" Yang's position as the wife of a presidential nominee candidate enabled her to bring some justice to a sexual predator and to empower women to speak up as one step in their journey toward healing from perinatal sexual abuse. In the context of our work, we must ask the question: to speak up *where*? If social media mommy group ground rules against discussing "controversial" topics are enforced to *not* scare moms-to-be, is there any place for stories like Yang's? How might social media discourse and the circulation of traumatic birth stories possibly help heal the gap in patient-practitioner communication that birth plans set out to close some forty years ago?

Samantha Wallace (2020) offers us hope by extending our understanding of the social media #MeToo movement. #MeToo was founded by activist and sexual harassment survivor Tarana Burke (2018). Burke first used the hashtag on Myspace in 2006 to raise awareness of the pervasiveness of sexual harassment and assault in today's society. If you are unfamiliar with #MeToo, you might visit Samantha Bee's YouTube review, a popularly accessible source that engages with the movement's founder in a productive way.[6] Wallace adds to the #MeToo conversation by asking us to consider #MeToo in light of the rhetoric of certainty.

Wallace (2020) prefaces her work with three foundational claims: (1) "Listening to survivors is a good idea," (2) "language is both a tool for articulating one's experience and a system that organizes knowledge and how we come to know it," and (3) "language is also a site of social struggle" (1–2). Which narratives are allowed in societal discourse, and how they enter societal discourse, necessarily shapes our understanding and de/valuing of the subject of those narratives as well as their authors. #MeToo is a particularly powerful discourse move because hashtags, in and of themselves, create a socially constructed community, affording agency to those who perceive themselves to be part of a particular (marginalized) group. "Too" further constructs that community as an affirmative response in kind (it happened to me, *too*) (2). "Me" serves as an actor, the object to whom something (sexual violence) has been done but who, through the act of speaking up, regains their subject position and power (3). Through "declarative, affirmative language," it provides survivors an opportunity to express experiences "authoritatively, straightforwardly. That is *without qualification*" (4). It grammatically, formally, rhetorically, and epistemically constructs a solid survivor *ethos* (4).

While Wallace (2020) makes the case that there is power in the testimonial certainty afforded to sexual abuse survivors invoking #MeToo, she asks that we complicate our interpretation of the #MeToo movement and explore the ways in which it productively makes room for "uncertainty": "Reading for uncertainty pursues accounts that might not correlate with existing templates for stories of sexual violence, including those that exist in marginalized or fringe areas. Theorizing uncertainty opens up space for complexities, ambiguities, and incongruities within these accounts" (6). "Reading for uncertainty," then, asks us to pay attention to stories like those of Evelyn Yang, who suffered abuse at the hands of her prenatal care provider while she was pregnant—stories that don't necessarily fit into the dominant mode of rape culture (3).

Wallace (2020) compares the "uncertain" employment of #MeToo with Swedish-based #talkaboutit (#prataomdet): using autobiographical stories to raise awareness of "grey experiences" (7). Grey experiences are "indeterminate, negative, predominantly (hetero)sexual situations residing in a continuum from consent to assault" (7). The #talkaboutit campaign calls attention to the complexities inherent in these preponderant grey encounters and our inability (unwillingness) to make sense of them because the discourse used to define and describe them does not align with the "standard" (black and white) narratives of sex, violence, trauma, and healing (7). The risk in embracing uncertainty is in dismantling a certain (socially accepted) survivor *ethos*; the benefit, however, is in empowering those in grey area purgatory to tell their stories, to create a *nuanced* discussion of sexual and gender-based dialogue that includes complicated birth stories. Sharing such complicated stories provides a benefit to the survivor by "experiencing caring by being listened to and acknowledged, a sense of belonging, letting go, making sense of it all, being empowered, helping other women, and providing a voice" (Beck 2006, 454). It also may prevent future mothers-to-be from having to distraughtly muse: "To care for me: Was that too much to ask?; To communicate with me: Why was this neglected? To provide safe care: You betrayed my trust and I felt powerless; and The end justifies the means: At whose expense? At what price?" (454).

At what price, indeed.

CONCLUSION: THERE'S NOTHING BINARY ABOUT BIRTHING

That we accept that women's suffering as an immutable fact—like the weather—that we cannot control but can only predict, is the very thing that makes women seem hysterical and overreacting when we speak up about it. But we're not. And when you don't listen to us, we're not the only ones who pay the price. Our national failure to take women seriously is a public health crisis. (Friedman 2020)

This chapter has delineated that there is nothing binary about birthing, that un/consciously pitting women against medical practitioners in our discourse does nothing to further health objectives for parturient mothers or soon-to-be-delivered babies, and that making space for media circulation of always complicated and sometimes troubling birth narratives means moving our maternal knowledge forward in difficult but productive ways. Yet, delivery room expectations and experiences are only one of the binary-bound parental decision-making contexts in which women with narratives defying the romanticization of birth and the glory of new motherhood are silenced. Chapter 3, "We Have Never Been Normal: Postmodern Postpartum Experiences and Their Discontents," takes on the problematically employed code of silence surrounding postpartum depression.

3 WE HAVE NEVER BEEN NORMAL: POSTMODERN POSTPARTUM EXPERIENCES AND THEIR DISCONTENTS

"Irresolvable stress can lead to depression."

"Knowing that you are doing a good job is important for coping with stress."

"Unfortunately, such recognition is not often expressed."

"Their decisions can endanger human lives."

While these quotations come from a story covering an *Environmental Health* study of pilots and workplace health (Schmidt 2016), they could easily be attributed to the working world of the new mom. Preparations begin *at least* sixty to ninety minutes before the day's first departure, perhaps with some small talk but most definitely with the hashing out of—or intense negotiations through—what the day will hold for "the crew." Then there's the assessment of the physical environment and mental work of documenting things that need to be addressed. (There's some nonessential disorder, but the day must go on.) There's probably some ruminating on what went wrong yesterday, but, simultaneously, the challenges of present weather conditions must be accounted for in how they might affect the day's plans. Then there's the additional (over)preparing for obstacles that might be met along the way.[1] And that's just "preparing for takeoff": "The goal is to get everyone and everything lined up to attain that all-important on-time departure" (McFly 2016). But there are no on-time departures in the precarious work of parenting tiny human life. The cargo is far more complex—and ultimately unpredictable.

The *Deutsche Welle* story relates that around 12.6 percent of pilots in the study evidenced signs of depression. According to the Cleveland Clinic

(2018), 50–75 percent of new moms experience "baby blues" and up to 15 percent experience a "more severe and longer-lasting depression." Fifteen to 75 percent is a significant leap and invites scrutiny of the classification systems defining depression.

The Cleveland Clinic (2018) defines "postpartum blues" or "baby blues" as a condition that begins one to four days after delivery, comprising "frequent, prolonged bouts of crying for no apparent reason, sadness, and anxiety." Treatment is described as follows: "All you'll need is reassurance and help with the baby and household chores."

"Postpartum depression" (PPD), on the other hand, is "far more serious." "There will be 'highs' and 'lows,' frequent crying, irritability, and fatigue, as well as feelings of guilt, anxiety, and inability to care for your baby or yourself." PPD can begin days or even up to a year or more after delivery. Recommended treatment includes psychotherapy or antidepressants (Cleveland Clinic 2018).

There's also "postpartum psychosis" (notably depicted in the film *Tully* [IMDb 2018]). Postpartum psychosis is defined as a severe form of PPD. Onset and duration of symptoms mirrors that of PPD, though they may also include "severe agitation, confusion, feelings of hopelessness and shame, insomnia, paranoia, delusions or hallucinations, hyperactivity, rapid speech or mania." Hospitalization and treatment with medication are recommended (Cleveland Clinic 2018).

In addition to those postpartum disorders already mentioned, a small number of new mothers may experience postpartum obsessive-compulsive disorder, postpartum post-traumatic stress disorder, or postpartum/peripartum bipolar disorder, well described by the Anxiety and Depression Association of America (2018).

It is particularly noteworthy that the early symptoms of the more concerning postpartum disorder—PPD—are, in reality, nearly indistinguishable from the "baby blues" that the majority of new moms experience in the first few weeks after delivery. The binary we seek to complicate in this chapter is just that: "simple" baby blues versus "serious" PPD, or, in other words, the binary construction of the classifications of a "normal" postpartum state versus a "nonnormal" mental and emotional aberration. This binary constructs an unforgiving theoretical line that new moms are warned not to cross. Yet, we argue that in real-world maternal experience, the chaotic feeling of postpartum sadness is a *normal* outcome of labor and delivery: because *nothing* is "normal" in the postpartum period—it is a period of constant mental, emotional, and physical change. As detailed in our pregnancy-risk chapter (chapter 1, "It Was Never about the Coffee"), it is this very dynamic of the constantly changing body that both makes it impossible to map onto black-and-white binaristic systems and represents risk and uncertainty because of this "in-betweenness" that *is* pregnancy. Thus, the overly simplified diagnostic systems of psychiatric medicine will necessarily fall short of capturing the ever-changing state of the postpartum mind-body as it works to reestablish its own baseline "nonpregnant" state. Yet, there is a real need to help women who are in subjective distress or moments of crisis. Where, then, is the happy medium in a classificatory system that can helpfully direct women to the appropriate resources yet can still allow for the *natural* and *normal* fluidity of the postpartum woman?

We encourage normalizing that continuum of postpartum feelings and behaviors because, indeed, postpartum maternal decision-making can cost human lives. The diagnostic binary of "normal" baby blues sadness versus "abnormal" PPD reinforces mental health stigma. New moms want to be labeled "normal"—not "mentally ill"—and will sub/consciously approach postpartum discussion and diagnostic medical visits with the aim of circumventing such labels at the cost of receiving help that could improve her and her baby's quality of life. Because PPD includes symptoms such as "inability to care for your baby or yourself" as well as a "hopelessness" that could lead to suicide or infanticide, it's well worth analyzing the network of nodes affecting the discourse surrounding these diagnostic practices, including how such diagnostic tests themselves feed into this problematic postpartum binary.

IS IT MORE THAN BABY BLUES?

The Cleveland Clinic (2018), as is common with other health-care organizations in neoliberal societies, inherently puts the onus on the suffering new mother to recognize potential mental health issues in herself. At the six-week postpartum visit common to US birthing contexts, her doctor may ask the following two questions:

1. Over the past two weeks, have you felt down, depressed, or hopeless?
2. Over the past two weeks, have you felt little interest or pleasure in doing things?

If the exhausted new mother can muster the courage to say yes (when relevant), the doctor may administer a more in-depth depression screening tool; however, the idea that asking for help would be an admittance of failure with dire consequences was a mythos that pervaded my own first pregnancy.

A friend in my doctoral program communicated the following to me over a collegial dinner: "Be careful what you admit to your doctor about the baby blues. You don't want your baby taken away." We are both highly educated and ascribe to a holistic understanding of well-being. Yet, as a mother and a mother-to-be, living in a society that blacklists mental illness, we internalized the fear of unwelcomed intervention in the most vulnerable of times: the delivery of and first days of caring for fragile new offspring. The level of vulnerability inherent in admitting the need for mental support shortly after the trauma of expelling a new life from one's loins—admitting you are struggling to care for a child you created and carried for nine months prior, that your mind is failing when your body succeeded—cannot be understated. The physician-administered screening tool, then, is a disruptively unparalleled request for exposure from someone the mother has entrusted with the care of her most intimate bodily experiences. Furthermore, the overwhelmed new mom must ask herself: do I trust the *ethos* [2] of the diagnostic tools my health-care provider will use to assign my place on the "ab/normal" postpartum continuum?

Postpartum Screening Test as Actant

The rhetoric of many PPD diagnostic tools provides a compelling case for the patient to lie given the perception (via societal stigma) that consequent outcomes are set in stone. In other words, it doesn't take a PhD to understand which answers will label you as problematically mentally disturbed and incapable of caring for yourself or your child versus being a trooper through the trials of new motherhood. We must also necessarily recognize the inherent privilege of being PhD holders in this situation. Being a professor comes with a certain level of cultural clout; underserved demographics, however, remain infinitely more vulnerable in the face of Child Protective Services and, therefore, to the perceived or real consequences that may come with being labeled dangerously depressed. Enter the plethora of self-diagnostic tools available online—an anonymous way to self-check one's supposed psychological aptitude at "normal" motherhood.

Consider the Postpartum Depression Test from Psycom (Remedy Health Media 2018):

I feel like a failure as a mother and guilty for not being happy around my baby.

True
False

The thought of harming myself has occurred to me.

True
False

I feel anxious and panicky for no good reason.

True
False

Psycom is clear to offer the caveat that "only a licensed mental health professional or doctor can give a formal diagnosis of postpartum depression," but also that "you should only answer true if you have been experiencing the symptom nearly every day for at least 2 weeks." Is the takeaway, then, that if "the thought of harming myself has occurred to me" every other day instead of every day, it's just "normal" baby blues? The answer choices, which must be registered according to a true/false binary, mirror the larger ab/normal postpartum sadness binary. There is little to no nuance here to guide and encourage the potentially suffering new mother into deeper discussion with her health-care provider.

The virtues of collective intelligence notwithstanding, the internet is notorious for proffering poorly constructed advice for the sake of expediency; there must be fewer rhetorical frameworks guiding us toward unhelpful answers in the formal diagnostic tools used by our health-care providers, right? That brings our discussion to the Edinburgh Postnatal Depression Scale (EPDS) (Psychology Tools, n.d.), considered the gold standard in diagnosing PPD (D. Levine 2017).

The EPDS was designed for pregnant women and new moms to identify their risk for perinatal depression. It is also used to identify general depression in the larger population, and it's easy to see why. The EPDS provides a bit more nuance in its Likert scale (e.g., "No, not at all," "Hardly ever," "Yes, sometimes," "Yes, very often"), but it has been criticized, among other reasons, for its lack of specificity to the postpartum period. One question, for example, asks the quiz taker to assess how much "things have been getting on top of me." We can think of dear mom friends who would likely respond, "I haven't been able to cope at all"—with laundry, since 4 and 6 were born. Though we offer this example somewhat in jest, other issues plague the test. Quiz takers are asked to determine how often in the past seven days they have "felt sad or miserable," with no recourse for communicating or assigning weight to other factors that might be contributing to said sadness or miserableness. Another question provokes the quiz taker to rate how often they have "blamed [themselves] unnecessarily when things went wrong." There's a lack of clarity in the terms "blamed," "unnecessarily," and "wrong" here (a standard problem with self-report inventories in general). What defines the assignment of "blame" in this case? More importantly, how does the quiz taker know whether the assignment was "necessary" or, at some level, "unnecessary"? Isn't the ability to recognize responsibility in "wrong"-doing a sign of health and maturity?

Applying rigorous rhetorical analysis to such screening techniques may confound our understanding of the results they're meant to reveal: a sense of subjective emotion, the patient's perception of their current situation. Yet, researchers have suggested, time and again, that the scale needs to be "shorter, easier to use and more specific to identifying PPD" (Cohen quoted in D. Levine 2017)—harking back to the more productive rhetoric of *standardized* or *hospital* birth plans. Dr. Lee S. Cohen[3] is a key player in initiatives led by health-care practitioners to improve the diagnosis of postpartum disorders; Cohen suggests that "there has been rapid growth in the development of a variety of web-driven screening tools for many mental health issues, but 'to date there has been little attention to the use of technology to better diagnose and treat PPD'" (quoted in D. Levine 2017). Essentially, Cohen is advocating for the benefit of technological actants in targeting more productive diagnosis of postpartum disorders.

We present our analysis of the EPDS and other widely circulated PPD screening tools to extend this conversation and to suggest, like Cohen and Dr. Donna Stewart,[4] that such tools are actants. That is, we suggest, from our unique perspective, that such tools can play an active part in dismantling the postpartum binary of ab/normal sadness. A well-designed web screening or app has the potential to influence the new mom to trustingly, and truthfully, explore her complex postpartum feelings and to seek help when needed if the technology itself takes part in critically framing a nuanced picture of the postpartum experience of sadness. Both Cohen and Stewart, however, point out that there's little utility in developing additional diagnostic tools if *treatment* cannot also be elevated in similar ways. Stewart asks, "Why screen if you don't have the services? . . . That's where the gap is" (quoted in D. Levin 2017). According to Cohen, however, using big data to enhance the *ethos* (the credibility and authority and, thereby, effectiveness) of screening tools is the first step, which can be followed by technological actants that come in the form of "treatment delivery tools—if you score a certain number, you have a link to a treatment tool—[coupling] specific screening with effective delivery of treatment, for getting women well and doing it in a timely way" (quoted in D. Levine 2017). Both practitioners push for constructing a more complete picture of the ethical nodes in postpartum decision-making.

In other words, the creation of such screening and treatment tools may become important nodes in the networked *ethos* of contemporary maternity advice, but they contribute little to positive, actualized results if the women who need them do not have access to them. Enter the node of note for this particular book: social media mothering groups and the circulated discourse (or lack thereof) surrounding PPD.

KAIROTIC IMPLICATIONS: PPD AS SOCIAL MEDIA DISCOURSE

Though one might expect that PPD is as stigmatized in social media mothering groups as it is in geographically bound discourse communities, it is a surprisingly common subject in both general and specialized mothering groups alike. What's most significant here, however, is not the amount of discourse dedicated to postpartum disorders but the rhetorical notions of *kairos* (a favorable moment for decision or action) and hedging (a rhetorical strategy used to make statements less definitive or forceful) that nearly universally affect new media mothering group discussion of postpartum disorders. Both rhetorical moves contribute to more deeply entrenching the binary of "normal" versus "abnormal" postpartum sadness.

Consider a post from a specialized feeding group in which the original poster (OP) delivered a PPD "rant." The OP details how her child's doctor discovered results from a test conducted months earlier indicating the OP was at risk for PPD. More testing (i.e., paperwork) is now necessary to confirm that diagnosis—a diagnosis that had been made months earlier but not shared with the OP. Worse yet, when the OP follows up with *her* doctor, the staff person she speaks with concludes her situation isn't an emergency. The staff person recommends the OP connect with her doctor later and abruptly ends her conversation with the OP.

While the OP evidences no hedging in announcing the acuteness of her symptoms, she does demonstrate rage at the delayed course of treatment: *kairos* is clearly at play. While some commenters may continue the discussion by noting their surprise (delight) at pediatrician involvement in the fight against PPD, most will cry "unacceptable!" at a physician's laxity in not *immediately* informing a patient of a high score on a PPD screening (given that early intervention is critical for the health and well-being of mother and child); the physician has thwarted the OP's opportunity to act on "a favorable moment for decision or action." Ultimately, commenters' cries constitute multiplied collective vocalizations for "self-advocacy!"

In this representative vignette, one commenter explicitly points out that obstetricians, primary care providers, and pediatricians are not experts on mental health—it's not their job—so new mothers need to take mental health care into their own hands. Indeed, many commenters advise skipping the typical ob-gyn or primary care provider routes and going straight to a therapist, "not tak[ing] NO for an answer," and being "super pushy" when it comes to mental health needs. We note particularly the neoliberal tones to these responses: your Optimal Mental Health (as a facet of Optimal Motherhood) is *your* responsibility alone, and responsible citizens should perfectly maintain this "resource." Thus, while the collective empathy among commenters might bring relief to the OP by reassuring her righteous indignation, there is much to consider given the concerns already raised in this chapter: Do new moms have the expertise to diagnose their own postpartum disorder symptoms and the confidence (let alone energy) to "push" for their own mental health needs while tending to the lives of their newly formed little ones?

Another *kairos*-relevant trend in social media mothering group discourse about postpartum disorders concerns the tendency of new moms to reach out only *after* they have been suffering for a significant period of time. Such OPs in generalized and specialized social media mothering groups begin their threads in line with what follows: "I've been feeling this way for a long time and . . . ," "I started noticing symptoms of deep worry and sadness months ago . . . ," "I've finally been diagnosed but . . ." ("but" being a classic marker of hedging). These admissions are often met with condolences from well-meaning empathetic commenters who project personas situated somewhere between cheerleader and chastising parent. Commenters are often quick to say, "Good on ya for getting help!" but also, implicitly or explicitly, "Why did you wait so long?" unintentionally reinforcing the opposite side of the binary. These unintentional reprimands come in the form of comments using the imperative, "You need to get another doctor"; comments that reference the OP's supposed misunderstanding of the situational urgency, encouraging she take action "ASAP"; and comments that invoke repetition and exclamatory punctuation, such as "Call back!! Call back!!" When such vulnerability is met with reprimand, it's reasonable to conclude that many OPs will be hesitant about posting postpartum issues in the future; the expectation has been set that she is damned if she does and damned if she doesn't. If she doesn't seek help, she faces the physical, mental, and emotional challenges that consume those with PPD alone—or with the reproof of her online village. If she does seek help, she faces the internally or externally imposed stigma attached to the label of a depressed and otherwise unfit mother.

Social media mothering group commenters are surprisingly quick to share, in detail, what particular psychotherapeutic or medicinal interventions worked for them in their own battles against postpartum disorders— but only in comments (rarely, if ever, as original posts), suggesting that discourse about mental health disorders and treatment is reserved for threads that will not show up in the mainstream feed of social media mothering groups. This discourse choice embodies rhetorical hedging on a larger scale by relegating a particular subject of contemporary maternal decision-making discourse—postpartum disorder treatment—to a particular (and particularly limited) space: comments only. This choice might appear to be at odds with the chorus of women crying for heightened awareness and self-advocacy when it comes to postpartum disorders. However, rather than suggesting that women suffering from postpartum disorders be responsible for outing themselves and proclaiming their disorders more prominently in their social media worlds, perhaps what we're suggesting here is creating an alternate but equally prominent place for such discussion, as in the mentoring programs being initiated and actively advertised by some specialized feeding groups (see chapter 4, "Breast/Fed Is Best: Whose Algorithm Is Feeding My Baby?"). Consciously creating such a conspicuous space for this work supports the normalizing of the differential continuum of postpartum feelings and behaviors.

Moms' Best Friends: Guilt and Shame

As mentioned, the postpartum disorder discourse of social media mothering groups—often uncomfortable and conceivably controversial—may be unintentionally reinforcing the larger nodes of guilt and shame that feed postpartum disorders. Original posts inquiring about members' experiences with postpartum disorders are often hedged with language such as "Is this allowed?" "Please don't judge me!" and "I hope I'm not alone." Such introductory phrasing (negatively) colors the reading of what comes next in the given post. Posts commonly include those inquiring whether there are other online mothering group members suffering from depression and/or anxiety. Just as commonly, these posts are hedged with language wondering whether such inquiry is "allowed" and whether other mothers feel like they are "doing this thing wrong." Such posts communicate guilt via the perception of having committed an offense, which is inherent to the question of what topics might be off limits for discussion in a social media mothering group. Shame is also evidenced in such posts—feelings of humiliation or distress at having done something "wrong" or foolish and the expression of disquieting desire for other moms to own up to feeling like less than Optimal Mothers or to a general feeling of failure at mothering.

Where do such guilt and shame come from? We have already explored the deceptively complex *ethos* of health-care providers' frameworks for responding to issues of PPD as well as general trends in mothering group social media discourse that mirror a real-world reluctance to discuss postpartum disorders in concert with larger social stigmas surrounding mental health care. We must also acknowledge memes and other technological actants that circulate alongside or through postings of members of social media mothering groups (in groups that function as formative villages in contemporary mothers' parenting decisions). Consider the following text circulated on a birth doula / sleep consultant page in late 2019:

> If you cried this week because the exhaustion was so physical your limbs felt like lead.
> If you felt stretched, pulled between the needs of different children, and guilty that you simply didn't have enough energy.
> If you're struggling with depression or anxiety and wondering when you'll start feeling yourself again.
> If you're just holding on, juggling work and life and your relationship and lurching between coffee and wine.
> Remember this: to your children, you are the world.
> You are the world.
> (COPE 2019)

Though the text is seemingly positive in its implicit refrain of "you matter," the underlying message is, "you should put up with the exhaustion, the never-ending guilt, the harrows of depression and anxiety, because, well, baby." Baby is privileged over mom by this technological actant, which purposefully or not so purposefully feeds the narrative that suffering through PPD or anxiety is the expected course of martyrdom for the new mom. Martyr is the *expected* persona a postpartum mother must perform. Silently suffering through life-depleting sadness, a sadness that causes you to question your identity and self-worth, is presented as a satisfactorily *normal* requirement of new momhood. What we need to recognize is that performing the persona of martyr is not merely physically damaging but also mentally and emotionally damaging for the postpartum mother; this *pathos*-laden, emotionally gut-wrenching, viral post exemplifies this damage, pinning the suffering new mother, inescapably, into current binary discourse (valiant martyr vs. failed depressive) surrounding postpartum sadness.

Another example of a technological actant—one that doesn't tiptoe around its insistence that guilt (the kind of guilt that fuels postpartum disorders) is both useful and part and parcel of new motherhood—is a viral post from June 2019, circulated by Taylor Kulik (figure 3.1).

> Too often in our culture, providing information is perceived as "mom-shaming." Now, I'm not saying that mom-shaming doesn't happen, because it does! But sharing info is not shaming. The content I share, harmful impacts of sleep training and punitive discipline, tends to trigger people, and I GET IT. I've been hesitant at times to share what I really want to here out of fear of offending people.
>
> I want to talk about why you might feel triggered. Maybe you feel guilty. I know I do. I mess up daily—I yell, I lose my patience, whatever it may be. And I feel guilty. But is this a bad thing? Are we so afraid of the discomfort of guilt that we are willing to deny information that could be helpful to our children? I am on a Brené Brown kick lately, & I want to share how she explains the difference between shame & guilt:
>
> "Shame is a focus on self; guilt is a focus on behavior. Shame is, 'I am bad.' Guilt is, 'I did something bad.'" She goes on to explain that "shame is highly, highly correlated with addiction, depression, violence, aggression, bullying, suicide, eating disorders.
>
> "Here's what you even need to know more: Guilt is inversely correlated with those things. The ability to hold something we've done, or failed to do,

USE GUILT
TO FUEL
GROWTH.

@taylorkulik

up against who we want to be is incredibly adaptive. It's uncomfortable, but it's adaptive."

So, no, I don't think that feeling guilty is bad. I've realized that it can be a helpful, productive part of the adaptive process. If you are feeling triggered by information someone is sharing, ask yourself "why?" If you are feeling guilty, accept that feeling, & do something. Whether it's learning more, hearing someone else's perspective, or making an effort to do better next time, act on it & make positive changes! What if we could all have difficult, vulnerable conversations? What if we could admit our mistakes & work to improve them? I think we might create positive changes in the world for not only us, but future generations.

And at the end of the day remember that you are enough. You are a good parent.

There's a lot to unpack here. The post, in fact, ends with a point we agree with: "What if we could all have difficult, vulnerable conversations? . . . I think we might create positive changes in the world for not only us, but future generations." Where we might beg to differ is in the simple statement that "sharing info is not shaming" and that one can necessarily, with ease, compartmentalize shame as a selfish act of self-focus or that one can just as easily categorize guilt as a productive feature of flexible behavior. *How* one goes about sharing information, especially in social media mothering groups, absolutely can and does result in mom-shaming—a shame that is not purely self-fueled but influenced by a network of actors and actants expressed in infinitely complex ways.

The language of "triggering" and "offending people" deserves careful unpacking too, but, more importantly, we need to consider how "guilt" is synonymized with "being triggered" and how that problematically neutralizes or otherwise misrepresents a primary criterion in diagnosing a clinically serious mental illness: PPD. Notwithstanding the problematic ways that "trigger" has been co-opted from PTSD diagnostic criteria (and postpartum PTSD is an increasingly recognized condition) into vernacular language, the term is also invoked here to intentionally instigate feelings of maternal inferiority (with the idea that this feeling of inferiority could, hopefully, motivate ambitions toward Optimal Motherhood). Indeed, the viral post seems to announce that there will be guilt in new motherhood, and the only responsible course of action is to accept that that guilt will be painful but necessary for growth into an Optimal Mother—that if we just think about our behavioral choices as new mothers hard enough and long enough, we will avoid the pitfalls of PPD and, importantly, that guilt might, in fact, be indicative of real ineptitudes. The culture of Optimal Motherhood oozes from this passage.

In fact, the inherent message of "dwelling in discomfort" only further evidences the kairotic problem discussed earlier in this chapter: across social media spaces, women are suffering far too long in silence because of a perceived notion that the guilt, shame, and sadness they are battling are, at best, nothing more than a little baby blues, and, at worst (as indicated by Kulik's viral post), indicative of true failings. Discourse like this, which claims that the experience of shame and guilt is a "normal" part of the postpartum experience but that sadness beyond a quick bout of the baby blues is not, erases opportunities for productive postpartum recovery, meaningful discussion, and a collective movement past the norms of Optimal Motherhood. It is only when mothers (and the society that reinforces the norms of Optimal Motherhood) undermine this binary and internalize the idea that feelings of postpartum dysphoria are not so "different" after all that women may become more willing to talk about their postpartum feelings and walk the path toward understanding what all parents want to believe (and, arguably, need to believe to persist): "you are enough. You are a good parent."

CONNECTING ONLINE AND OFFLINE NODES

Observing social media mothering group discourse afforded productive insight into the slices of postpartum life members were willing to share among (presumably) trusted group members. Institutional review board and ethical internet research guidelines, however, left us little leeway for most powerfully representing the raw and unfettered perspectives of new and veteran mom participants, the type of data that would confirm the problematically binary-bound representation of postpartum sadness that we observed in said social media mothering groups; therefore, as explained in the book's introduction, we interviewed a convenience sample of mothers and health-care practitioners regarding their thoughts on PPD.

The Moms

"Did you discuss postpartum depression and other like disorders with your doctor or anyone else?"

Interviewed moms commonly felt the need to state that they did *not* have PPD when answering whether they discussed the issue with doctors:

"Yes, they brought it up while I was pregnant and then after at any and all follow-up things. They would ask the screening questions, but I never had that with either boy."

"We had some education at our hospital prior [to] giving birth. I had someone from [the] hospital to check in with me after I was done. A lot of people asked me 'how are you,' so that was helpful. I felt SO hormonal and had too many tears, but I never got depressed."

"Yes, they asked me at my ob-gyn. I didn't have it, but they asked me about it. I didn't have time to be depressed with twins. I didn't have time to think about my own feelings, honestly."

The third mom's response is of particular interest given that she rhetorically situates PPD as a nonissue in tension with lack of time and a privileging of her children's wants and needs over her own as a mother. She admits to dishonest, or at least nonexistent, engagement with her own feelings because she perceived her children to be more significant stakeholders in this particular decision at this particular time. Her narrative speaks to an important conclusion of this book: enveloping (or being enveloped in) the rhetoric of Optimal Motherhood problematically erases the mother in the mother-child parenting relationship and, thereby, precludes productive maternal decision-making. Such a rhetorical move should be considered in the construction and delivery of PPD diagnostic actants like the previously discussed diagnostic questions in clinic room conversation and the EPDS.

Even when interviewed moms (reluctantly) admitted being diagnosed or suffering with PPD, the agency for open discussion was placed on the health-care practitioner rather than being initiated by the mom (an opposing pattern to previous "self-advocacy" social media findings): "Yes, with [my third child], I had postpartum depression, and I had to be medicated. I wasn't intending on talking to my doctor, and he brought it up, and he said I needed medication, and so I finally gave in." The inclusion of "I finally gave in" is of particular rhetorical significance. The interviewee implicitly indicates she was fighting an ongoing battle against being diagnosed with—or at least against taking medication for—PPD. She did not want to be labeled in the binary of aberrant sadness or otherwise be complicit in this intervention, one that signaled she needed assistance to function as a stable care provider, something she had presumably already been succeeding at twice over.

The *ethos*, or credibility and authority, that other parties hold in postpartum mental health-care decisions was blatantly presented in the interviewed moms' answers: "I did not [discuss postpartum depression . . . with my doctor or anyone else]. And I did experience some postpartum depression, but I grew up in a house that wasn't progressive around these issues, so we didn't talk about it—otherwise my mom would be mad. The doctor asked, but I brushed it off because my mom was in the room." In this instance, a young mother's dependence on (or perhaps fear of) her own mother as an authority in her decision-making process inhibited her ability to openly and honestly discuss her postpartum mental health-care concerns with her medical practitioner. The doctor was not able to effectively intervene in the patient's suffering with PPD given the patient's mother's physical presence and invisible emotional *ethos*. There is an interesting tie to social media mothering group shaming and silencing here.

Receiving a poor, shaming, hurtful, or otherwise negative reaction to a post soliciting parenting advice—or even *fear of* receiving a poor reaction, having silently observed discourse in the watchdog community—can disempower new and vulnerable moms (particularly young ones) from bringing such important decision-making discourse to their medical practitioners. Rather than working together to come to an ethically informed and community-supported best-practice decision, nodes in the network of contemporary maternity advice have severed literal lifelines. What if the mother had been more concerned for her daughter's mental well-being? What if the doctor had asked the mother to leave the room? What if the patient were able to muster the courage to have the discussion despite the odds stacked against her? *What if the agency lies in the network as a whole rather than in one person or entity? Our interviewee well articulates what is at stake in this proposed agential shift:* "I did not [discuss postpartum depression . . . with my doctor or anyone else] and mostly because it did not come up. I had a couple of friends with it. I don't think I knew anyone who was clinically depressed who needed assistance. I personally did not experience it. It's terrible, and it taints your whole experience." The last sentence of this quote— "It's terrible, and it taints your whole experience"—realistically captures the exigency of this book as a whole. We must work to recognize how difficult contemporary maternal decision-making is and how social media mothering groups designed to be supportive villages too often become platforms for polemics that misrepresent complex decision-making realities in the form of black-and-white binaries. Then, and only then, can we begin to envision ways to reframe these communities. These communities could empower mothers to take advantage of the human and technological actants converging in social media, as well as assemble an instrumentally significant *ethos* of happy and healthy parental decision-making that cares for the mom as much as or more than those around her. But there's still stigma, as evidenced in the following moms' answers.

"Do you feel there is a stigma around this conversation?"
As supported by our observation of discourse in contemporary social media mothering groups, interviewed moms seemed to agree that issues of PPD are being talked about, but probably not enough yet. In response to the question

"Do you feel there is a stigma around this conversation? Why or why not?" the interviewed moms answered as follows:

> "I don't feel like there is so much, but I didn't experience PPD, but I've seen so many people share openly about it, and I think that's something that's common now. I know it's something that's hard to admit and come to terms with and it becomes less of a stigma."

> "I feel like there's less of a stigma around it. I haven't personally encountered someone experiencing [an] intense form of it. I feel like there was more stress and anxiety about 'will I have it?' beforehand. My doctors all built me up to believe I was going to get it, so it kind of took away from the 'this could be joyous' attitude. Instead, I was expecting something worse."

What is intriguingly common to these two responses is the implicit passing of responsibility to those suffering from PPD to do the work of lessening the stigma. The first respondent clarifies that she "didn't experience PPD" but that it's "hard to admit and come to terms with and it becomes less of a stigma," thereby structurally juxtaposing the circulation of first-person narratives of suffering with the lessening of the stigma. The second respondent juxtaposes "less stigma" with personal encounters of intense PPD, implying that it is the intensity of suffering that determines whether the stigma is lessened or strengthened. An additionally revealing comment in the second respondent's answer is the assertion that her doctor prepared her for the worst and made her believe that she would suffer from depression in her postpartum period. This was a particularly disabling discussion, according to the respondent, because she was hoping to indulge in the "joy" of the perinatal period; instead, her medical practitioner, presumably one of the figures with the most influence in her perinatal decision-making, caused her to feel the opposite of joy in expecting "the worst": inevitable PPD.

The intensity of language used by social media mothering group members as well as interview participants is duly worth noting:

> "Yes. I do. I feel like a lot of women feel like they have postpartum[5] and they're not a good mom and people don't want [to] talk about it. And taking medication feels like you're failing and that's really hard."

> "Yes. I do." Full stop. "Not a good mom." "You're failing."

"Absolutely, and I think part of it is the normal stigma of talking about mental illness. So many people have this attitude of, 'why would you be depressed; you just had the best thing in the world: a baby . . . you couldn't possibly have depression,' and people brush it off as being tired."

"Absolutely." "Normal stigma." "You couldn't possibly have depression."

"YES. People pretend it's not happening, especially on social media. People just post happy things on social media."

"YES." "People *pretend it's not happening, especially on social media*" (emphasis added). While we might argue with this respondent that people on social media *are* talking about postpartum depression, another interviewee brings up a productive (if implicit) distinction between "understanding" and "feeling":

"Yeah, I do. I feel there's a stigma. I think that women are becoming more and more understanding, but in society there's a stigma."

While women may be becoming more knowledgeable about and generally more aware of PPD (its symptoms and causes), how it is *perceived* (and how it is *talked about*) is another story.

"Are there related topics you wished were being discussed that are not being discussed by moms and/or doctors?"

The fact that topics related to PPD were not being discussed was evident in social media mothering group discussions of PPD as well as in interviewees' responses to the question "Are there related topics you wished were being discussed that are not being discussed by moms and/or doctors?"

"My peds office is great with talking about everything. My OB was good, too. She didn't tiptoe around anything. I like that. My sister is the opposite, so I hope that doctors are good with not tiptoeing around sensitive topics."

"I wish postpartum was more aggressively discussed."

"In general, I wish that people were more comfortable asking their pediatrician or ob-gyn questions. I think people feel like they have to figure it out themselves (I was that way). 'What are ways that I can manage this?' I also think they should ask the new mom serious questions in private without their mom/husband being there."

There is direct reference to the American bootstrapping *ethos* in the respondents' answers to this question as well as a clear delineation of PPD as a "sensitive" subject that deserves "aggressive" attention on the part of medical practitioners. "Tiptoeing" is a particularly apt description given the attention we want to put on not only *what* is discussed in social media mothering groups but *how* it is discussed. Silence can be particularly damaging for various reasons but talking *around* sensitive subjects may be equally if not more damaging.

The Nurses

We wanted to include the voices of real-world medical practitioners, both doctors and nurses, in this project, particularly in regard to the discussion and practices surrounding diagnosing and treating PPD (their satisfaction levels with current engagement and recommendations for future areas of research). Not unexpectedly—given the complicated legal context of contemporary medical practice liability—we were unable to find doctors willing to comment; however, a convenience sample of nurses wished to make their voices heard.

"Do you feel there is a stigma around this [postpartum disorders] conversation or practice?"

When asked to comment on the non/existent stigma surrounding postpartum disorder discussion and diagnosis, nurses seemed to agree that although the stigma was lessening, it was still an important factor in women neglecting postpartum mental health care:

"Yes—there is in general. I think that people think of it as a weakness. People always say 'just be happy.'"

"It's lessening, but yes, there is definitely a stigma. People feel shame surrounding the subject so they don't want to talk about it. They feel bad because they should."

Nurses offered language concerning "weakness" and "shame," complementing findings from face-to-face interactions and observations of online moms concerning how postpartum disorders are contextualized in everyday conversation. One nurse went on to contextualize "stigma" specifically as a matter of needed ongoing education:

Oh yeah, for sure. With any type of mental illness, there's so much stigma and shame. Moms might not be educated about their hormones, but there is a scientific reason for you to feel this way. There's a lot of guilt. "I have a new baby, why do I feel this way?" and they get buried in this guilty feeling.

I had someone in the ER who came in with postpartum, and she was saying, "I can't even look at my daughter" and thought, "What's wrong with me? Why do I feel this way? I'm fine, I don't need help." People don't want to seek out help, but they need to utilize resources.

Considering that the nurses in our study (and other medical practitioners) advocate for ongoing education regarding postpartum disorders, we felt it would be pertinent to ask the following question: "How do you discuss and/or diagnose depression and other like disorders with your pregnant and postpartum patients?"

"How do you discuss and/or diagnose depression and other like disorders with your pregnant and postpartum patients?"

One nurse echoed the kairotic concerns discussed earlier in this chapter: "It has a lot to do with how they're attaching or bonding with the baby, which I think is a late cue, but it's the most measurable. It's a huge indicator." Criticism of the "measurable" nature of this variable aside, we call attention to the nurse's mention that ineffectual bonding is a "late cue," which accords with our observations of the *untimely* nature of current postpartum discourse.

Another nurse noted the shame inherent in answering the typical postpartum "quiz": "From my time, there are a lot of pre- and postnatal screenings; however, there is a lot of shame in answering those questions. Nurse practitioners and doctors sometimes need to push past these screenings to get the answer, and the shame can make that really hard." The nurse further implicated patients' partners in ongoing postpartum disorder work: "Also, sometimes the partner is a co-parent that also encourages a discussion of depression."

Though these short answers provide compelling evidence that complements interpretations of findings discussed earlier in this chapter, one nurse's lengthier personal narrative proved equally if not more valuable:

Oh my gosh this is such a great question. I have struggled with my own general depression since I was in college. And we need to talk about it more, and it needs to be less of a stigma all around. It's a HUGE part of my discharge teaching. I always talk about discharge teaching, but I talk about it before they walk out the door. We will get the history of the patient beforehand (depression, anxiety: we flag when moms have had depression in the past) so we know beforehand if it's something we need to look out [for]. I try to bring it in matter of factly so that it doesn't feel so heavy.

It's SO common.

I always ask, "Have you ever had medication, counseling, suicidal thoughts?" and I talk about it with the dad present. Or if I need to ask in a gentle way, I say "Have you ever heard of postpartum blues?"

It's REALLY common, even if there's no history, and I don't think that's known. There's a dramatic change of hormones from moms after they give birth. The placenta was FULL of hormones that grow the baby, and the hormones drop after, and you'll cry a lot for a week or two.

There are SO many times where I bring up "post baby blues," and moms get tears in their eyes. For about every 10 I bring it up, 6–7 moms nod their heads and agree.

I also think it's difficult because a lot of times, during the 9 months [of pregnancy], everyone checks in on the mom, but when the baby arrives they forget to check in with her and just focus on the baby.

It's always smart to have a good tribe with you that can help and encourage you.

We ALWAYS screen new moms. It can happen up to a year postpartum.

The nurse's conflation of baby blues with PPD and her insistence on the commonality of PPD are particularly revealing. While other health-care professionals might balk at the idea of conflating the definitions of these clinical conditions, the rhetorical move here is to emphasize that these new mothers are not struggling alone ("It's SO common. . . . It's REALLY common"), that they are experiencing symptoms that can be explained in a medically sound and accessible fashion ("The placenta was FULL of hormones that grow the baby, and the hormones drop after, and you'll cry a lot for a week or two"), and that there is a shift in the focus of discourse after the baby arrives ("but when the baby arrives, they forget to check in with her and just focus on the baby") that significantly affects the mother's mental health. Even the nurse's awareness of tone in the delivery of this information ("I try to bring it in matter of factly so that it doesn't feel so heavy. . . . Or if I need to ask in a gentle way, I say 'Have you ever heard of postpartum blues?'"[6]) offers so much to the discussion of how *ethos* can and should be built around the circulation of parenting advice for contemporary mothers.

"Are there related topics you wished were being discussed that are not being discussed by moms and/or doctors?"

While there is so much to learn from *how* such advice is rendered and circulated, we felt compelled to ask the nurses, too, whether "there [are] related topics you wished were being discussed that are not being discussed by moms and/or doctors"; in other words, we wanted to know about what was not being talked about in addition to what was being talked about. The nurses we interviewed generally did *not* reiterate the need to talk about postpartum disorders or otherwise highlight postpartum disorders as a completely neglected topic of discourse among health-care professionals and their patients, as had the new moms we interviewed for this study; rather, they had some specific suggestions:

"Maybe postpartum sex? Also depression should continue to be a topic of conversation to normalize it."

"There is literally 0 percent chance that vaccinating your child will give them autism. Vaccinate your kids."

"Yeah, I wish domestic abuse. They ask it once and they should ask it multiple times because no one is actually [supposed] to answer that with one question. They need to make the person feel safe and have the partner leave the room."

"Social media. It can create a negative image."

Of particular interest to this book is the final suggestion, that social media needs to be a more prevalent topic of discussion in all postpartum discourse.

CONCLUSION: BLURRING THE LINES

The discourse that circulates via social media mothering groups can be variously heartening and troubling. Baby Forum's "What It Feels Like to Have Baby Blues, PPD, No PPD" infographic (figure 3.2), for example, does

WHAT IT FEELS LIKE TO HAVE

BABY BLUES	PPD	NO PPD
Sleep Deprivation makes you emotional	**Sleep Deprivation** makes you angry	**Sleep Deprivation** makes you tired
Bonding with Baby doesn't happen immediately	**Bonding with Baby** doesn't happen at all	**Bonding with Baby** happens shortly after birth
The Changes in Your Life make you feel overwhelmed	**The Changes in Your Life** make you feel worthless	**The Changes in Your Life** make you feel excited
You Cry Tears of sadness	**You Cry Tears** of frustration	**You Cry Tears** of joy
Your Mind is foggy and unclear	**Your Mind is** full of bad thoughts	**Your Mind is** forgetful and distracted
Your Worry about un-important things	**Your Worry** if you are fit to be a mother	**Your Worry** if baby is pooping enough
After a Few Weeks you start to feel better	**After a Few Weeks** you start to feel worse	**After a Few Weeks** you get into a good routine

For More Info Visit:
www.RUNNINGINTRIANGLES.com

Figure 3.2

Source: Vanessa Rapisarda quoted in kmswear22, June 13, 2018, at 6:10 a.m., comment on emccaskey (2018).

damage in rigidly insisting that "bonding with baby doesn't happen at all" under PPD; such false statements enhance the guilt and shame that confirm a new mother's desire not to be labeled with aberrant sadness, and stymie complementary help-seeking behaviors.

The infographic is hyper-determined, stylistically (in its iteration of vertical columns of vastly contrasting colors). It doubles down on its insistence that baby blues, PPD, and absence of depression are discrete categories, though the reality is that these feelings and behaviors all exist on a continuum of normal postpartum experience that can certainly at times become debilitating or need treatment. It also reinscribes the dangerous binary that a new mother's body and brain (self-worth) are tied exclusively to the baby. Rather than technological actants and human actors that further establish existing binaries in postpartum disorder discourse, we need to ensure new mothers making mental health maternity decisions know that an experience that seems to blur existing mental health diagnostic lines is normal and that there is no trophy for waiting out the symptoms of PPD—in the same way that there are no "winners" in the gamifying of infant feeding decisions, discussed in chapter 4, "Breast/Fed Is Best: Whose Algorithm Is Feeding My Baby?"

4 BREAST/FED IS BEST: WHOSE ALGORITHM IS FEEDING MY BABY?

"Are you uptight? You must be uptight. Just stop being uptight and you'll be fine."

Minutes after delivering my second child, the postpartum nurse asked whether I would be breastfeeding. With all the calmness and clarity I could muster in that moment, I matter-of-factly related that breastfeeding my first child had been a challenge. Incessant crying; weight loss; supplementation; endless cycles of Supplemental Nursing System at the breast, followed immediately by a bottle and pumping; mastitis and a 105 degree fever twice (or was it three times?); lactation cookies, teas, and supplements galore; no answers from lactation consultants, pediatricians, ob-gyns, primary care providers, or anybody else who was supposed to be able to tell me why breastfeeding wasn't working for us. An eleven-month feeding journey ended with me in a deep depression.

And the postpartum nurse felt it was prudent to tell me I was just being uptight. That *not* being uptight would solve my breastfeeding issues with baby #2. I think it was in that very moment that I realized this book was necessary and that identifying the multiplicitous actors and actants in the network of contemporary maternity advice is an important step toward better understanding how maternity advice *ethos* is evolving in this moment in time. Not only *what* we're saying but also *how* we're saying it matters, because that advice is circulated in problematically oversimplified ways in our on- and offline villages—to the potential detriment of new moms everywhere.

To that point, one of the most obviously contentious new parenting decisions is feeding. Perhaps your reaction to the previous sentence was, "No it's not. Breast is best!" or "No it's not. Fed is best!" Ergo, our assertion that new maternity decisions are problematically binary-bound and extend the cultural phenomenon of "mommy wars."

THE "MOMMY WARS"

The term "mommy wars" is decades-old nomenclature for the battleground that is new motherhood. It was first used to describe the perceived ideological disparities in how working moms and stay-at-home moms choose to parent their children. Some trace the origin of the term to a 1989 *Texas Monthly* article. Jan Jarboe's "The Mommy War" explicated her personal, experiential understanding of the "natural antagonism" between mothers who worked outside the home and those who did not (quoted in Milkie, Pepin, and Denny 2016, 55). Others trace the origin of the term to Nina Darnton's 1990 *Newsweek* article "Mommy vs. Mommy." Darnton, a journalist, interviewed working mothers and stay-at-home mothers. She reported that working mothers perceived stay-at-home mothers to be "spoiled and uninteresting," while stay-at-home mothers perceived working mothers to be "materialistic and selfish" (quoted in Moore and Abetz 2016, 50). These frameworks of individual competition paralleled mass media representations of motherhood at the time. Late 1980s films such as *Baby Boom*, for example, depicted the trials of many mothers entering the public sector and labor force for the first time in the late 1980s and early 1990s (Milke, Pepin, and Denny 2016, 56). Since that time, "mommy wars" has remained a rhetorical and sociocultural conundrum.

The term received new attention in a 2015 advertisement produced by Similac (figure 4.1), a company that makes infant formula: "There's something going down on the playground. Don't they know that everyone has their own way of parenting? But when it comes down to it, we're all on the same side. Help us put an end to the judgment by sharing this video with every parent you know. Join the conversation on http://www.facebook.com /Similac#SisterhoodUnite."

The ad plays up stereotypically clashing parenting subtypes: the formula feeders, the breastfeeders, the working moms, the attachment parents—even the playground dads. Toward the end of the video, a baby in a stroller is

Figure 4.1
Screenshot from Similac's "The Mother 'Hood" commercial.
Source: Disney (2015).

unintentionally launched down a hill, and the whole ensemble scrambles to ensure the baby's safety, resulting in a rom-com-style happy ending with the collective realization that "we are parents first." The goal is admirable: put an end to parental judgment. Convince parents we are all on the "same side," the side of raising safe and protected children. But academic[1] and lay community responses to the ad were decidedly mixed: "One of our mothers then brought up the point that these are caricatures of actual mothering subtypes. They are extremes, and we as a society can get a little sensitive to things like this. A lot of mothers get offended very easily when someone tells us they do not agree with our parenting philosophy. Why? Because deep down we are all doing the best we can, making the best decisions for our children and there is nothing in this world more personal than that" (MOMentous Moms 2015). The noted "extremes" are the most important subject of this book. In seeking to dismantle those extremes, the Similac advertisement may well be, unintentionally, reinforcing their acceptance. The advertisement in and of itself became a viral actant, garnering over eight million views on YouTube (Norris 2015) and inviting viewers to sub/conscientiously identify with or against a multimodal representation of a particular parenting *ethos*:

"Oh look, the breast police have arrived."

"Looks like some moms are too lazy to breastfeed."

"Someone came with their nipples blazing."

"Oh yeah, well, I pump during conference calls!"

Our goal here isn't deep rhetorical analysis of Similac's well-intended text. Our goal is to point out that feeding is one particularly popular node in the dynamically complex network of contemporary maternity advice. If a single ad from an infant formula company can get that much attention, who else or what else is influencing our infant feeding decisions?

SOCIAL MEDIA AND INFANT FEEDING DISCOURSE

In an informal poll of a social media mothering group that asked participants to name popular new media sites they visited for parenting advice, over three hundred commenters pointed to YouTube, Kellymom.com, BabyCenter, and The Bump as well as Google searching, message and discussion boards, social media support groups (Facebook, Instagram), online friends, mothering blogs, and parenting apps. Participants supplemented these online resources by seeking infant feeding advice from health-care practitioners and support staff such as midwives, lactation consultants, ob-gyns, pediatricians, and hospital prenatal educators. Others were sure to mention lay human resources such as mom friends, family, and life partners as well as print resources such as parenting books and magazines or literature from and participation in community educational support groups sponsored by nonprofit, medical, or governmental organizations, such as the American Academy of Pediatrics.

This list of actors and actants that may influence new moms in their infant feeding decisions is necessarily long and involved; we are choosing to focus on explicating thematic discourse patterns in social media mothering groups as sites that often involve the circulation of materials mentioned above, technological actants whose *ethos* may be compromised or otherwise complexly layered and difficult to ascertain (or at least easy to ignore before hitting "share"). For a more complete understanding of how infant feeding discourse is composed and circulated on social media, then, we must necessarily illustrate how these technological actants function within these discourse communities before returning to discussing the input and outcomes of the human actors.

The Technological Actants

Popular cultural narratives tout the "unequivocal" evidence of breastfeeding benefits (American Academy of Pediatrics, n.d.). That is why *infant formula cans*, too (under the auspices of the World Health Organization, n.d.), attempt to influence women to breastfeed. The following suggestions and warnings are found on the label of the formula can shown in figure 4.2:

IMPORTANT NOTICE: BREAST MILK IS BEST FOR BABIES.

Before using an infant formula, ask the advice of your healthcare professional.

PRECAUTION: Powdered infant formulas are NOT sterile and should NOT be fed to premature infants or infants who might have immune problems unless directed and supervised by your baby's doctor.

WARNING: DO NOT USE MICROWAVE TO PREPARE OR WARM FORMULA. SERIOUS BURNS MAY OCCUR.

The World Health Organization hails breast milk as "the ideal food for infants," claiming that breast milk is, universally, "safe, clean, and contains antibodies which help protect against many common childhood illnesses." Furthermore, the organization claims that breast milk will provide "all the energy and nutrients that the infant needs for the first months of life" (World Health Organization n.d.) These sweeping generalizations are problematic in and of themselves; however, touting unqualified claims regarding the still-contested link between breastfeeding and intelligence or breastfeeding and weight[2] is even more problematic when the one thing scientists seem to agree on in this regard is "the magnitude and extent to which breast milk feeding is beneficial varies across studies" (Berger et al. 2020). For more details on the factors that confound "good data" in neonate and pregnancy recommendations, see chapter 1, "It Was Never about the Coffee." It will

Figure 4.2
Safe handling instructions found on infant formula.
Source: "Parent's Choice Advantage Non-GMO Infant Formula," https://images.app.goo.gl /FoVWKvFRT9SDQ1Hp9.

suffice here to state briefly that double-blind randomized trials have not been done on formula-fed versus breastfed babies, so, as with so much in parenting, little is certain. In light of this, it is rather shocking to observe the prevalence that "breast is best" has garnered in society, such that few modern mothers will *not* have heard it, when compared with the actual paucity of evidence in support of this statement.

More importantly, a quick social history of infant feeding methods reveals what we have found to be true over and over again while writing this book: the common denominator is the illusion of choice presented to women as representative of freedom in liberated, Western nations (more specifically, the United States and Canada) that in fact hems women in with a narrow range of unrealistic options. That is, what seems to be the liberated woman's due is in fact a false binary presented to her instead of the buffet of options that actually exist. Her freedom to choose is in fact her constraint by falsely represented, oversimplified options. And, because of neoliberal politics and risk aversion, women feel isolated and alone in choosing—devoid of the robust communities of women that many other cultures find helpful to new mothers—and the stakes are high in a culture of Optimal Motherhood. Make the wrong choice and you demonstrate that you don't love your baby enough. Whether we examine 1880s' discourse urging women to nurse their own babies (rather than hire wet nurses), 1970s' discourse about the medical perfection of infant formula, or 2010s' discourse of "breast is best," the result is the same: institutions (often male-dominated ones) urging women to do what said institutional authority believes is best for their babies. Even the most seemingly female-friendly of these movements exhibit the wiliness of the patriarchy as it wends its way into even the most pro-women campaigns. For instance, many women express great frustration with La Leche League's insistence on breastfeeding as a means of forcing women—via neoliberal guilt and shame—to do particular things with their bodies. Of course, the league was formed as part of a general cultural movement to take back women's understanding of baby feeding from male-dominated science that had promoted formula widely in the 1950s, implying that men knew more about infants than their mothers. As with birth plans, the allure of "choice" offered to "liberated" postfeminist women is in fact their jailhouse. Neither choice truly has women at its center, both options promise a one-size-fits-all mechanism that doesn't align with women's and baby's nuanced needs, and both insist on a binary decision that need not be posited as such.

Such steadfast adherence to the historical lineage of binaristic thinking that has dominated parental decision-making is why the World Health Organization hastily claims "inappropriate marketing of breast-milk substitutes continues to undermine efforts to improve breastfeeding rates and duration worldwide" on their website and why "BREAST MILK IS BEST FOR BABIES" is splashed on formula cans (see figure 4.2). What is so powerfully evidenced in contemporary social media mothering groups, however, is the impact the rhetorically prevalent presence of such alphanumeric and visual messages has had on new moms. Consider Facebook marketing.

WHAT ROLE DO COMPANIES HAVE IN MARKETING PRODUCTS TO FACEBOOK USERS?

In chapter 2, "Take Back the Delivery Room: Narrative Control, Traumatic Discourse, and the #MeToo Labor Movement," we broached the subject of object actants (birth plans) and their role in laboring mothers' control in the birthing process; here, we revisit the idea of women exerting control over maternal decision-making in the face of object actants—in the form of social media advertising. Interestingly, unless a person is shown an ad for Facebook on their Facebook feed, Facebook is not in charge of showing a user a specific ad. Most of the ads shown to users on their feed come from a service called Ads Manager, which is a product of Facebook. Ads Manager makes it possible for a company to target users based on a multitude of factors.

We interviewed Amanda Loeffler, a search engine algorithm designer for Acura, and she provided information on how companies target users and then broadcast their ads to a person's Facebook page. Companies can use any and all of the following to target users for ads: Facebook interests, job titles, location, "lookalike" properties, and even life events. On Facebook, ad targeting is specifically limited to information that people share on their own accounts, but even then, companies have a lot to work with. We dug into Ads Manager with these concepts in mind.

We were able to create an ad campaign through Ads Manager, accepting no terms and not going through a vetting process; we simply connected via a personal Facebook account and were able to look through all of Facebook's terms for creating an ad.

Ad Manager's "Special Ad Audiences" option targets "lookalike audiences," or audiences that behave similarly to people who have already interacted with an ad. So, if a person on Facebook (user1) shares a lot of the same interests with another person on Facebook (user2) , user2 will be targeted as user1's lookalike. In our case, if a woman (mom2) in a mothering group becomes Facebook friends with another woman in that same group who does a lot of online shopping for her baby's needs and "likes" those brands on her Facebook account (mom1)—and mom2 shares those "liked" interests— ads for products related to what mom1 bought could show up on mom2's account.

Ad Manager's "Location Audiences" regards how the location of an ad can be manipulated to reach different audiences. As long as the audience radius is within at least fifteen miles of the location specified for the ad, Facebook can target whole countries, individual cities, and even areas marked as free trade, app store areas, and "emerging market areas." Facebook can dig even deeper, targeting only people who live in a city, people who have traveled there, or people who are traveling there in the future. Travel or experience companies could use this feature to market excursions to people they know will be visiting a certain location soon.

Finally, Ad Manager's "Detailed Targeting" Facebook describes this option as targeting "people who have expressed an interest in or like pages related to [interest]" (Facebook quoted in Powell 2021). Figure 4.3 is only a snapshot of some options on the list, but there are hundreds to choose from. Many parents on mothering group pages would most likely be targeted as individuals who are interested in children or parenting, thus allowing companies that use Ad Manager to target these people directly based on what kinds of posts they like, their life events (recently gave birth, recently adopted), or anything that would fit them into a mold these companies could target.

In the end, Facebook is the connection between companies and people, profiting from ad campaigns run by businesses that want to make more money. Companies use the information presented to them through Ads Manager (for a price) in order to reach larger audiences of potential buyers. All the information collected must be public information, so private mothering group pages are safe from advertisements, *but the members themselves are not*. Any interests targeted by liking products posted in private groups or friending active Facebook users from those groups can be used to target individuals on their personal feeds for ads. So, what control do maternal decision-makers have over these potentially influential technological actants that show up on their personal Facebook feeds?

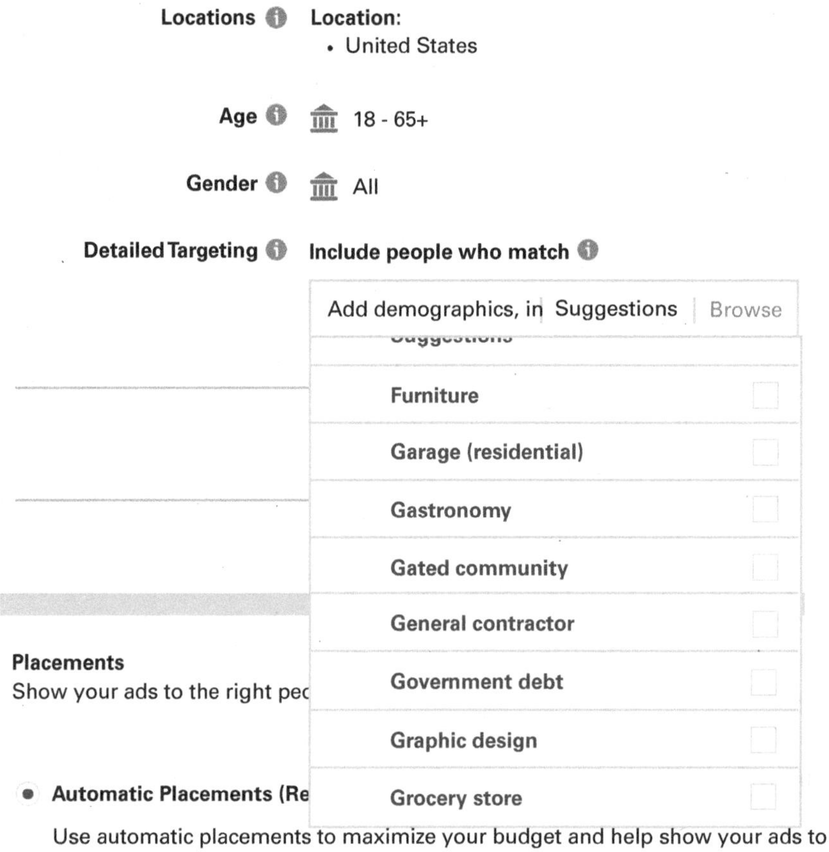

Locations ⓘ   Location:
· United States

Age ⓘ 🏛 18 - 65+

Gender ⓘ 🏛 All

Detailed Targeting ⓘ   **Include people who match** ⓘ

Add demographics, in	Suggestions	Browse
~~Suggestions~~		
Furniture		☐
Garage (residential)		☐
Gastronomy		☐
Gated community		☐
General contractor		☐
Government debt		☐
Graphic design		☐
Grocery store		☐

Placements
Show your ads to the right pec

● **Automatic Placements (Re**

Use automatic placements to maximize your budget and help show your ads to

Figure 4.3
Screenshot illustrating Ad Manager's Detailed Targeting, from personal Facebook account.

WHAT CONTROL DO INDIVIDUAL USERS HAVE OVER THE ADVERTISING PRESENTED TO THEM?

Individuals have the ability to control their Facebook "interests" and who they interact with, which in turn influences the types of ads they see on their Facebook feeds or on any other websites they visit.

We took to our own personal Facebook pages to show examples of how a user can change their preferences and view different ads on their feed via "Sponsored Content." We recently noticed a "Sponsored" advertisement for Huggies (figure 4.4). By clicking on the blue arrow highlighted on the image, users can either choose to hide ads they do not want to see or ask Facebook why

Huggies
Sponsored · 🌐

···

Natural Care Wipes are soon to be Natural Care Sensitive Wipes! Still the same wipes you know & love, just with a new name.

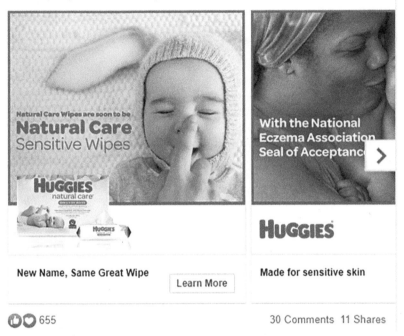

Natural Care Wipes are soon to be
Natural Care
Sensitive Wipes

HUGGIES
natural care

With the National Eczema Association Seal of Acceptance

HUGGIES

New Name, Same Great Wipe   Made for sensitive skin

Learn More

❤️👍 655   30 Comments 11 Shares

Figure 4.4
Screenshot of sponsored advertisement for Huggies, from personal Facebook account.

they are seeing a certain ad. By hiding ads, a Facebook user signals a decreased interest in that product, making it more likely that the user will not see that ad again. The advantage that companies have is that even if an ad is hidden, *users cannot preemptively hide ads they don't want to see.* A user can hide an ad only after they have seen it, ensuring that the ad is viewed before it is disregarded.

Regarding Facebook's "Advertising Requests," we previously explored what interests and properties go into a person seeing an ad. Here, Huggies is telling us we are seeing this ad because we match their "advertising requests" (figure 4.5). This could mean anything; maybe they know that we viewed one of their ads previously, that we speak English, that we are over eighteen, or that we live in the United States. If a user clicks the "Make changes to your

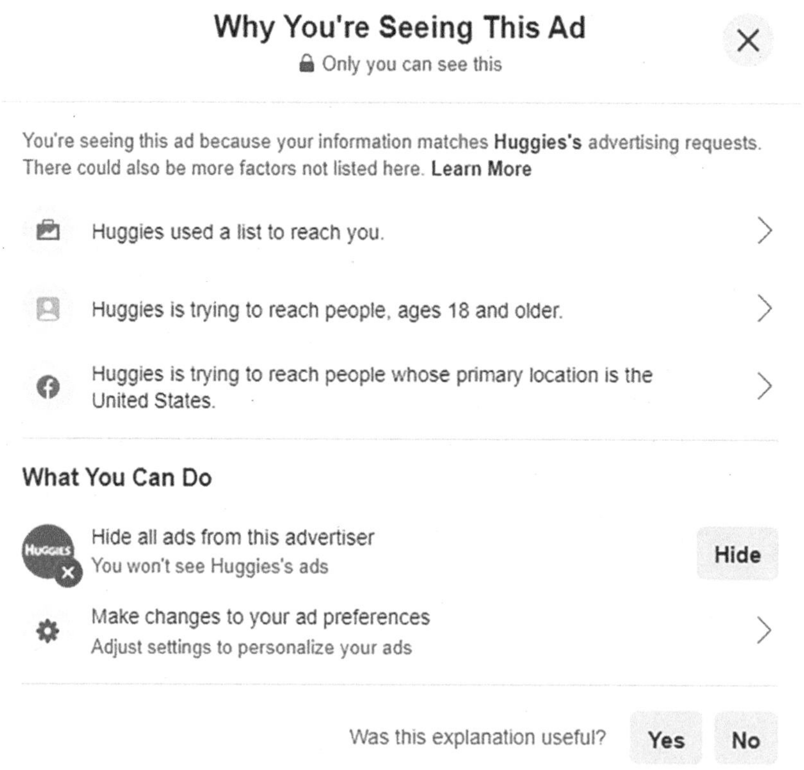

Why You're Seeing This Ad

🔒 Only you can see this

✕

You're seeing this ad because your information matches **Huggies's** advertising requests. There could also be more factors not listed here. **Learn More**

📑 Huggies used a list to reach you.   〉

👤 Huggies is trying to reach people, ages 18 and older.   〉

ⓕ Huggies is trying to reach people whose primary location is the   〉
United States.

What You Can Do

Hide all ads from this advertiser
You won't see Huggies's ads   **Hide**

⚙ Make changes to your ad preferences   〉
Adjust settings to personalize your ads

Was this explanation useful?   **Yes**   **No**

Figure 4.5
Screenshot of "Why You're Seeing This Ad" explanation for Huggies advertisement, from personal Facebook account.

ad preferences" button, they can see what interests of theirs led companies to show them ads (based on pages and ads they previously interacted with), a list of businesses that have interacted with their information in the past week, and the information they provided in their profile, which is fair game to advertisers.

Once an individual has seen an ad, they can opt to never see that type of ad again by changing their ad preferences and the information they make public to Facebook and, thus, to advertisers. This is *one* opportunity for the mothering group member to exert agency in the social media–informed maternal decision-making process.

IN WHAT WAYS ARE FACEBOOK STRATEGIES DIFFERENT FROM OR SIMILAR TO OTHER SOCIAL MEDIA STRATEGIES?

Facebook owns Instagram, so any ads a person sees on Facebook will likely also be on their Instagram feed. Instagram states that they only share information that they are given permission to share, but what most users don't know is that this entails all of the information Facebook can access based on the user's demographic, interests, and any lookalike information collected. This adds up to quite a lot of personal information that goes into targeted ads.

Many social media sites (like Twitter) have strategies similar to Facebook's but may be even more specific when they narrow down their ad search results. Twitter searches user interests like Facebook and Instagram to benefit ad campaigns, but there are even more specific options on Twitter's version of Ads Manager. Twitter's "Recommendation" is a tactic we have yet to see on any site besides Twitter. Since Twitter is more engagement based than Facebook and other social media sites, they rely more on mentions and hashtags for spreading information. Through these methods, Twitter can track what people and what hashtags a person follows in order to better serve them with ads they will respond to. Twitter also has a "lookalike" function for targeting interests, but offers little information on how they target lookalike audiences.

Facebook appears to be the most transparent about what information they use and where they are getting it from to serve us the ads we see; we might, then, find Facebook's *ethos* to be more persuasive than that of Twitter or Instagram. Yet we must consider not only marketing policies and procedures but also the algorithm that optimizes the Facebook News Feed.

"ALGORITHMIC AMPLIFICATION OPTIMIZED FOR OUTRAGE"

Facebook is not designed to encourage users' perusal of personal pages; rather, it is designed to encourage users to engage with their News Feeds. If what people actually read on Facebook is their News Feed, then "what people actually read on Facebook" is determined by an algorithm. This algorithm does not give all Facebook users an equal voice; rather, native content that optimizes engagement and paid advertising are inherently amplified. While

Facebook may claim that their News Feed algorithm is "content-agnostic," it remains true that only users selected by Facebook's algorithm get a voice in the News Feed.

Jon Evans (2019) relates that "'optimizing for engagement' all too often means optimizing for outrage, for polarization, for disingenuous misinformation. True, it doesn't mean favoring any side of any given issue; but it does mean favoring extremes, the conspiracy theorists, the histrionic diatribes on all sides. It means fomenting mistrust, suspicion, and conflict everywhere."[3] Evans's statement powerfully illustrates the key concern of this book: social media mothering groups' binaristic discourse and how not only human actors but also technological actants are feeding into the problematic circulation of these polarizing opinions. While Facebook ensures human intervention in algorithmic choices to filter out—as required by law—"hate speech, abuses, or dangerous medical misinformation" (Evans 2019), the site bears no responsibility in ensuring a continuum of necessarily complex positions are represented or in filtering out merely misleading or otherwise problematic "fake news." Facebook is complicit in the circulation of *ethos*-compromised fake news and its role in contemporary maternal decision-making.

"Fake news" and "false news" are terms, often used interchangeably, to describe the following: "disinformation, misinformation, hoaxes, propaganda, satire, rumors, click-bait and junk news" (Pierri and Ceri 2020, 18). While "fake news" is nothing new, its proliferation via social media has drawn academic and popular audience attention in recent years. On social media, the technological barriers to crafting and circulating fake news are low. Couple this with the human tendency toward naive realism and confirmation bias (inherently believing your position is the only right position and seeking out only those sources that confirm your existing beliefs), and the phenomenon of out-of-control fake news circulation on social media makes perfect sense. When we add in social identity theory and normative social influence, meaning "users tend to perform actions which are socially safer, thus consuming and spreading information items that agree with the norms established within the community," we get a more complete picture of how social media mothering groups operate as echo chambers, "characterized by extremely polarized opinions as they are insulated from opposite views and contrary perspectives"

(19). Each social media mothering group has chosen their position on the qualities of Optimal Motherhood and will remain unyielding to the other.

The Human Actors

In our coding of posts and comments from self-identified "formula feeding support groups," we found, not unsurprisingly, PFF (pro formula feeding) posts and comments, with the occasional MFP (moderate feeding position) post. Those groups that identified with "science," "evidence," or "woo free" tended to offer PBF (pro breastfeeding) posts. Again, this is not surprising. What is, if not surprising, certainly worth note is not *what* is being espoused (PFF vs. PBF) but *how* women enter these conversations on social media mothering groups. In terms of the binary discourse and "team-based" rhetoric that drives our analysis in this book, we note that infant feeding conversations tend to be "defensive" of the mother's choice. This is opposed to the pattern we note in mothers' tendency to take an "offensive" position against their opponents in the infant sleep approach debates on social media (a dynamic we further explore in chapter 5, "Precious Little Sleep™: Total Risk Aversion, Neonate Sleep, and the Erasure of Maternal Needs").

More specifically, in social media mothering groups organized around formula feeding, there was a clear defensive pattern of (1) decrying the suffocating judgment they had received for their choice (or lack thereof) to formula feed, (2) articulating the pervading guilt and/or shame they feel in performing or discussing that choice in front of/with other moms or healthcare practitioners, and (3) the complementary need to cling tighter a formula feeding community and to shout louder regarding their identity as new mom and formula feeder.

Consider this composite post representing the defensive position expressed in infant formula feeding support group discourse on social media, with commonly used language in quotation marks. An original poster (OP) may open her post by noting how the pressure to make the *right* parenting choice is perceived to be "EVERYWHERE." This is immediately followed by noting any choice of nonconformity begetting feelings of guilt and shame—that there is no choice that will prevent the OP from feeling "less than" or "not as good." The OP targets breastfeeding as a particularly troubling concern.

The core of the message breaks down the OP's discontent with the constant pressure to breastfeed and the false assurance that it will be easy and comfortable. The OP ends the post by labeling the pressure as "inescapable." (Group discourse espouses that every article, every video, references it—explicitly or implicitly. Well-intentioned people constantly inquire about your feeding plans. Health-care professionals "push" it.) First-time moms may qualify the overwhelming pressure of these choices as an especially repressive burden because they feel they *have* to search out information to be prepared. They have to understand the fiercely touted pros and cons of the two, binary-bound infant feeding approaches (among other maternal decisions) if they are ever to live up to the ideals of Optimal Motherhood.

Such an OP implicitly suggests that she has received the message that new parents are inherently unequipped to deal with modern-day parenting decisions and that if she wishes to be a competent parent, she *must* enter the matrix of maddeningly obstinate "opinions" regarding parenting "choices." Unfortunately, comments on such posts in social media infant feeding support groups commonly convey that (1) you will be judged, (2) you "can't win," and (3) nobody else's "opinion" but your own matters (with at least one commenter offering the caveat "as long as baby is healthy and happy"). These comments seem to reinforce that the judgment is indeed as inescapable as the OP perceives, that parenting decisions are a game (one that is perennially rigged against you), and that there are *no* reputable sources (that will not reinforce your guilt and shame) besides your own gut. There is a clear theme of "defeat" (or entrapment) as well as a need to "defend" one's choice to formula feed among such posters.

While there are examples of "neutral" information-seeking posts in formula feeding support groups, these types of posts were more frequently found in pro breastfeeding social media mothering groups. That is, because breastfeeding is perceived as the gold standard for infant feeding worldwide, we did not find the same prevalence of guilt- and shame-laden rhetoric in pro breastfeeding group discourse (or among breastfeeding discourse in more generalized social media mothering groups). This does *not*, however, mean that breastfeeding moms are not on the receiving end of guilt or shame. There are countless media stories and social media mothering group messages about breastfeeding moms being asked to cover up or leave public spaces. You've probably also read stories about the criticism faced by those who choose to breastfeed longer than the first year. On September 17, 2019, Cara (@caraandthecubs) made a notable #extendedbreastfeeding post:

> I wasn't going to post this picture. I'm aware that the fact I still breastfeed my almost 4 year old makes some people feel weird. . . . Feeding older children is a lot more common than people realise; it's just usually done behind closed doors because older children feed more seldomly. . . . The feeling of having them both curled up on my lap is indescribable, but they are quickly outgrowing it, and soon I will look back on these photos wistfully and remember how my body comforted and nourished my boys. #naturaltermweaning #normalizebreastfeeding #extendedbreastfeeding #tandemnursing.

Many supportive comments followed, such as "Oh my! How precious! You are an amazing mama!" But judgment also followed: "Why still allow the 4-year-old to do this when they can have normal meals [that] provide the same level of nutrients?" and "Very disturbing." Judgment was countered, expectedly, with fierce but slippery slope defenses: "Exactly! Women need to take back control of their bodies; it's no one else's business how a woman feeds her children" and "What's good for your children is good for you. No one else needs [to] have an input." Our point here isn't for readers to quibble over the relevancy of breastfeeding a four-year-old as an example of common breastfeeding kickback; our point is to note that extended breastfeeding lies on the complex continuum of maternal feeding decisions and that publicly performed acts of breastfeeding, too, encounter mothering shame and stigma.

Also consider the negative connotations now attached to the term "lactivist." "Lactivism" was a movement born in the 1970s that was designed to counteract corporate greed, to fight a formula company that put women and babies in developing countries at risk; Nestlé unethically pushed formula in regions that lacked access to clean water, at prices that caused the poor dependent on it to water it down, resulting in infant diarrhea and malnutrition, among other critically concerning outcomes (Goldberg 2015). Now, however, the term "lactivist" is associated with "self-righteous extremists preying on innocent mothers in the name of science and good parenting" (Bartick 2015). It is not a term of endearment. Rather, it is an insult.

What this all seems to add up to is an endless cycle of guilt and shame surrounding infant feeding choices, choices that are presented as black and white online: you are team breastfeeding or you are team formula feeding. The loyalty is fierce and the criticism is harsh, even when (as previously noted in this chapter) the science is shaky. In reality, feeding *practices* exist on a complex continuum because, "for many, the current WHO recommendation of six months of exclusive breastfeeding is simply not realistic and can discourage mothers from even initiating breastfeeding. *Instead we should follow a woman-centred approach where mothers are empowered to set their own realistic targets*" (Komninou and Fallon 2016; emphasis added). If a "women-centered" approach is the goal, we need to first understand the competing framework that represents a key node in the circulating *ethos* influencing infant feeding decisions: baby-first initiatives.

BABY-FIRST VERSUS WOMEN-CENTERED

By now you've seen the articles: "The Failure of Baby-Friendly Initiatives" (Braff 2019), "Baby-Friendly Hospitals Can, Paradoxically, Be Unsafe for Newborns" (Strauss 2016), "Nurses Are Speaking Out about the Dangers of the Baby-Friendly Health Initiative" (Fed is Best 2018), and other similar titles. The authors of these articles cover issues tackled in a March 2020 study published in the *Journal of Pediatrics*, "Outcomes from the Centers for Disease Control and Prevention 2018 Breastfeeding Report Card: Public Policy Implications" (Bass, Gartley, and Kleinman 2020). The purpose of the scholarly study was to compare the success of "in-hospital breastfeeding initiation" with breastfeeding outcomes from baby-friendly hospitals. The study's authors concluded that while in-hospital breastfeeding initiatives generally had positive breastfeeding results, baby-friendly certification and facilitation did not. As a reminder, the Baby-Friendly Hospital Initiative was sponsored in 1991 by UNICEF and the World Health Organization with the goal of ensuring "that all maternities, whether free-standing or in a hospital, become centers of breastfeeding support" (UNICEF 2005). To achieve "baby-friendly" designation, a hospital *cannot* accept free or low-cost breast milk substitutes and *must* follow these ten steps:

1. Have a written breastfeeding policy that is routinely communicated to all health care staff.
2. Train all health care staff in skills necessary to implement this policy.
3. Inform all pregnant women about the benefits and management of breastfeeding.
4. Help mothers initiate breastfeeding within one half-hour of birth.
5. Show mothers how to breastfeed and maintain lactation, even if they should be separated from their infants.
6. Give newborn infants no food or drink other than breastmilk, unless medically indicated.
7. Practice rooming in—that is, allow mothers and infants to remain together 24 hours a day.
8. Encourage breastfeeding on demand.
9. Give no artificial teats or pacifiers (also called dummies or soothers) to breastfeeding infants.
10. Foster the establishment of breastfeeding support groups and refer mothers to them on discharge from the hospital or clinic. (UNICEF 2005)

This probably all sounds well and good given the perceived unequivocal benefits of breastfeeding,[4] except when the risks outweigh the benefits to the infant *and to the mother*. Serious criticism arose from the academy in the 2010s (and we dare say, informed complaints arose much earlier): near-fatal or fatal sleep, suffocation, and fall incidents (Feldman-Winter and Goldsmith 2016); sleep deprivation leading to perinatal anxiety, depression, and other mood disorders (Theo and Drake 2017); infants suffering from dehydration (Bass, Gartley, and Kleinman 2016); and other nutritional deficiencies while *breastfeeding outcomes were not being achieved* (Bass, Gartley, and Kleinman 2020). Our goal here is not to present a Romper article as sound science or to holistically criticize baby-friendly initiatives and breastfeeding; rather, our goal is to further evidence that an all-or-nothing approach to parenting decisions is unrealistic and often punitive to new mothers, that science has not provided a clear answer, either—though human actors have acted as much. Therefore, qualitatively understanding our complex human condition and complementary discourse conventions is integral to empowering women in the precarious position of making contemporary maternity decisions often sans geographically bound village and clear-cut *ethos*-informed advice.

(A FEW OF THE MANY) COMPLICATING FACTORS IN INFANT FEEDING DECISIONS

There are a host of complicating factors that should be considered nodes (actants or actors) in the networked *ethos* of contemporary infant feeding advice. Consider Andrea Freeman's (2019) work in the book *Skimmed: Breastfeeding, Race, and Injustice*. Freeman relates the story of Annie Mae Fultz, a Black Cherokee mother who gave birth to the world's first identical quadruplets on May 23, 1946. Fred Klenner, the white doctor who delivered the quads, stole the privilege of naming the girls, began doing controversial experiments with vitamin C on the girls, and "began negotiating with formula companies that sought to become the newly famous Fultz Quads' corporate godparent. The company with the highest bid would be the first to target Black women with a formula advertising campaign." Freeman goes on to tell the story of Tabitha Walrond, a young Black woman who was unable to successfully procure a Medicaid card for her child because of governmental red tape. After enduring a complicated delivery in August 1997, she was quickly dismissed from the hospital with the assurance that she would be able to successfully breastfeed her son. However, she struggled with breastfeeding and her son lost weight. Since she did not have a Medicaid card for him, she could not afford to take him to a doctor. Within eight weeks he died of inadequate nutrition, and Tabitha was charged with second-degree manslaughter. According to Freeman, "The factors that contribute to Black women's low breastfeeding rates are manifold, complex, and interconnected. They include *race-targeted marketing, unequal distribution of resources* for new mothers, and *historical and present discrimination*. Underlying these factors is the symbiotic relationship between the US government and formula corporations that gives the government a stake in the formula industry. This partnership harms women and infants in all communities but has a disproportionately negative impact on Black women and children" (2019, 6; emphasis added). Labor studies ultimately show that it is, in fact, working conditions—not female un/willingness—that have a significant impact on infant feeding decision.

Kimberly Seals Allers (2019) productively continues the conversation in "Six Things I've Learned about Making Breastfeeding Accessible for All." Allers relates that conversations typically center on middle-class white women, but that, instead, we need to "look to the margins": "The picture of breast-feeding needs more hourly workers, retail employees and recognition of the unique challenges for schoolteachers and health-care professionals. We must also look at women's lived experiences."[5] She calls for us to look at the "lived experiences" of the multitude of women who make up the network of contemporary mothers, precisely what we call for in this book: acknowledging the complexities of maternal decision-making that too often show up on social media as binary-bound choices when, in reality, infant feeding choices are practiced on a spectrum—with many mothers breastfeeding, pumping, *and* formula feeding their infants (the invisible-to-social-media art of combination feeding).

Allers (2019) also calls us to pay attention to "social stressors": "When mothers are stressed about getting *Instagram* perfect, when mothers are stressed about being 'productive' (as if mothering is not important work), when new mothers are stressed about returning to work in 10 days, it is no wonder American women report having insufficient milk." She draws attention to what we have termed social media's seeming insistence on performing Optimal Motherhood: the working mother must work as if she does not have children to tend to, and the stay-at-home mom must not reveal that her stay-at-home mothering is work. Consider, too, that American women have been screaming into the void about unfairly short (or nonexistent) parental leave policies (depending on a leave policy is, after all, the by-product of neoliberal isolationism given that contemporary American mothers generally lack a parenting village to fulfill this need).

The third item on Allers's (2019) list is "Anger and division won't get us anywhere" (are you getting the impression that Allers has concisely summarized the many themes of this book?). She iterates that if not full-blown "mommy wars," then divisiveness, at least, clearly colors our conversations with one another; yet "turning anger onto mothers who have had different experiences instead of turning that anger into coordinated action to help all mothers will not move modern motherhood forward." Let's use that angry energy, instead, to advocate for lactation management education for physicians, resources for funding hospital lactation staff, and mandatory at-home postpartum visits as standard practices of care.

She further asks us to turn our feelings of ill will away from formula proper and toward the *marketing* of formula: "Everyone knows infant formula needs to exist. The issue is the unethical and inappropriate marketing of breast-milk substitutes that undermines women and puts corporate profits ahead of infant health" (Allers 2019). Formula companies make up a $70 billion+ industry, one that succeeds only when breastfeeding fails.

Further considering marketing and the circulation of discourse surrounding feeding, Allers (2019) asks us to reconsider championing "Breast is best" as a slogan. Allers asserts that "'Breast is best' is scientifically accurate, but where is the mother in that phrase?" As stated previously, we would challenge Allers's assertion of the scientific accuracy of "breast is best," though we heartily agree with the relevance of her question: "Where is the mother in that phrase?" As we demonstrate again in chapter 5, a significant common denominator in these discussions is the disembodiment of the mother, who discursively becomes a tool for the baby and little else.

Finally, Allers (2019) tackles guilt, shame, pressure, and privilege: "Lastly, there is a dangerous thread in breast-feeding conversation that needs to be addressed head-on, big-girl-panties style." Allers calls on all to consider that the sharing of information is *not* inherent mom-shaming: "I don't subscribe to the concept that mothers are too weak to understand credible information. This idea that mothers are too fragile for facts is rooted in patriarchal structures." Again, we would emphasize it's not the "what" that's being shared but the "how." Complicated context, honesty, and care are all important to the delivery of maternal decision-making discourse.

From the Mouths of Moms and Health Professionals

Our interviewed moms felt the pressure:

"There's weird mom-group pressure."

"Yeah, [shame or guilt from] the church I was attending at the time."

"People always judged and said 'Are you thinking about what's appropriate' in terms of asking how long I'll do it."

Our interviewed nurses reported the pressure:

> "I have had patients tell me that they felt pressure from doctors, the internet, blogs, [and] other moms to feed their newborn one way or the other."

> "If my mom and grandma had bottle-fed I would probably do the same thing with no thought. [It] also depends on socioeconomic background (breastfeeding is free)."

> "I think also frequency and exhaustion play a huge role in feeding decisions. I often hear moms talk about fatigue and ask the question, 'Can't I get a break?'"

> "Body image can also sometimes factor in."

So how can we get the larger discourse community to acknowledge the complicated variables that play a role in the *ethos* of contemporary maternal decision-making?

Perhaps it is about focusing on perinatal women-centered education and care that acknowledges not just the "what" in the delivery and circulation of discourse but also the "how." One performative aspect of this is online mentoring.

Mom Mentorship

In an informal poll regarding difficult parenting decisions complicated by misinformation or conflicting information, members of a five-thousand-plus evidence-based social media parenting support group listed the following as issues: feeding solids, diapering, sleep training, breastfeeding, induction, vaccination, co-sleeping, special needs, circumcision, attachment parenting, and childcare (among other less frequently mentioned concerns)—with sleeping and feeding each receiving multiple mentions in various forms.

It should be no surprise, then, that one formula feeding group we observed has begun a mentorship program to help members wade through the seemingly infinite amount of available information and well-intentioned (or not-so-well-intentioned) advice, to offer members a trusted guide for their infant feeding journey. The program's stated foundational goals are to "share your experience or learn valuable skills from someone in your group." How the mentorship program works is explained in four steps:

1. Create a profile in which you explain who you are and your desire for facilitating or receiving mentorship.

2. Find a "partner" by browsing profiles and reaching out to someone who could be a good fit for you.
3. Discuss mentorship goals with that partner—and know that you will have the support of weekly Messenger prompts to encourage your collaborative progress.
4. Reach goals: "Achieve something exciting, or enjoy the deep satisfaction of helping someone else be successful."

In many ways, the rhetoric parallels that of a dating app; in a positive light, this affords an avenue of relationship building for those mothers who are lost in the binary-bound discourse of social media mothering groups. Where the *ethos* of one digital actant has failed (social media mothering groups as discourse arenas that undermine their own intentions of creating connections—pitting players for "team breastfeeding" against those for "team formula feeding," for example), another actant has been assembled within the larger network of digitally circulated motherhood advice (connecting and building trust among more and less experienced human actors), giving lifeblood to the *continuum* of infant feeding choices.

To play devil's advocate, wouldn't mentorship within a given "feeding type" group come with the danger of further distancing the "formula feeders" from the "breastfeeders"—compounding the binary, if you will? This is where the scholarly perspective on mentorship is of particular importance. The group takes care to invite all to participate ("anyone who has experience and a skill to share can offer support in the Mentorship program") but qualifies their answer to "Who can become a mentor" with "Your mentor's advice is their own opinion, and not that of Facebook or your admin(s). All participation is voluntary, your mentor's advice is not meant to substitute professional advice." Not only does the mentorship structure assemble a networked *ethos* that relies on both the credibility and authority of "professional" advice as well as the "experience" of a veteran mom mentor, but it also, structurally, nurtures critical and complex maternal decision-making that is otherwise muted in the seamless harmony of most "safe" social media mothering group spaces.

That is, many social media mothering groups (as stated elsewhere in this book) ban "controversy" and seek to operate as a "safe" space of support for those navigating twenty-first-century maternal decision-making. Safe spaces are predicated on performing sensitivity and inclusivity (Arao and Clemens 2013). This seems well and good *except* that these safe spaces, then, in the banning of "controversy" and the privileging of sensitivity, tend to become echo chambers for uncritically examined and homogeneously elevated binaristic thinking. Instead, we might lean into Arao and Clemens's (2013) understanding of "brave spaces," spaces where courage and risk taking lead to learning across complex differences and critical reflection on our own perspectives. We believe brave space growth can occur productively for twenty-first-century mothers in the context of mentoring within social media mothering groups. It's easier to be brave by growing in relationship with a *trusted* veteran mother, setting concrete educational goals and challenging each other's binaristic maternal decision-making matrices. In short, this provides a productive pathway where disagreement can be navigated without reinforcing the outrage and defensiveness that characterizes Optimal Motherhood. As a node in the networked *ethos* of contemporary maternity advice, mentoring may afford a ripple effect that then positively influences the algorithms and other technological actants currently swaying social media mothering group discourse toward an entrenching of (rather than the desired dismantling of) oppressive Optimal Motherhood.

CONCLUSION: EATING AND SLEEPING

While this chapter has worked to describe and define maternal infant feeding decisions as problematically bound in defensive binaristic discourse, chapter 5, "Precious Little Sleep™: Total Risk Aversion, Neonate Sleep, and the Erasure of Maternal Needs," illustrates the intractably offensive nature of social media mothering group discourse on infant sleep. Regarding feeding methods, women are tasked with picking the most wholesome, nutritious choice and, thereby, with the notion that they are, in fact, capable of shaping a perfectly healthy human being; in the sleep debates, women are laden with the sense that they will always be somehow responsible for the death of their neonates. To this end, chapters 4 and 5 demonstrate perhaps most palpably the ways in which motherhood in the white, middle-class Western world has become a force of productive citizen-shaping whose greatest burden is laid on the mother, who must navigate a series of seemingly impossible binary decisions in the space of (increasingly digital-only) communities that form around such polarized choices.

Correctly install your car seat, 'cause we're about to go for a ride.

5 PRECIOUS LITTLE SLEEP™: TOTAL RISK AVERSION, NEONATE SLEEP, AND THE ERASURE OF MATERNAL NEEDS

I don't know exactly what I expected to happen when I laid my two-day-old down in her crib for the first time. At the time, I generally acknowledged my lack of certainty regarding any part of her care—I vividly recall being handed my daughter for the first time after her birth and saying, "Oh, no. You can't just hand me a baby without teaching me how to hold one first!" My husband and I had not been around children much, and, because I was an only child, one could assume I had precisely *no* knowledge about infants. So, cluelessness was already rather old hat to me, a forty-eight-hours-old mother. But, I had assumed, there were at least *some* givens. A wise friend had told me, "Babies sleep. They eat. They poop. That's all they need. It'll be okay." "But how?" was my resounding chorus in those early, exhaustion-filled days—as my body screamed for rest and recuperation but a new, external being also screamed at me to meet its needs. How to make it sleep? Interestingly, I did not ask myself this question on the end of the second day of her life. For once, something seemed obvious. People sleep in beds; therefore, put the child in a bed. Voilà!

So why was she suddenly screaming herself hoarse?

When I look back on this memory, nothing is clearer to me than the universality of moments like this. Of course, at the time, I felt so vastly alone—literally groping in the dark, clutching this creature that hadn't been screaming at me just forty-eight hours ago. I was armed with nothing more than a vast and desperate desire to meet its needs but had little know-how and few people (at four in the morning, anyway) whom I could turn to. I see now, in the clearer light of day (and several years' remove), that this must be the plight of nearly every mother in the United States, where communal infant care is a concept conceived only in its uniformal rejection when the topic of postpartum doulas or hospital infant nurseries arises. In the modern-day United States, land of bootstrapping success and self-made riches, mothers are expected to fend for themselves, and almost any suggestion of help for new mothers is, if discussed at all, discussed with a sort of disdain for the laziness implied (especially among white, middle-class mothers). These mothers, it would seem, have not escaped their Victorian legacy as backbone and soul of a house, especially when it comes to child-rearing. It's no wonder, then, that women, awake and desperate with the "little stranger" (as Victorians called newborns) in the middle of the night, turn to the internet for solutions. More than perhaps any society the world over, American women are denied a collective community of concern directed toward their infants.[1] We are expected to go it alone; yet, humanity finds ways to connect, and, in our present moment, the ever connectivity of the internet is a convenient (if, as we shall discuss, fraught) means of finding communal advice in a trying time.

This chapter addresses the realm of infant sleep. Sleep is such a basic necessity that, as the opening anecdote to this chapter demonstrates, it might be surprising to some (nonparent) readers that heated debates—wielding images of dead babies—surround this deceptively simple question: *how* (as I failed to ask in my early days of maternity) should infants sleep? While pregnant, I asked many questions; somehow, this was not one of them. The act of sleeping, for me, in my late twenties, was so natural, so embedded in the way that I consciously chose to *forget* the tumult of the world—its manifold existential and pragmatic dilemmas—that to denaturalize sleep as such, to recontextualize it as a process that I must teach to another human, simply did not occur to me.

As we say, we think many mothers find themselves in this position; however, with the increasing tone of Optimal Motherhood—in which mothers are tasked with doing everything perfectly for their babies—we have simultaneously observed more and more pregnant mothers researching and making such determinations *before* they give birth. Increasingly, since the growth of large interest-oriented Facebook groups circa 2013, posts like the following abound: "Hi! I'm due in about 2 months, and I definitely know that the way

I want to sleep with my infant is X, but I'm wondering how I do Y while that happens?" This is a departure from the previous (and still prevalent) posts that look like this: "Hi! My 6-month-old isn't sleeping anymore the way we have been approaching things, and I'd like to adjust our sleep model." Thus, we see more and more mothers preparing for birth in advance, making ideological determinations based on assumptions of how they *know* they will feel before they enter a state of personhood (motherhood) that they have never encountered before.[2] This, of course, does not only apply to first-time moms. As any parent of more than one child will tell you, every child is its own new and surprising adventure.

TO SLEEP, PERCHANCE TO DREAM . . .

The way communities of mothers approach maternal decision-making—like how to get a baby to sleep—is rather overdetermined by assumptive patterns (to draw from Emily Martin [1987]) about how babies are "supposed" to sleep to begin with. It is, in fact, this issue with which most of infant sleep discourse is preoccupied, as opposed to being focused on pragmatic guides. Such pragmatic guides do exist, but being rather simple stepwise practices (such as "cry it out," to which we will return), they make up much less of the volume of discourse than actual discussion of *which* pragmatic mode is "best." As with any discussion of health-practice decision-making, "best" in these conversations tends to be defined by an assumed polemic of "natural" versus "interventional" (although never, as we will elaborate on later, with a focus on the mother's own needs for sleep). The term "natural," here, represents the chosen term of communities advocating for certain practices (and against others)—that is, this term does not necessarily represent what *we* as authors see as natural, and, instead, represents a collective view of a certain set of stakeholders. As feminist scholars of science and technology, we question the concept or term of "natural" to begin with, as much as we are skeptical of the implied binary it establishes of "natural versus unnatural." To that end, our use of the term "interventional" is our own and strives to destabilize this binary by not replicating it but gets, we think, at the heart of the alternatives women see for themselves—to let "nature" "naturally" shape feeding, sleeping, and birthing practices or to claim agency in changing some aspect of this (formula feeding or medically assisted births, for instance).

This chapter began with a longer anecdote than some of the other chapters in this book, because while formula and epidurals are rather obvious interventions in what seems easier to call "the natural state of affairs," so-called natural sleep seems harder to define. Again, while we fundamentally resist the notion that concepts of the natural are helpfully invoked in medical praxis and decision-making, nevertheless, it is abundantly obvious that five hundred years ago women had to labor through childbirth without mass-produced drugs or assistive technologies (the forceps not having been invented until 1735) and that lactated milk of some form or another (the mother's, a wet nurse's, a goat's, or a cow's) constituted the only available food source for neonates. Thus, while we stake no claims as to the "bestness" of such "natural" options—and while we resist invoking the notion of "nature" and the "natural" throughout this book—we assert that locating the figure of the "natural" in these two cases seems simpler than doing so in terms of infant sleep.

Did sleep somehow look different in the Western Renaissance than it does today? We have far less data on a subject like this—one so *natural* to human existence—purely because it is so natural. By adulthood, sleep is a habitual practice that we do fairly automatically, and the entrance of a "little stranger" has the tendency to suddenly render unfamiliar that most familiar and comforting part of life. Childbirth is much more momentous, certainly rarer than our daily slumber, and food availability has simply been documented in recipes much more widely than discussions of something so ubiquitous as sleep that, ironically, we've been left with much less evidence on the history of a practice that makes up about 30 percent of every human life. Another issue with knowledge preservation in this field has to do with class. Wealthy women may have had servants to care for their babies, and undereducated servants throughout history were not equipped to record their best practices. The same would be true for lower-class mothers who did *not* have hired help. Men—educated, wealthy men—were the main preservers of history and cultural practice up until at least the mid-eighteenth century (to give a liberal estimate), and while they may have been invested in documenting birth practices over which they may have at times presided, it would be difficult to imagine them being interested in the nuances of household female labor such as newborn care. We do have cradles and drawings, of course, which can tell us something about at least the *aims* parents had for infant sleep, but much less about a family's actual practice at four in the morning in 1542 when their newborn awoke for the tenth time. Did they stay in the cradle then? That's the million-dollar question. Thus, with little historical evidence to guide us, and with unclear and often conflicting evidence about what constitutes the healthiest sleep for babies,[3] mothers today turn to crowdsourcing information online to determine what is "best." And in this space of digital crowdsourcing, in the gap left by scientific clarity, the choice between the two seeming possibilities of infant sleep methods—alone or with others—has become arguably one of the most polarizing of maternal health decisions that we observed for this study.

In fact, when seeking permission to study various issue-specific parenting groups, we encountered intense aggression—including curse words—from one of these social media infant sleep groups because our study did not take a stance on the issue of child sleep. Unlike in, say, feeding groups (already a contentious space full of debate and defensiveness), our "on the fence" or neutral position in regard to sleep was itself vilified as complacency with the harm of children (it is worth noting that both sides of the sleep debate exhibit this dynamic, so the specific group alignment of the speaker in this case is irrelevant here). What could seem like two neutral options has become quite politicized in these groups. As opposed to feeding debates, in which both groups appear to feel vilified by the other (formula feeding moms claim they are seen as providing subpar nutrition to their children, while breastfeeding mothers argue that they are shamed for feeding in public), both sides of sleep debates conversely spend most of their efforts decrying the *other* side as harmful. This is perhaps one clue to the intense and often vitriolic nature of sleep debates: where feeding debates are defensive—defending personal choices—sleep debates often tend to be *offensive*, proclaiming *other* choices as wrong, cruel, or even deadly.

Consider this public Facebook post from Cultura Colectiva (2018)[4]: "It all dates back to when they were babies . . ." The post prominently features a *pathos*-laden image of a crying baby: furrowed brows and face reddened in rage, scream lines emanating from a mouth agape (figure 5.1). We are meant to embody the place of the invisible parent, physically (and, by proxy,

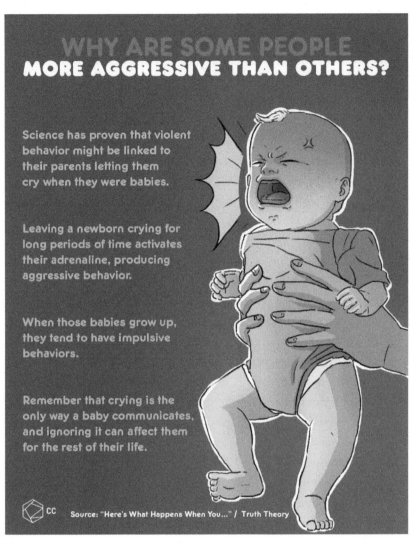

Figure 5.1
Image of crying baby from Facebook post.
Source: Cultura Colectiva (2018).

mentally/emotionally) holding the enraged child at a distance. The top center text invites parents to read on to answer the question "Why are some people more aggressive than others?" (as if the answer isn't already obvious in its visual rendering).

The answer text attempts to couple the *pathos*-heavy imagery with an appeal to *logos*: "*Science* has *proven* . . ."; however, the text immediately undermines this *logos* with a "might": "Science has proven that violent behavior *might* be linked to their parents letting them cry when they were babies" (emphasis added). The poster attempts to recover some credibility, or *ethos*, by listing a source—"Here's What Happens When You . . ." / Truth Theory—but those willing to do additional research will find the appeal to authority to be suspect. What is of most interest here is the way the post's replies tend to largely overlook these weak logical and ethical appeals and, instead, illustrate the instinctual emotional reactions that tend to characterize infant sleep debates circulated on social media. The binary-bound conversations in these comments speak to the fiercely aggressive and notably offensive nature of this particular node in contemporary maternal decision-making discourse.

For example, we noted that the sleep debate, perhaps more than any parenting issue covered in this book, employed the use of expletives, from both sides: "Wow . . . I can clearly see by the amount of comments here that we are getting more and more damaged children into adults (me being one of them). Hold your baby when they cry! They don't understand this new world! They only have one way to tell you something is wrong. Fucking heartless miseducated bunch. Cry it out is wrong and dangerous to a baby 😢" and "This is such BS. Just another way for the kids to take control over their parents even more. LMAO. 😂😂😂"

Proponents of the cry-it-out or safe-sleep approaches were quick to cry "nonsense":

"BS. This is why there [are] so many Brats out there."

"Hence: ENTITLEMENT."

Both sides, then, are offensively (sometimes implicitly and sometimes *explicitly*) blamed for humanity's mental and emotional ills: on the one hand, coveting of convenience, bratty behavior, and overall entitlement if a mother has elected to co-sleep; on the other, rage and attachment disorders if a mother has chosen safe sleep. The screaming child in the figure is apparently unavoidable. Combing through the comments also reveals disparaging declarations of co-sleeping and attachment parenting's supposed causal relationship with the lack of self-control and the "overly sensitive" nature that besieges contemporary citizens in this regard.

Like safe-sleeping proponents, who are blamed for a child's brain damage through prolonged stress, co-sleeping proponents are further blamed for physical abuse: shaken baby syndrome. For example: "Posting shit like this leads to the propaganda that you cannot leave a child alone at all, which is the number one cause of shaking baby syndrome[—a p]arent under the pressure that they cannot leave or calm down or decompress or give it five fucking minutes to calm down themselves." This commenter may have been unique in their invocation of shaken baby syndrome, but there was no shortage of commenters quick to insinuate that co-sleeping results in the deaths of babies:

> He does love a [cuddle], but it is still dangerous. There was a mum and dad not so long ago [who] killed their 2-and-half-year-old because he rolled on him and didn't know and killed him; so, it is dangerous xx. . . . I[t] doesn't matter. One time you can go into a deep sleep! I get that you don't like seeing him upset. . . . You might not agree with it, but [it] isn't your decision to make😘😘

The commenter not only problematically juxtaposes kiss-throwing emojis (meant to convey general feelings of love and affection) with imagery of a dead baby but also matter-of-factly strips maternal decision-making agency from the mother she discourses with in this exchange.

Co-sleeping proponents exhibit an offensive approach as well. One commenter blatantly calls out cry-it-out paradigms as child abuse: "I believe it's a form of child abuse. . . . Not sorry I said that." We see this aggression mirrored in diction and syntax, with co-sleeping parents metaphorically yelling at cry-it-out parents in all capital letters:

YOU CANNOT SPOIL A BABY.
YOU
CAN

NOT
SPOIL
A
BABY.

They were also not afraid to use full stops, adding to the urgency of their anti-cry-it-out message:

> You. Can't. Spoil. A. Baby. By. Giving. Affection. And. Meeting. The. Need. Of. Being. Held.
> Period.

Rhetorically, the commenter situates letting an infant cry themselves to sleep not as neglect of a want but as *neglect of a need*.

We can't resist repeating what one commenter offered in jest: "Going by the comments, I'm guessing you were all left to cry. . . ." In all seriousness, another commenter pointed out the larger exigency driving our inquiry into these social media mothering group conversations: "Gotta love all the mom shaming on this post." Mom-shaming seems ever more systematic in sleep debates. The science may be muddy, but the discourse is clear: we are trenchantly loyal to our "teams" in these binary-bound maternal decision-making contexts.

Thus, two seemingly neutral choices—baby sleeps alone, or baby sleeps with mother—in these debates tend to become the following: if you let your baby sleep with you, you are risking its life through potential suffocation or rollover; and if you let your baby sleep alone, you are not meeting its needs, and your child will be traumatized from withheld nurturing and affection. In this way, the sleep debates, perhaps more than any we cover in this book, demonstrate in clear language the double bind in which modern maternity finds itself. Women are bad, risky, dangerous, and unloving no matter what they elect in terms of sleep. Whereas in the feeding debates women are posited as not doing *enough* (to nourish the infant or to cover up their bodies), the sleep debates cast mothers as already *doing* that which is either emotionally or physically harmful, and they must choose one. There is no opting out of sleep, after all, and the message women resoundingly get online is that if they elect to protect the life of their baby (so the conversations run), they are ipso facto electing to neglect the emotional health of their baby—by abandoning it to physically so-called safe sleep. On the other hand, if they elect to protect the emotional needs of their baby (so the debate terms go), they have by proxy chosen to subject their baby to the risk of death through supposedly "natural" co-sleeping. The sleep debates come down to "natural" versus "safe" and sheltering the physical versus mental lives of their babies, and this is perhaps why they (structured as implicitly castigating choices other than one's own) remain trenchantly *offensive*—directed outward at *other* mothers' choices in support of the primacy of their own.

GETTING BACK TO SLEEP

We've mentioned mothers electing to make these decisions while still pregnant, and it is worth keeping an expectant mother's fears and anxieties in mind while reading through the discourse we provide and analyze below. The message of safe sleep is deceptively simple: sleep with your baby, and you willingly risk the baby's life. The mental and emotional stakes of this particular maternal decision are as significant as or more significant than the *ethos* that informs them, though it is the credibility and authority of such monolithic institutions (like the National Institutes of Health [NIH]— and its interpretations of "solid" scientific data) that pervade much of the source-slinging in these debates in social media mothering groups. In 1994, the National Institute of Child Health (NICH) launched the Back to Sleep campaign, which sought to lower sudden infant death syndrome (SIDS) death rates by encouraging families to follow the "ABCs" of safe sleep; that is, infants should sleep **A**lone, on their **B**ack, and in a **C**rib (National Institute of Child Health and Human Development, n.d.).

Figure 5.2, produced by the NIH, shows the inverse correlation between back-sleeping and SIDS rates; however, such data has often been contested, even by those who promote back-sleeping.

For instance, the diagnostic criteria of SIDS have often been conflated with those of infant suffocation, when they are, in fact, two separate conditions. By definition, SIDS is intended to refer to any infant death that *cannot be* linked to any obvious cause (suffocation included; LaFrance 2016). While

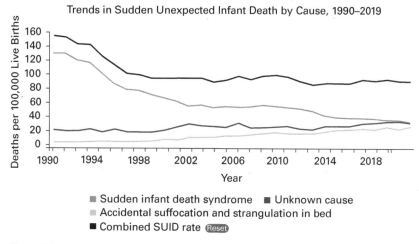

Figure 5.2
CDC Chart: SIDS, suffocation, and strangulation deaths per 100,000 live births.
Source: CDC (2021).

this doesn't mean that the data represented in the NIH graph is *untrue*, it does mean that it very well could be misleading or confounded, depending on which infant deaths were selected for inclusion in this study and how.[5] This does not change the fact that infant suffocation rates during sleep may very well have improved since the Back to Sleep campaign; it simply means that this is not necessarily what *this data* itself *proves*. And it is *this data* that is dispersed widely to mothers, proclaiming the risk of co-sleeping.

Aside from this, the pervasive culture of risk hypervigilance, outlined in the introduction to this book, certainly pervades the world of infant sleep. If the sleep debates are *offensive* and the feeding ones are *defensive*, then this is likely related to the fact that while feeding decisions seem to be wrapped up in seeking out the *best* food choice, sleep choices seem to be wrapped up in avoiding the *worst* (i.e., most unsafe) options. Consider, for example, the NICH's Interactive Safe Sleep Room (figure 5.3).

The NIH places a polite but perplexing insistence on the flexibility and adaptability of these guidelines as shown on the landing page preceding the interactive room—"Please note that this room is for teaching purposes only. You can adapt the recommendations to rooms of any shape or size in your

Figure 5.3

NICH's Interactive Safe Sleep Room welcome message.

Source: National Institute of Child Health and Human Development (2020).

home"—especially given the stringent dos and do nots the viewer is visually bombarded with upon entering the Interactive Safe Sleep Room (figure 5.4). Though the viewer is prefaced with a gentle "this is for your edification only; you can adapt this advice as needed in your own home," the repetition of the general prohibition sign carries significant weight as a technological actant in this digital discourse. There is no room for arguing against the most unsafe sleep options: no tobacco, marijuana, alcohol, or drugs. No toys or bedding in baby's crib. Make no mistakes in adjusting nursery temperature. Most importantly, do not feed, comfort, or bond with baby in a chair, because you might fall asleep. One hardly needs to "select icons to learn more." The message here is clear: death lurks for your baby everywhere.

The digital rhetoric of the interactive Chair of Death is worth particular note (figure 5.5). "Couches and armchairs can be *very* dangerous for babies" (emphasis added), though we are meant to believe they are just as much standard fixtures in most nurseries as are teddy bears and blankets neatly stacked on nightstands and next to proudly displayed safe-sleep pamphlets, of course. This particular type of "surface" is not merely dangerous but *very* dangerous—not because of definitive scientific inquiry and outcomes but because a hypothetical caregiver "may" fall asleep while on this surface. The

Select icons to learn more.

Figure 5.4
NICH's Interactive Safe Sleep Room "dos" and "do nots" message.
Source: National Institute of Child Health and Human Development (2020).

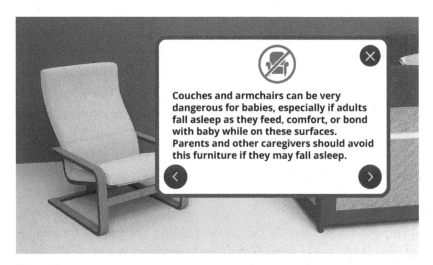

Couches and armchairs can be very dangerous for babies, especially if adults fall asleep as they feed, comfort, or bond with baby while on these surfaces. Parents and other caregivers should avoid this furniture if they may fall asleep.

Figure 5.5
NICH's Interactive Safe Sleep Room couches and armchairs warning message.
Source: National Institute of Child Health and Human Development (2020).

straightforward technical diction of "surfaces" and "sleep area" situated alongside extremist mandates like "Always place baby on his or her back to sleep" leave little room for maternal decision-making agency, if we are to believe the *ethos* of the Interactive Safe Sleep Room. Yet it is the "ifs" and the "mays" that nod to the complex continuum of real-world infant sleeping practices that we wrestle with in this chapter.

The trouble is—all values aside—babies get *mad* when they are first put in their cribs by themselves (see Exhibit A, the anecdote at the beginning of this chapter). They also simply seem to prefer curling up on their stomachs or sides—the anecdotal prevalence of this tendency giving rise to the vernacular "fetal position." The difficulty of following this safety protocol, then, should be apparent. Sleep-deprived parents are tasked with doing two things fairly universally acknowledged to make babies cry foul and are asked to do so under pain of (potential infant) death. So, to facilitate safe sleep, mothers generally institute one of several measures taken from classical conditioning methods in behavioral psychology: graduated extinction or plain old extinction. Graduated extinction involves placing a baby in their crib to sleep, walking away, and returning (if the baby is crying) in two minutes, patting (but not picking up) the baby (possibly not speaking to it), and then leaving again—to return in increasingly longer intervals until the crying has stopped. Pure extinction involves not returning at all. Both methods are often referred to as cry it out, although we frequently observed that those who support "sleep training" object to this label, saying it misrepresents the practice. Because of this controversy, we will defer to the less contested term of "sleep training." Sleep training is almost a prerequisite for safe sleep as babies get old enough to protest, and so the terms "safe sleep" and "sleep training" are almost interchangeable concepts at times.

Yet even mothers who sleep train eagerly—and certainly those who do so under duress "for the baby's safety"—hate being in the thick of the process. This is true in spite of safe-sleep proponents often proclaiming that "for babies, crying is a normal response to settling down at bedtime" (Zero to Three, n.d.). Scrutiny of such terms as "normal" aside, hearing one's child cry and choosing not to respond is difficult. Here, then, is a real fallout of the sleep debates: many mothers themselves report crying as they listen to their baby's cries but believe they must endure this emotional turmoil to protect the baby's life. Thus, on any given night, hundreds of mothers across the country are agonizing over a decision that they believe protects physical life at a high emotional cost on the part of the maternal-fetal dyad. The matter could also be framed chronologically: mothers agonize over the temporary (potentially sincere) agony of their child in order to achieve long-term security.

Images in various social media mothering groups promoting safe sleep merge *pathos* and *logos*—the emotional heft, that is, of the statistics of infant death, often promoting stories of "loss moms" to persuade other mothers to adopt safe-sleep habits. For obvious reasons, it seemed unethical to us to reproduce stories posted of mothers whose children had died; however, such threatened and implied risk of infant death pervades public health rhetoric on this topic.

Images like figure 5.6 work to jar mothers into sudden awareness, operating on the implicit notion that mothers naively do not believe their own bodies to be a risk to their infants, and, therefore, must be shocked into awareness of the riskiness of their arms and bodies, all potential infant suffocation vectors (Cook Children's Health Care System, n.d.).

Figure 5.6
"Help promote safe infant sleep," Cook Children's website leading image.
Source: Cook Children's Health Care System (2020).

If the message of safe sleep is a "simple" matter of life and death, then the message of co-sleeping or "natural" sleep is this: allowing your baby to sleep anywhere other than next to you is cruel and unusual—nay, "unnatural." If the logic of safe sleep wields the persuasive heft of big data, paired with the *pathos*-laden fear of child death, then the logic of supposedly "natural" co-sleeping cuts rather straight to the core of targeting maternal guilt. Consider "A Letter from a Sleep-Training Baby," written in a popular mom blog, *Alternative Mama* (it is worth reproducing in its entirety):

Dear mommy,

I am confused.

I am used to falling asleep in your soft, warm arms. Each night I lay snuggled close to you; close enough to hear your heartbeat, close enough to smell your sweet fragrance. I gaze at your beautiful face as I gently drift off to sleep, safe and secure in your loving embrace. When I awaken with a growling stomach, cold feet or because I need a cuddle, you attend to me quickly and before long I am sound asleep once again.

But this last week has been different.

Each night this week has gone like this. You tucked me up into my cot and kissed me goodnight, turned out the light and left. At first I was confused, wondering where you'd gone. Soon I became scared, and called for you. I called and called for you mummy, but you wouldn't come! I was so sad, mummy. I wanted you so badly. I've never felt feelings that strong before. Where did you go?

Eventually you came back! Oh, how happy and relieved I was that you came back! I thought you had left me forever! I reached up to you but you wouldn't pick me up. You wouldn't even look me in the eye. You lay me back down with those soft warm arms, said "shh, it's night time now" and left again.

This happened again, over and over. I screamed for you and after a while, longer each time, you would return but you wouldn't hold me.

After I had screamed a while, I had to stop. My throat hurt so badly. My head was pounding and my tiny tummy was growling. My heart hurt the most, though. I just couldn't understand why you wouldn't come.

After what felt like a lifetime of nights like this, I gave up. You don't come when I scream, and when you do finally come you won't even look me in the eye, let alone hold my shaking, sobbing little body. The screaming hurt too much to carry on for very long.

I just don't understand, mummy. In the daytime when I fall and bump my head, you pick me up and kiss it better. If I am hungry, you feed me. If I crawl over to you for a cuddle, you read my mind and scoop me up, covering my tiny face with kisses and telling me how special I am and how much you love me. If I need you, you respond to me straight away.

But at night time, when it's dark and quiet and my night-light casts strange shadows on my wall, you disappear. I can see that you're tired, mummy, but I love you so much. I just want to be near to you, that's all.

Now, at night time, I am quiet. But I still miss you. (Alternative Mama, n.d.)

The hyperbolic image of a mother's "soft, warm" arms as more a part of her infant's needs than her own body with its own needs kicks off this "letter," and we ought not to overlook its rhetorical heft. Instantly, situated as this document explicitly is, as an argument staged as part of the co-/safe-sleep debates, the mother's arms are converted from potentially deadly weapons (which safe-sleep advocates depict them as) to necessary gifts that only an evil mother would deprive her child of (as a promotion for co-sleep). From the very opening of this letter, before maternal guilt is invoked through the more obvious route of the baby's sadness and needs, the more insidious vehicle of the mother's own body is used—thereby implying that this body rightly belongs to the baby, before and preeminent to its existence as the mother's own vehicle for existence. Moreover, this statement pushes back against safe-sleep debates that cast the maternal body as a threat. As we have seen with so many other issues in this book, however, instead of circumventing this binary and refusing to map the maternal body onto it (risk/no-risk), the rhetoric in this letter doubles down on it, insisting that the maternal body is *morally owed* to the baby, thus creating an arguably more urgent binary with the maternal body (deadly threat/required sacrifice). The direct references to the baby's feelings proclaim quite literally that the mother ought to feel bad for not sleeping with her baby. Moreover, the implicit reference to maternal-body-parts-as-baby-tools builds rhetoric into this letter that lessens the reader's ability to eschew its presumptive patterns. It instead insidiously doubles down in binaristic opposition to the perceived debatant (safe-sleep advocates). A mother can decide, perhaps, that she disagrees that her baby feels this way when she leaves it, because the baby, posited as an actor, has a subjective perspective the mother-reader can reject in this rhetoric. Yet, the "soft" and "warm" ascribed to her arms are presented as statements of fact—seeming to appeal to *logos* even as they are in fact *pathos* (simple tugs at the heartstrings)—and rope the reader into accepting its logic and thereby making it seem like less of a narrative possibility to reject the later claims (which borrow from the seeming objective *ethos* of these statements) that this flesh is also simultaneously a vital necessity to the baby by rhetorical proxy. Flesh is, indeed, soft, and warm, but it need not stand to reason that this softness and warmth belong at a child's disposal or that the mother whose heart beats the warmth and softness into these appendages be disembodied and sacrificed as creature comforts to an infant.

The double bind that Gilbert and Gubar (1979) so famously noted decades ago, in which women must choose between being either monstrous (and deadly) or angelic (and necessary to others' happiness) rings out in these various messages. It hardly matters which option mothers pick—they're damned either way, either painted as murderesses in the making or condemned to a life of self-abnegating servitude. Several parts of the letter, in which the infant reminisces over the disembodied body of its mother, continue this pattern: the "smell" of the mother's "sweet fragrance," her "beautiful face," and her "heartbeat" are also invoked as *logos*, while they insidiously rope the reader into the pathetic fallacy of the maternal-guilt-as-mirrored-infant-desire *by virtue of their being stated as fact*.

"When I awaken with a growling stomach, cold feet or because I need a cuddle, you attend to me quickly," the imaginary infant continues. The sudden shift in tense here from past-tense reverie to present-tense statement could easily be dismissed as the rushed and necessarily informal writings of the sort of mom blog from which this letter comes; however, as scholars of rhetoric, we would urge reading such an abrupt shift in tense more intentionally. "You attend to me quickly" reads, in tone, much more like an imperative demand than the previous tone of wistful reverie. And it is this demand—the imperative placed on the mother's body—that we most particularly note in this letter, built insidiously into the "soft, warm" arms of the mother. The infant's claim that its cries stop only because of overwhelming pain ("my throat hurt so badly") certainly presents a loaded explanation of neonate motivations that can never be fully known. Such a description places rhetorical emphasis less on the infant itself and more on the absentee mother who apparently refuses to "hold [the infant's] shaking, sobbing little body," especially when juxtaposed against the infant's observation that the mother seems to care for the baby during the day when it cries, implying her unjustified need for sleep (and/or value of safe sleep) at nighttime. The inverse image of co-sleeping proponents is clear here. If, on any given night, there are hundreds of mothers who endure present emotional pain to stave off future physical harm, then there are—likely in equal number—mothers who nightly elect to nurture the supposed emotional needs of their infants via co-sleeping to stave off supposed long-term emotional suffering from poor attachment.

THE THIRD POLARITY: MATERNAL GUILT

Or, as reality would often have it, mothers may not have a strong opinion on the matter, but pull their babies into bed in moments of midnight exhaustion, opting in the moment for the safety and comfort of sleep, only to awake and believe that they have done the unthinkable: endangered the lives of their babies for the sake of short-term gains. The logic of these guilt patterns (driven home by the sleep debates in digital communities) of course neatly sidesteps the biological reality that mothers *must sleep*. And it is the mother that is left out of these debates. The arguments about infant sleep are, importantly, not just polarizing or representative of another example in a series of false binaries, but like the other issues in this book, they leave the mother out of the equation. Her needs are not at issue; they are not a factor in the debate. The basic biological need for maternal sleep under pain of death is notably absent from *all* stances in the sleep debates.

In fact, the very existence of these debates on the intensely urgent rhetorical scale on which they now exist demonstrates the true imperative that mothers live under, which is *both* exigencies. All mothers desire emotional *and* physical health for their children, yet regardless of their own positionality along this sleep continuum, they are told insistently and loudly that they cannot achieve both. They cannot engage in the easier practice of sleeping with their children without, by virtue of this act, embodying the evil mother who has risked her baby's life for her own selfish needs. They cannot practice safe sleep without metamorphosing into the heartless mother who allowed her baby to cry and did not comfort it. The only solution that *might* serve both ends (of never letting a baby sleep alone but also never sleeping with it) would be a mother holding a sleeping baby while she herself is seated and to, miraculously, never fall asleep herself (recall the threat of the Chair of Death in the interactive sleep room).

If this sounds absurd, then we would urge the reader to believe that it is as tragic as it is ridiculous, for this is the road more or less traveled by most parents—who cannot endure the guilt on either side of the co-/safe-sleep debate and, thus, draw from their own depleting energy resources as the only route that frees their consciences. Of course, the reality is that most people eventually fall asleep in these setups and awake to the same (or worse) guilt, as one of the few statistics agreed upon by *both* co-sleeping and safe-sleeping communities is that the greatest number of infant deaths happen while the parent falls asleep with the baby while on a couch or in a recliner.[6]

MY KINGDOM FOR A NAP

The fear induced by this third polarity (i.e., attempting to uphold both goals) has allowed for the advent of a number of for-profit sleep websites and coaches. Largely, the advice to be had by such "sleep coaches" or "sleep manuals" is that of eliminating "sleep crutches" (e.g., don't rock the baby to sleep) and variations of instituting schedules, routines, and sometimes cry-it-out methods. That these are rather obvious resources, readily available in crowdsourced communities, speaks to the desperation of mothers to perform Optimal Motherhood and to achieve these apparently mutually exclusive goals of perfect infant emotional and physical health, bolstered by external validation. The website Precious Little Sleep, for instance, offers a range of resources, including a podcast, a book, "survival guides," and paid consultation appointments. This website is just one of many offering pay-to-play (or, more aptly, pay-to-stop-playing-and-sleep) services to help women juggle their many existential goals as mothers, all while being affirmed by an infant sleep guide available through a variety of platforms.[7] Indeed, most of these companies notably use terms like "institute" and "coach" in their brand names, indicating the neoliberal impulse that instincts and rhythms can be simply taught to babies, if we adults could only get the curriculum right. For the very wealthy, the labor of sleeplessness can simply be outsourced with the hire of a night nurse rather than worked around. As scholars of gender and embodiment, we find this to be perhaps one of the most disturbing trends: the imperatives about sleep put women in such a binaristic double bind that paying for a procedural solution or simply another body to deal with the issue seems necessary. We hardly need point out (but we will) that for women living in financially precarious circumstances (disproportionately BIPOC women), such options are not possible, and they are essentially sacrificed to the binary gods. We would posit that this may be why this binary persists: if paying for a solution seems to be the only way of escaping the polarity of being either a deadly or an unloving mother, then it seems mothers without the financial means to easily do this *must* reject the evidence of the other side to uphold their own belief in their worth as a mother. Considering that most sleep coach packages start at somewhere around $200, and with no guaranteed results, this is likely the case for a great many mothers.

WHOSE EVIDENCE IS IT, ANYWAY?

Both popular websites and social media discourse evince these polarities in which anyone (infants, public health experts, and so forth) may emerge satisfied—except the mother. Even the names of sleep-based parenting groups on Facebook evidence the value-based judgments made preemptively against *other* groups: Biologically Normal Infant Sleep, for instance, in its name promotes co-sleeping by implying that anything else is *ab*normal, and it suggests that such a view is backed by science with the inclusion of "biologically." Terms such as "Safe Infant Sleep" readily promote certain value judgments against an ideological image of a reckless mother endangering her children, and most groups similarly append a qualifier such as "evidence-based" to bolster the claims implicit in their names.

Once promoted as a pathway toward better health outcomes through clinical testing, evidence-based medicine has done much for Western healthcare practices since the 1990s; however, it tends to occlude considerations of practices that could be useful but are outside the purview of a large-scale study. What's more, what counts as "evidence" is a controversial issue among scientists themselves, being of course the very reason the peer-review process exists. Among the lay public, such scrutiny of data—and whether it "counts" as evidence—tends to fall more along the lines of already-extant ideological belief (Braman et al. 2012). Thus, one of the major proponents of co-sleeping, an anthropologist from Notre Dame named James McKenna (2012), can be touted as a "quack" by those in the safe-sleep field, whereas safe infant sleep studies can be decried for their lack of controlling variables by those in the co-sleep field.

As we have mentioned, arguments that appear to be about data are rarely so—as data itself is messy and convoluted, full of human choices made by human actors at all levels and guided in its early stages by extant human biases. We would be remiss not to remind the reader that technological actants are also at play: the algorithms of Google, the marketing of Facebook, and the multimodal rhetoric of a birth plan, formula can, or Interactive Safe Sleep Room. It is as common to see arguments over what "counts" as data supporting one side or the other as it is to see arguments about which side is "best"—and, in fact, we would argue that there is likely no difference between best-practice arguments and arguments about which evidence "counts" in the era of evidence-based medicine, as seen in the following example. A typical exchange often appears thusly:

Pro-co-sleep mother (CSM): Here is a link to an article by James McKenna.
Pro-safe-sleep mother (SSM): James McKenna is not a scientist.

CSM: He is an anthropologist, and he can explain what is natural for babies. In Africa, babies normally sleep with their moms.

SSM: "Naturally" babies died a lot. Look at the mortality rates in Africa.

CSM: Here is an article showing the brain damage that occurs to babies when they are allowed to cry without comfort for extended periods.

SSM: This study was done on infants in orphanages and cannot be applied to infants in loving homes. Here is a study showing the rates of SIDS death correlated with co-sleeping.

CSM: That study did not separate for SIDS vs. suffocation deaths, thereby confounding the data. Here is an infographic on how to practice *safe* co-sleep.

SSM: There is no safe co-sleep.

While, as noted in our book's introduction, our institutional review board did not allow us to use exact quotations and conversations from mothers in this book out of concern for women's privacy, we nevertheless gathered data and surveyed conversations to build representative samples like this that speak to the rhetorical pathways of these debates. In general, we observed that several things fairly consistently defined these arguments.

First, it is worth observing what *isn't* said. Neither party raises the question about whether "Africa"—and Africa is almost always invoked as a non-differentiated mega-entity rather than represented with nuance as many different societies with different societal practices—ought ethically to be or even factually *can* be used as a metonym for "natural" practices. The ethics of this practice (of referring to Africa as a means of accessing some untouched human nature) is dangerously close to nineteenth-century fantasies of the exotic primitive, a tool that was readily harnessed to fuel scientific racism through the course of the century, and we think must be identified here for the problematic rhetorical tool that it is. The scientific hypothesis that any one country represents an earlier state of human development (again, a nauseatingly dangerous sentiment, we argue) is empirically dubious. Such a null hypothesis is, frankly, impossible to assess and verify and could only ever be weakly supported by the tools of anthropological comparisons—precisely the field of study eschewed by approximately 50 percent of the actors in the infant sleep debate.

In fact, another significant "unsaid" in this debate is that even the co-sleeping mother (CSM) who supports and circulates McKenna's work does not defend him against claims of being "unscientific." Anthropology, and medical anthropology more specifically, is typically allowed to fall to the wayside, a necessary casualty of this debate. Rather than defending the anthropologic principles *built into* the very issue at the core of this debate ("naturalism") and upon which the entire argument relies, even CSMs tend to simply shift stances and to argue from a different perspective that appears more "scientific"—such as promoting articles about brain damage from crying.

What *is* said in this exchange follows many of the patterns outlined previously in this chapter: debates over what constitutes "natural" sleep, with concomitant arguments surrounding whether natural or interventionist approaches are "best." While Africa as a conduit to the "natural" is an unspoken given on both sides, the casual disregard for ostensible indigenous practices (seen in comments about how "naturally" babies died in these communities) is often quite explicit in safe-sleep arguments, presenting not only an interventionist view but one that privileges first-world contexts as a foundational point of its argument. That is, for many families around the world, a separate infant bed is not economically or spatially possible (to say nothing of norms or preferences). To disparage infant death in such communities as evidence of unsafe praxis thus upholds a sense that such communities are culpable for such deaths, taking no other contextual factors into account. Significantly, it exploits such possible nonvoluntary reasons for co-sleeping to promote a view of Western sleep habits as superior, again reinforcing a narrative of developing-world primitivism. As with so many other binaries discussed in this book, then, whether "natural" sleep is touted by co-sleepers as evidence of a "primitive natural" state or by safe sleepers as evidence of a primitive and backward society, the common denominator is an exploitation of difference that reinforces extant xenophobic biases for self-serving purposes.

Qualitative rhetorical examples aside, we found remarkable scientific *literacy* on both sides of sleeping debates. While there is a tendency to attach the ad hominem of "woo" (for more info about this term, see our introduction) to any practices self-identifying as "natural," the exchanges we observed in fact fell in line with extant thinking about scientific communication in the West, which notes that low scientific literacy is not at issue in debates like these. Rather, as indicated by the fact that *both* parties discount the study design of the research promoted by the other, this conversation (and the many hundreds that it was constructed to represent) reveals a surprising degree of critical thinking about quantitative research design, used, significantly, to facilitate the in-group/out-group thinking that predetermined acceptance of study conclusions.

Tellingly, the conversation ends with the reassertion of the initial point—there is no such thing as safe co-sleeping, and, even if evidence is provided to support this claim, it tends to be the same evidence already marked as specious by the interlocutor. The circularity of these conversations, we hope, is clear. If we were to reduce the conversation down to its rhetorical moves, it might figure like this:

> **Pro-co-sleep mother (CSM):** Shares evidence of perspective 1.
>
> **Pro-safe-sleep mother (SSM):** Dismisses evidence based on *ethos* of evidence creator.
>
> **CSM:** Upholds *ethos* of evidence creator, followed by an appeal to the "natural."
>
> **SSM:** Debunks the *ethos* of the "natural" by invoking *pathos* (dead babies).
>
> **CSM:** Rhetorical pivot that preemptively dismisses the evidence they predict the opponent may submit; this evidence reaffirms the *ethos* of the "natural" with counter-*pathos* (brain-damaged babies).
>
> **SSM:** Notes flaws in study design and applicability. Presents counterstudy.
>
> **CSM:** Notes flaws in study design and applicability. Presents best practices for their own stance.
>
> **SSM:** Denies that there can be a best practice to begin with.

If we appear to be belaboring the point, this is because even academics often lament that laypeople "simply won't listen to Science" (with a capital "S") when "the data is clear." We hope to suggest, through this detailed, if repetitive, rhetorical analysis, that such lamentations begin from the wrong assumption. It should be clear from this rhetorical translation that both sides are, in fact, urgently addressing and invoking scientific perspectives. Rather, the debate has much more to do with what data one accepts, and, beyond casual lamentations, any academic will acknowledge that the messiness of study design and data analysis is the very reason scientists themselves debate evidence and conclusions. If we can, then, let go of the notion that simply continuing to point to data will somehow lead us to an exit point from this dizzyingly circular debate, we might begin to piece together what the argument is really hinging on. Its very circular nature, pinging back and forth between two poles of impasse, reveals the answer, we think; already-extant beliefs and biases are the real subject of this argument, and science becomes a proxy tool to justify both perspectives.

CONCLUSION: CORPORATE RESPONSIBILITY

Looking outside the predetermined polarities of this debate, imagining a better future for women in regard to infant sleep perhaps relies more urgently than any other issue in this book on returning to a community of women—eschewing neoliberalism's individualization of responsibility. If a woman is to take safe sleep seriously (and we here neither advocate nor disavow the perspective, but simply make allowance for that potentially being a woman's decision), she simply will need more than just herself and her partner (if one exists) in her support network to help with the baby while she sleeps. Making this possible would mean, of course, a radical difference in the way our *society* invests in maternity leave and makes allowances for basic social supports for families. The answer, in this regard, then, seems both more obvious and more insistent: neoliberalism's side effect of isolating women from community is perhaps as much the culprit for unsafe infant sleep practices as are exhausted moms who fall asleep with their babies. For, such moms might not unwillingly fall asleep with them if they were not expected to handle infant sleep alone. Man-hours and limited human energy reserves are key here, and it is the job of neoliberalism to obscure those simple facts and make it seem as though merely trying could make Optimal Motherhood so.

Thus, far from demonstrating a lamentable lack of scientific literacy, sleep debates, and others like them, in fact reveal that science—particularly where differential data is to be found—is invoked to promote a priori personal perspectives, rather than vice versa, as evidence-based practices would seek to do. While this has been found to be the case in a wide array of scientific communication fields, we would argue the broad cultural zeitgeist of note in this book—that is, the insistence upon Optimal Motherhood—fuels such frantic efforts to declare, in advance (sometimes even in advance of childbirth), what is "right." This perspective must then be defended rigidly, for to acknowledge failure would be to self-identify as a sub–Optimal Mother. Well may it be, then, that mothers fling data back and forth at one another, demonstrating a remarkable ability to critique study design only when it suits them, for the argument was never about data to begin with—it was about self-worth and validity (and if that can be bought at the price of a $280 email consult at Preciouslittlesleep.com, those mothers who can buy it, likely will). Chapter 6, "Can I Get a Tweak? 11 DPO FRER FMU," however, provides us a light at the end of the tunnel: an exemplar of an online mothering community that functions to safeguard the self-worth and validity of its members amid incredible maternity trials including infertility and pregnancy loss.

6 "CAN I GET A TWEAK?": TOWARD A POLITICS OF FEMALE BIOLINGUISTIC AGENCY IN THE AGE OF NEW MEDIA

We have chosen to approach the end of our book at the beginning. Up until now, we have tracked pregnancy and maternity in basic chronological order, from gestation to delivery, to postpartum and neonate life. Given that structure, it probably comes as some surprise that we have chosen to *end* with conception. But in many ways, ending with conceiving performs very nicely the biomimicry we see between intellectual and gestational labor. Both a book and a baby start with a concept(ion), and neither is really ever "finished." When a pregnancy ends with birth, it is truly a beginning rather than an end—the beginning of a life, the beginning of a new family structure, the beginning of someone's maternal identity. So, too, do the ideas brought forward in a book live on beyond themselves in the lives and minds of audiences, who, we hope, are encouraged to think, feel, and act differently based on the concepts developed (gestated, if you will) and borne forth (laboriously) in the book. In such a way, the ending of the book may very well be considered the conception of new ideas and possibly new, later books. The present book certainly does not serve as an ending, we hope, but an opening for readers to reimagine motherhood, free from the limiting binaries we've been told are our only choices. The end of this book, we hope, will plant the seeds for the renaissance, or rebirth, of maternity in neoliberal societies that are tainted with the legacies of the Cult of True Womanhood, risk aversion, and the controlling impulses that walk alongside that risk aversion.

Beyond this, the concept of, well, conception performs nicely an idea that has been integral to all the chapters of this book: the notion that words affect lived, embodied, realities. Judith Butler (2011) goes so far as to say that words and discursive categories such as the ones we've highlighted over the course of this book fundamentally bring bodily categories into being. As she explains regarding human gender norms,

> Consider the medical interpellation which (the recent emergence of the sonogram notwithstanding) shifts an infant from an "it" to a "she" or a "he," and in that naming, the girl is "girled," brought into the domain of language and kinship through the interpellation of gender. But that "girling" of the girl does not end there; on the contrary, that founding interpellation is reiterated by various authorities and throughout various intervals of time to reinforce or contest this naturalized effect. The naming is at once the setting of a boundary, and also the repeated inculcation of a norm. (7–8)

The same, we would argue, goes for regulations and norms surrounding Optimal Motherhood. Once a risk and the risk-controlling regulation are spoken, they become the material realities under which mothers live; thus, the word is made flesh in these dynamics, and, in a society still in many ways guided by the Victorian legacy of the Cult of True Womanhood, the womb and the word coalesce all too easily into one another. And, indeed, Butler (2011) has noted that the very words of "matter," such as bodily matters, derive from the words for "womb"—the organ that brings matter into being.

Under the present system, the words that speak the womb into being are those of fear and control that *seem* to serve women's interests by suggesting best practices according to evidence-based medicine. Yet, as we hope we have shown, these best practices act as a stranglehold on mothers rather than empowering them. And the very act of their communication matters: these rules are set out in language. They are spoken, and written, and spoken about ad nauseum, resulting in an overdetermined, intensely polarizing, material reality for mothers—one in which they must choose, fight, and strive to win their own sense of value and worth as mothers. The teams are predetermined, and once spoken into being, mothers' only choice seems to be to pick one team and fight for self-worth. The outcome of this game, as we have tried to demonstrate in this book, is predetermined. No one wins when the messy realities of life and data science are construed as neat binaries—ones with the extremely high stakes of seeming to love your child enough. Instead, the system as a whole serves to rob women of the abundance and resilience that mothers could provide to one another *if* they could only break free from these patterns.

In some ways, it is an ethnographic coincidence that we observed the most productive move away from these suffocating strictures in a community devoted to *pre*-mothers: women trying to conceive. Yet, at the conclusion of this project, we are more motivated to say that there are no rhetorical (and therefore no bodily/material/enwombed) coincidences. It is no longer surprising that the moment of creative and productive *potential* is the one in which women have found it easier to begin again and to make a womb of their own words—before it enters the predetermined realm of pregnancy, birth, and maternity.

In many ways, the stakes and stakeholders in pre-conception communities are vastly different from those of women who are already pregnant or have delivered their children, because, of course, there is not yet an infant/ fetal life in the equation. But this is precisely the point. In beginning to sketch out a way that women might move away from Optimal Motherhood and see beyond its boundaries, we found the most helpful parallels in the adjacent group of women *seeking* to enter the ranks of mothers but who were not yet among them, and therefore were more easily able to craft a vision of maternity *outside* of the polemics and power dynamics that affect mothers.[1] That is, without a fetus/infant yet in play—whose needs can supersede those of the mother as well as erase her value, and for whom the mother must be Optimal—these would-be mothers, we observed, were able to develop a robust, supportive, *non*binaristic community.

What may seem like a tangential example, then, compared with the themes tackled in the previous chapters, is in fact urgently relevant. Optimal Motherhood, as we have shown, is so deeply embedded in white, Anglo culture that its roots go back almost 160 years, if not further. Optimal Motherhood so completely pervades our most basic assumptions of what parenting, families, and child development look like, that even researchers and experts are naive if they assume they can see outside the bounds of what defines our most basic normative concepts. So, instead, we looked to a related, but differently staked, example—in this case, instances of women *trying* to become mothers. As we mentioned, without a fetus/infant to obsessively fixate over regarding risk factors, and without this obsessive focus on risk factors leading to a desire for control, key ingredients are absent from the recipe for Optimal Motherhood. This prematernal space, therefore, may just well be a key component to productively reimagining motherhood according to completely different and new ideals. We believed looking at this group might provide us hopeful material toward envisioning a new future, allowing our readers to come away with hopefulness and brimming with creative ideas for a new culture of motherhood. In hindsight, we think these observations did just that.

This closing chapter presents an ethnographic study of digital spaces created for and by women actively trying to conceive. With their own lingo, unique and complicated menstrual cycle charting methods, and pregnancy test "tweaking" processes, these groups build community around reproduction and structure it with evolving, crowdsourced linguistic signifiers that change in accordance with group-identified needs. These various group activities, we argue, structure a community capable of sustaining hope via rhetoric that emphasizes presence instead of absence, incorporates its own initiation process via expansive and nonintuitive lingo, and provides endless data cycles to be mined for meaning from *within* the group of stakeholders, instead of by external authorities. All of these processes function as protective devices, shielding the groups from internet trolls and requiring newcomers to integrate themselves into the group slowly as they learn the terminology, a process that acts as a sort of built-in initiation ensuring simple commitment to the community atmosphere of the group (and without more historically common group initiation behaviors such as hazing or hierarchical enforcement).

By analyzing these groups, which exist in a demimaternal space (or, perhaps, we could say, a futuristic vision of motherhood), we are able to provide for the reader a reasonable assessment of what a future outside of Optimal Motherhood might look like and how it might function. By analyzing a parallel but not-yet-maternal space in digital media, that is, we are able to explore what a world of mothering outside Optimal Motherhood—outside of binary structures, risk aversion, and fear-based control—might look like.

UNDERSTANDING TWEAKS

Pregnancy test "tweaking" is a recent phenomenon among online communities. Using specialized apps and filters, members of tweaking forums alter the contrast and color saturation of photographed home pregnancy tests, attempting to discern a "pregnant" line at the earliest possible date. As Anna Prushinskaya (2015) said in her article for the *Atlantic*, "I joined this site because I wanted to 'catch' my pregnancy as soon as it happened." Home pregnancy tests, which even in their cheapest iterations can detect human chorionic gonadotropin (hCG) as early as ten days after ovulation, are thus being chromatically manipulated so as to—ostensibly—show faint lines to the naked eye even earlier than this. There are a few different tweaking processes, most of which are relatively straightforward. Tests can be enhanced by increasing the color contrast of a photo, inverting colors, or converting to grayscale (see figure 6.1, showing the original, grayscale, contrast adjustment, and color inversion, respectively).

Users typically start submitting images of home pregnancy tests for tweaking—lining up in the dozens and begging to be chosen first by overburdened community "tweakers"—as early as seven days after ovulation (or what would traditionally be considered a week before onset of menstruation). Tweakers are those who have taught themselves how to manipulate photo images of home pregnancy tests so as to "pull" (to employ their community lingo) a positive line at the earliest possible date. Experienced tweakers act as a community resource and are in high demand among these groups.

After a request is made, a tweaker agrees to take on the project of manipulating a given test. The test is then digitally manipulated and redistributed (i.e., reposted to the community forum) for group analysis. Originally, pregnancy test tweaking took place in online message board communities, and tweakers typically used specialized software capable of making adjustments to images (e.g., Adobe InDesign and Photoshop). Freidenfelds notes that "when these sites began several years ago, they were very much do-it-yourself efforts, but recently a number of tweaking apps for smartphones have become available" (2020, 182).

These apps increased accessibility of the relevant photo-adjustment tools, and by 2019 such apps, recognizing the community *ethos* inherent in

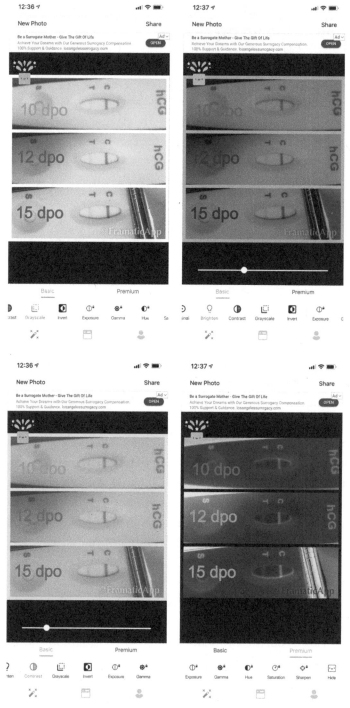

Figure 6.1

Examples of pregnancy test tweaking in Pregnancy Test Checker app: Original, grayscale, contrast adjustment, and color inversion.

Source: Nixon (2014).

the process (and that we lay out below), included message board and posting capabilities. Tweaking just isn't the same in neoliberal isolation, it seems, as tweaking apps quickly realized their photo-manipulation software was not desirable to users without social media interfaces. Here, then, we already see a vision of a future beyond Optimal Motherhood; and as we've hinted at throughout this book, this future requires true communal support, not neoliberal bootstrapping. One such app, Checker, as seen in figure 6.1, locates the various photo-adjustment tools readily at the bottom of the screen, with tabs that can navigate users to a community forum to discuss their results. The icon on the upper left (which can be activated or deactivated as the user desires) is a "baby dust" token—a good-luck phrase used in such groups. When the icon is tapped, a picture of an infant appears, and confetti flies around the screen, wishing the user a positive test.

Tweaking Terms

In traditional community tweaking practices, after a tweaker agrees to tweak a test, the photo-enhanced test is reposted for the group. Group members then collaborate on subjective analysis of what is traditionally considered an objective test, each weighing in on the presence of a line or lack thereof, using a complex set of group terminology that is nearly impossible for a random visitor to understand—for example, BFP, Evap, Wondfo, AF (see figure 6.2).

The tweaking process comes with its own lingo and terms, developed by the group itself, that inform the community about how to read the test. Complicated abbreviations indicate the concentration of urine used (fmu or smu), cycle day of testing (11dpo, for instance), and brand of test used (FRER, a commonly used test). Respondents then invoke equally complicated forms of (most frequently) "not pregnant" verdicts, a phrase that is oddly absent from these forums (more on this in the next section). Terms such as "dye run," "indent," and "evap" stand in place of the maligned "not pregnant." The following table lists some of the most frequently used terms. Similarly, advanced menstrual cycle charting techniques keep members apprised of the fortunes or misfortunes of their community members, as participants frequently provide real-time links to their charts posted in their signature lines. This data, too, requires "insider" knowledge to interpret and is markedly incomprehensible to anyone who has not been trying to conceive, or TTC, for some time.

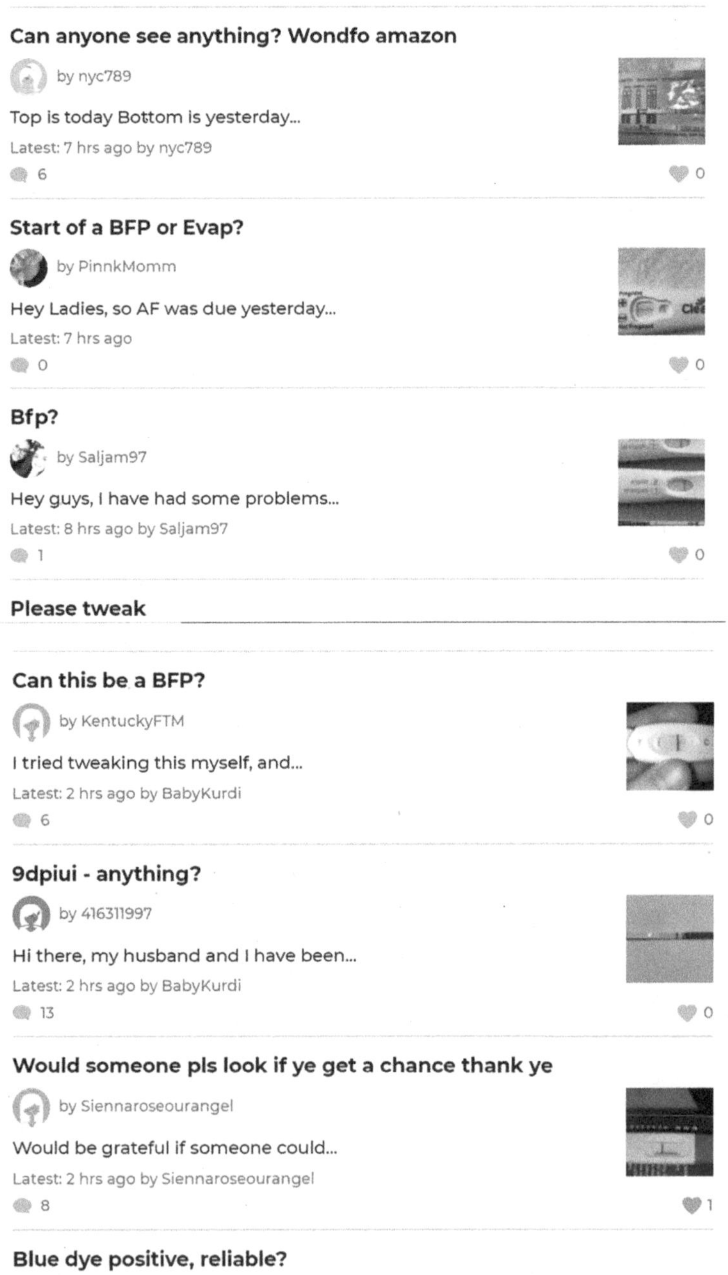

Can anyone see anything? Wondfo amazon

by nyc789

Top is today Bottom is yesterday...

Latest: 7 hrs ago by nyc789

6   0

Start of a BFP or Evap?

by PinnkMomm

Hey Ladies, so AF was due yesterday...

Latest: 7 hrs ago

0   0

Bfp?

by Saljam97

Hey guys, I have had some problems...

Latest: 8 hrs ago by Saljam97

1   0

Please tweak

Can this be a BFP?

by KentuckyFTM

I tried tweaking this myself, and...

Latest: 2 hrs ago by BabyKurdi

6   0

9dpiui - anything?

by 416311997

Hi there, my husband and I have been...

Latest: 2 hrs ago by BabyKurdi

13   0

Would someone pls look if ye get a chance thank ye

by Siennaroseourangel

Would be grateful if someone could...

Latest: 2 hrs ago by Siennaroseourangel

8   1

Blue dye positive, reliable?

Figure 6.2

Screenshot from social media pregnancy test tweaking group, illustrating complex group terminology.

Source: BabyCenter (2020).

Frequently used terms in the tweaking community	
TTC	trying to conceive
DPO	days past ovulation
fmu/smu	first morning urination / second morning urination
BFP	big fat positive
evap and dye run	various visual effects that may appear to indicate a "pregnancy" line but are in fact other, unrelated phenomena
FRER and Wondfo	pregnancy test brands
AF	Aunt Flo (menstruation)
BD	Baby Dance (sexual intercourse)

Users follow the unwritten rule of not submitting tests until seven dpo, or one week before a missed period, at which point home pregnancy tests typically advertise that they can accurately produce results; that is, at the point at which tweaking begins, most home pregnancy tests should be able to pick up something discernible to the naked eye—no tweak needed. To some extent, this is even acknowledged in the discussion boards; occasionally, when a positive test is posted, community members will eagerly respond with something along the lines of "I see it without a tweak!!"

Often, the test is tweaked anyway for posterity and celebration. Conversely, if a line is seen by the group after an early tweak, the response is virtually identical—"looks promising," respondents will say; "test again in a few days to confirm." So, whether a line is seen with the naked eye or through the tweaking process, the group response remains the same, which prompts the question of the need for the group and tweaking in the first place. Clearly, there is more going on in this process than simple photo enhancement. Instead, the community engagement seems to be the real end here.

What we're left with, then—when we realize that the photo enhancement itself is often not necessary but used anyway—is a pure dance of communal interpretation. In tweaking groups, collective *female* collaboration determines, as a group, the significance of health data for themselves. Thus, in this rather hidden world of tweaking, a group comes together to determine pregnancy test results ahead of schedule; but, really, considering that tweaking yields little more than the test itself, we find (1) a supportive community of women in a shared state of reproductive health choice-making that come together to (2) create their own interpretive system and rituals around it, and in doing so, (3) resist simplistic binary systems (pregnant/not pregnant). That is, a home pregnancy test would seem to yield only one of two results—pregnant/not pregnant—signified by a line or the absence of a line, and more than perhaps any binary discussed in this book, this basic biological binary would seem inescapable. One either is or is not pregnant. But this is not the case for tweaking communities, and their willingness to resist such a seemingly concrete binary was inspirational for us as we sought exit points from Optimal Motherhood binaries, which are, at least, more obviously arbitrary.

HOPE IS THE THING WITH PINK LINES

Stretching this binary variable into a spectrum—and the crowdsourced in-group lingo that goes along with it—serves many purposes. Significantly, none of these purposes reproduce the meanings of fertility data created by spaces of institutionalized authority. The words "not pregnant" are almost never used in these spaces. Tweaking is most prevalent in TTC groups, populated by women hoping for a positive test result (rather than being used by women who are *fearful* that they might be pregnant).

Tweaking communities push the boundaries of the binary choices offered to women by refusing to allow pregnant/not pregnant to be an either-or. Instead, for tweaking communities, one is always "maybe" or "almost" pregnant, as groups mine photographic data for one another and always, always avoid saying "yes" or "no" but instead say "test again to be sure." In establishing a collective vantage point that always looks to the future, is always hoping, and is hoping for futurity in a community setting, we see a way to begin to move past Optimal Motherhood. Perhaps the very fact that there is no discernible fetus in these equations has enabled these groups to be so forward-thinking, so conceptually flexible, but we would argue that mothers must find a way to apply this thinking to the different stakes of actualized motherhood.

Although Linda Layne has argued that home pregnancy tests are *anti*-feminist, because of this very process of using multiple tests not to "replace doctors' tests, [but as] an additional, prior step . . . represent[ing] yet another instance of increasing pregnancy related consumption" (2009, 66), we find that women in this context have risen above corporately constructed means of using the tests and instead have used them to build communal interpretive moves around what could otherwise be an isolating. Indeed, our findings line up neatly with those of HaCohen, Amir, and Wiseman (2018, 720), who found that the infertility-to-pregnancy transition for women often existed on a continuum rather than as a binary: "Three Types of narratives were identified: (1) The infertility overshadows the pregnancy and approaching motherhood, (2) the pregnancy leads to a dissociation concerning the infertile period, and (3) the two states coexist together along an integrated continuum. We suggested that the different narrative types may occur in diverse circumstances that entail integrating a crisis . . . into a constructive and meaningful life story." Significantly, we observed that women appear to find community within this continuum and eschew ostensibly biologically deterministic binaries that separate women into groups of pregnant/not pregnant (akin to the later maternal decision-making binaries of breastfeeding vs. formula feeding or co-sleeping vs. safe sleeping).

On the surface, then, tweaking could easily seem as though it *reinforces* binaries by simply making the results of a test available sooner. Actually, though, the resounding refrains of "test again" always impose a message of hope, continued group participation, and a focus on a future that is never quite captured in the pregnant/not-pregnant test binary. The tweaking community predicates itself on the presence of vitalizing community life instead of the signification of an absence of a pregnancy—with every hCG test interpretation. As mentioned, most community assessments of tests boil down to a consensus of "uncertain, test again tomorrow." If no line is seen by the group, the poster is typically met with encouragement to "test again in a few days."

Thus, this crowdsourced semiotic system allows for, and in fact embraces, Derrida's notion of deferral (1982). Philosopher Jacques Derrida claims that, since all meanings depend on other meanings ("in," for instance, depends on a concept of "out"), nothing means anything precisely (see the introduction for the importance of postmodernist philosophy to dismantling Optimal Motherhood). Like a set of dominoes, each meaning falls back on another meaning, as it were, such that there are no clear-cut binaries—ever, anywhere—for Derrida. Similarly, nearly all the rhetoric employed in tweaking, which, to reiterate, is always collaboratively engaged with, essentially serves to defer meaning, render the ultimate result of the test "inconclusive" by group standards, and so resist binaries altogether. The *ethos* of maternal decision-making, in this case, is not the sole province of the scientifically educated, evidence-based medical authority's opinion or even the test itself as an actant. Instead, through deferral, it is the communities themselves that assemble an empathetic *ethos* of hope outside of the otherwise hyperdetermined—and downright hope*less*—binaristic discourse of contemporary motherhood.

In fact, tweaking communities—so often populated by women who see themselves as struggling with fertility—reconstitute the entire system of presence/absence as a stable category. That is, by defining themselves *within* a tweaking community, where women often follow one another's cycles month to month, women who might be classified as "infertile" by traditional medical judgments instead use this externally defined absence of fertility to create an incredibly vital community *presence*. Significantly, it is viable pregnancy continued through to delivery that constitutes an unsustainable *loss* or *absence* to these groups as their numbers dwindle and members drop out. Thus, by using this group-constructed linguistic system alongside a set of visual techne, these women engage with one another to create their *own* meaning from their bodies from within the space of this vitalizing community.

The Cycle of Cycles

In addition to crowdsourced photo manipulation, users often include real-time links to their personal "cycle charts" in their signature lines. By clicking on the link included in these signatures, group participants contextualize their photographic data within a set of other visualized data points that serve to give more meaning to where in a fertility cycle a test might fall (see figure 6.3).

Significantly, all this aggregated and visualized data, sourced by individuals but interpreted by the group within the matrix of an individual's pregnancy test images, bespeaks a weighty *presence* in communion with other women, where meanings are made together instead of simply indicating the

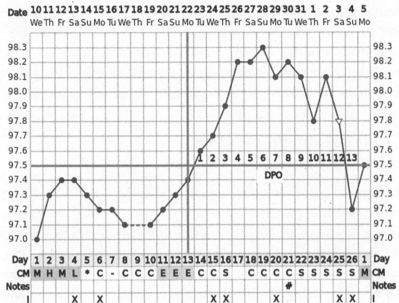

Figure 6.3

Example of personal fertility cycle chart often used a supplementary point of visual data in social media pregnancy test tweaking groups.

Source: Tamtris Web Services (n.d.).

presence or absence of pregnancy. Here, again, data is drawn out, contemplated, chewed on, and discussed in an interim space of "maybe pregnant," becoming its own category that resists what could seem like a quite apparent binary of pregnant/not pregnant.

And so in the shared new media space of tweaking groups, the cycle of "cycles" continues via communal *deferral* (to use Derrida's term). A cycle itself is obviously continuous, with no end point or goal; it is simply a process that continues on, allowing, again, for a vision that focuses on the future and on potential rather than judgments on one's Optimalness in the present or past. Through this constant deferral, carried on through cycles that mimic organic life much better than binaries, these communities mimic life itself (instead of the *un*life that anthropologist Emily Martin [1987] argues typifies attitudes toward infertility in our society). Life, in these groups, always exists in the moment just beyond our grasp: always never here, and always already somewhere beyond our cognitive, physical, and technological hold. It therefore can't be pinned down, constrained, controlled, or told what is optimal.

THE COGNITIVE DISSONANCE IN "CHEMICAL PREGNANCIES"

To this end, there is no better example of the problematic biopolitics of binary models of maternal options and the ways tweaking communities provide "a way out" of these concepts than their handling of what are called chemical pregnancies. A chemical pregnancy is defined as zygote loss before six gestational weeks. Conversely, pregnancy loss after this point is colloquially termed miscarriage. Whereas a chemical pregnancy is defined as such for its marked presence on an hCG home pregnancy test (a supposedly purely "chemical" marker of pregnancy), a visible embryo never appears via ultrasound (supposedly a *visual* representation of clearly "biological" life). The cognitive dissonance inherent in this binary is perplexing. Can a purely chemical entity cease to exist in any meaningfully *organic* (biological) way? How can a test demonstrating the existence of a certain biological hormone (pregnancy hormones) be classified as *only* chemical? What is at stake in using language that denies the biological factors (pregnancy) that cause this chemical reaction (hormone secretion)? Of course, it is tempting to argue that these categories are only medical terminology, necessitated for diagnostic or treatment purposes. Yet, women's lived experiences, especially as complexly expressed in social media mothering group discourse, suggest that there is more at stake in the insistence on discrete determinants of organic versus inorganic life.

In the online pregnancy and fertility communities we observed, for instance, women often push to define early pregnancy loss as "miscarriages," regardless of timing, and the idea of a "chemical pregnancy" is almost universally reviled. The negative tone of the term "miscarriage" is itself problematic in its suggestion of agency on the part of the mother as a "failed carrier." So, it is surprising that women seem to prefer this term over "chemical pregnancy." Given the two options on this binary—failed carrier of life or temporarily emitting chemicals—the fact that women would rather see themselves as "miscarried" is striking and, we think, telling. As Lara Freidenfelds explains, "By the twenty-first century, a diverse array of social, medical, and technological innovations came together to reshape pregnancy and thereby create a new experience of miscarriage" (2020, 6). Indeed, more recent ob-gyn best practices urge health-care providers to replace the term "chemical pregnancy" with "early loss," as the former "may not align with the image of the baby she bonded with after the positive pregnancy test" (Librizzi, Ilse, and Coyle 2016). Women express that this rhetoric leaves them feeling disembodied or depersonalized from their own awareness of their bodies' complicated bio*chemical* processes.

The complex interplay of "bio" and "chemical" here is palpable. The *chemical* hCG present in the *biological* blood of a woman's body comes together during zygote fertilization in an inextricably intertwined biochemical process that categorical medical classification cannot hold in tension. In attempting to pin down something as slippery and elusive as life's very origins—whether we mean fundamentally so, as in the chicken and the egg, or chronologically so, as in embryonic stasis at a certain time—we seek to define that which cannot be bound up in binaries, a state of personhood that exceeds simple classification. Women seem keenly aware of this in their own narratives, through the real fact of their body recognizing a biological pregnancy via chemical emissions, as well as through their aversion to the term "chemical pregnancy" and preference for what would seem the more obviously distasteful "miscarriage." Women in these spaces often insist that the biological and the chemical are *not* binaries but coexist fluidly. The "bio," the "chemical," the test, and the narrative are all nodes in the complex network of contemporary maternal decision-making discourse. Women in these communities take back control of the verbiage and place it on a productive continuum of agency more powerfully than anywhere else we observed in online social media mothering groups.

This extended example of the boundaries and definitions of the chemical pregnancy is helpful for a few reasons. First, increasing technology—which has made such powerful home pregnancy tests and also powerful photo-editing software that is intended to enhance even the pregnancy tests' abilities—has given rise to the problematic terminologies we have identified here. Even twenty years ago, pregnancy tests were not powerful enough to determine a pregnancy before it was undeniably "biological" in our traditional understandings. Lara Freidenfelds has devoted an entire book to exploring the phenomenon of pregnancy awareness by the mother at increasingly early gestational ages over time as well as the psychological impact this has on their experiences of their bodies. In *The Myth of the Perfect Pregnancy*, she notes,

> In earlier generations, it was exceptional for a woman to consider a pregnancy loss at six weeks to be a lost child, rather than a lost opportunity or possibility, or a fleeting hope of pregnancy reversed by a late period. Early miscarriages were not generally regarded as grave losses unless they were part of a pattern of infertility, signaling that a woman might not ever be able to have children. If a woman had reason to believe that she would soon have a successful pregnancy, an early miscarriage was regarded as little more than a temporary setback. Some women today continue to feel this way about early miscarriages, but they are far more likely to be censured than validated if they say so aloud. (2020, 4)

The way language and technology cycle back and forth to affect one another is important to consider as we think about how to move on from Optimal Motherhood.

Returning to tweaking, this act significantly calls attention to the ways we have attempted to approach biological life as a binary variable, a fact that we seem to rely on but also struggle against—as when a test with only two outcomes (positive or negative pregnancy) is manipulated and squinted at, revealing the continuous nature of life and its bio/chemical signifiers. To drive this point home, the case of a blighted ovum is a good counterexample, as it shows the inherent contradictions even from within the classificatory confines of medical rhetoric. A blighted ovum is a situation in which a gestational instance is visible on an ultrasound but no embryo is seen. Both chemical and biological markers of pregnancy are to be found, and yet, no "life" as we would seek to define it traditionally is definitively identified. This is the perfect example of the slippery slope that is our attempt to define something that will always defy definitions and technologies. What we want to highlight here is that even in the lay public, women *do* pick up on these inconsistencies and the biopolitical valences of these terminologies.

Redeeming the Failure of the Optimal Mother

As mentioned earlier, we note a fairly universal preference among women for classifying their pregnancy encounters as miscarriages rather than chemical pregnancies, in spite of the term "mis-carriages" seeming to more obviously imply faulty maternal action. Here, we particularly see these communities' upheaval of traditional medical rhetoric as providing a beginning point from which we might begin our own explorations of dismantling Optimal Motherhood.

For one, it highlights women's innate sense that prioritizing the pure biology of their bodies is problematic—as shown in the real-life example of pro-life protests and in the literary example of Margaret Atwood's *Handmaid's Tale*. By constructing communities of women, protected by their own self-created lingo that wards off outsiders and constructs redemptive community life in its very search *for* life, women have pushed back against these politics. Also, by a process of constant discernment of the *chemical* aspects of *biological* life, these online groups have developed their own means of resistance—they have taken it upon themselves to make visible what is all too often hidden in our neoliberal society: that technological actants have a real impact on the way we think, feel, and know our own bodies. Tweaking also serves to celebrate a broader range of women's experiences than traditionally allowed for, including supposedly inorganic/nonbiologically meaningful ("chemical" pregnancies) processes of that body. This acts as a radical disavowal of language and practices that erase women and mothers, and it importantly resists any moves that separate women into opposing teams of pregnant/not pregnant, unmedicated birth/medicated birth, formula feeder/breastfeeder, co-sleeper/separate sleeper.

Using the space of new media, then, tweaking communities created by and for the women they serve promote a linguistic system that valorizes female agency in a way that no lobbyist, political enterprise, or corporation could hope to do. Of course, we intend this chapter to provide ideas of what nonpolarizing data and discourse might look like in practice, and to consider ways that we can learn from such grassroots community movements in order to engage women's health-care campaigns and recommendations in productive, practical ways. So, yes, we are paradoxically arguing that while such grassroots endeavors cannot, by their very nature, be reproduced on an institutional level, we also ought to attempt to learn from exactly what makes this movement so productive and meaningful—how do female-created communities and the language and rituals they employ radically change women's experiences of their health and health-care choices? By way of closing and emphasizing this point, we provide just one more example—a corporately created alternative to tweaking communities.

PREGNANCY PRO

First Response's Pregnancy Pro is the first Bluetooth-enabled pregnancy test (figure 6.4). Women connect the test to an app on their phones, and they can choose from a variety of options to soothe or distract them while they wait for the results (figure 6.5).

Figure 6.4

"Pregnancy Pro," Bluetooth-enabled pregnancy test product photo and description.

Source: First Response (n.d.).

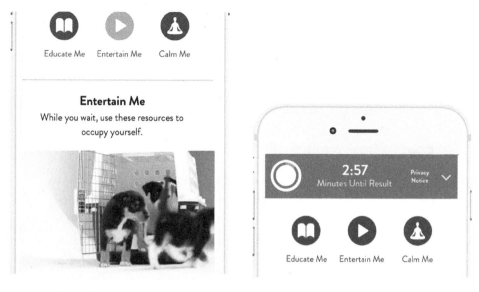

Figure 6.5
Screenshots from "Pregnancy Pro" app, while-you-wait-for-results options.
Source: Multivu (2016).

To begin, women tell the app and test whether they *want* to be pregnant, and the app adjusts its algorithms accordingly. Thus, depending on their answers to a series of questions on the app connected to the home pregnancy test, women will be guided to videos of puppies or rolling waves on a beach while they wait for the test to develop. The product and its "capabilities" are cringeworthy and, well, creepy. We would argue that this is because its verisimilitude to real compassion and companionship in a difficult moment descends into the uncanny valley. It may do what a real friend would, but it can never be more than a pee stick connected to a smartphone.[2]

These two routes hardly seem comparable. In one setting, groups of like-minded women help you interpret your fertility data using a communally created language, pictures, and rituals that serve needs the group itself has defined, combined with real-time reassurance and support from others like you who know your personal history. In the other, you get a corporate provision of the relaxing sound of crashing waves while you sit alone in your bathroom, scared that you're pregnant—or scared that you're not. For us, the preferential choice seems obvious. We would argue that it's fairly clear that the politics of the local—of female-centered and female-constructed understandings of reproductive states and a culture of grassroots resistance to institutionalized authority surrounding motherhood—are a powerful means to resisting the culture of motherhood in which the mother is erased.

CONCLUSION: A REBIRTH

By ending at the beginning, with conception, we invite readers to contemplate a new beginning—a clean slate, if you will—for maternity discourse previously embedded in intractably binary understandings of risk and the accompanying existential fear experienced by mothers forced to make such "risky" decisions for themselves and their offspring. Moreover, by ending on the topic of tweaking and chemical pregnancies, in which women control the shifting definition of when maternity begins (replacing current definitions with definitions that are more personally meaningful than necessarily medically meaningful), we also invite readers to invest in this beginning as a state

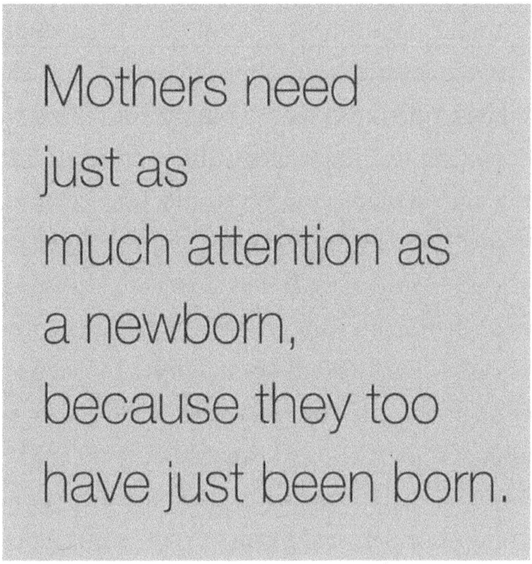

> Mothers need
> just as
> much attention as
> a newborn,
> because they too
> have just been born.

Figure 6.6
Pregnancy care center Facebook page post.
Source: Puget Sound Birth Center (2019).

of becoming rather than a destination. The word "matrescence" describes the transformation of a woman into her new identity as a mother, and we assert that this transformation is not unidirectional, simple, or mappable onto clear-cut binaries, but rather a broad spectrum, as vivid and diverse as the visible spectra that color the world as we know it. In allowing room for this miraculous, brilliant, and always-evolving, always becomingness of stewarding another person through life, often at the cost of one's own previously known physical and emotional identity, we allow for a richness of experience in which motherhood can exist as what it is: a thing of mystery and beauty that will never be fully quantifiable by big data. Data, indeed, should be informed by intersectional feminist thought (D'Ignazio and Klein 2020). Instead of data, we end, of course, on a meme (figure 6.6).

A VERY COVID CONCLUSION

The real problem with giving birth at the very beginning of a global pandemic, besides the massive fear and ridiculous isolation, is decision fatigue. Every single decision is weighty. You can't just pop out for a visit or get a massage or buy something. Every decision is so much work, a list of pros and cons, and the cons are "my baby could get seriously sick and possibly die." Is there any way I can swim safely with my baby? 6 articles later it seems like the experts all disagree and no one knows. Literally, "I could hold that railing as I walk down the stairs but my baby could die. Of course if I trip while holding her that's not good either. Which is worse?" I'm so freaking sick of it. New parents already have massive sleep deprivation and hormones are a mess—everything seems super hard under the BEST of circumstances. But when every single tiny decision is big, it leaves you incapable of making the decisions that are actually big. I'm at the point where not eating lunch is easier than deciding what's for lunch. Don't even get me started on big decisions. I'm exhausted. And by the time it's over, I won't have an infant anymore. I'll never get to spend 1 single day of her infancy free from this COVID suffocation. It's almost more than I can bear some days.

—Christine Spinetta-Ganguly, Facebook, June 15, 2020

This quote was posted on Facebook on June 15, 2020. In the thick of a global pandemic, this poster relates how COVID-19 further complicates the notion of parental "choice," how the black-or-white binary decisions of Optimal Motherhood are now seemingly shrunk to "would you prefer your infant to die this way or that?" None of us can accurately assess our own risk levels right now, because even the experts don't know precisely how this new virus works. And the mother? The life force held accountable for her own and her children's well-being bears the crushing weight of a million daily decisions that could, literally, result in harm or death to herself or her children. We've already covered in this book what such moments look like when the actual death of the child is a very slight risk—a minute possibility. It's not hard to imagine how any and all decisions are intensified with the increased actual risk of stewarding children through a pandemic. There is also the deep grief, the acute pain, that comes with realizing a pandemic-informed mother–new baby experience may not be able to be looked back on as "the happiest days of our lives." Parenting during a pandemic is an issue so new, so fraught with complicated variables, that we couldn't possibly do it justice in a single book chapter, yet we knew we would be remiss not to end our book by drawing attention to an issue so deeply entangled with notions of privilege, power, choice, and control—so deeply embedded in the decision-making discourse of the modern mother.

COVID-19 AND THE MOTHER OF ALL BINARIES: WORKING MOMS VERSUS STAY-AT-HOME MOMS

In July 2020, the Census Bureau conducted a survey concluding that women were three times as likely as men to leave their then current jobs because of COVID-19 childcare demands (Peck 2020). As US-based government authority figures assured us our fight with the coronavirus would be short-lived, women leaned into the long-standing narrative of maternal martyrdom: it was our maternal duty to reclaim the role of primary caretaker (a role easier to accept given that it was marketed as "temporary"); however, while a new school year usually sends children back to educational facilities and women back to the workforce, this wasn't the case in 2020. Before-school and after-school care programs were largely curtailed, remote learning contexts often required intense parental involvement, and in-person programs relied on the impossible standard of caretakers never slipping on strict health-care protocols as well as parents never needing to send their children to school sick (so parents could keep their jobs). COVID-19 intensified a historical continuum of problematic policies meant to fix a woman's place in the home: hiring biases, pay inequities, insufficient (or nonexistent) parental leave policies, exorbitant childcare options, and workplace facilities unconducive to infant-rearing needs (Peck 2020). In fact, some argue that the coronavirus will ultimately upend a *generation* of working moms: "Under the best circumstances, being a working parent feels like being an unwanted guest at the world's most tedious party, and what COVID-19 has done is essentially kick working mothers out of the room altogether" (Dickson 2020).

Our coronavirus-infected world, then, has doubly (triply?) confounded the working mom versus stay-at-home mom binary; while many mothers struggle to do it all (fulfill the roles of full-time parent, part-time teacher, *and* part- or full-time employee), those who have made a choice among roles are also suffering visceral consequences (see figure 7.1). Choose to work? Risk bringing home COVID to your children just to pay the bills. Choose to homeschool? Risk your own burnout while depriving your children of social-emotional growth. "The consensus is that everyone agrees this is a catastrophe, but we are too bone-tired to raise our voices above a groan, let alone scream through a megaphone. Every single person confesses *burnout, despair,* feeling like they are *losing their minds,* knowing in their guts that this is untenable" (Perelman 2020; emphasis added).

The mother's voice has, once again, been rendered silent—and "choice" has been rendered nonchoice. We see this zero-sum game evidenced in coronavirus wordplay: "But we don't even know if it's safe to send kids back to school!" "Why do you want teachers to get sick?" "You shouldn't have had kids if you can't take care of them!" and "Why aren't you enjoying the extra quality time with your kid?" (Perelman 2020). Sound familiar? That's because it is. It's the same old working moms versus stay-at-home moms debate—on steroids. We are reminded, with daily rising COVID-19 death tolls, that our parenting decisions are now directly (precariously) linked to control over our and our children's mortality. And there is nothing to gain from "choosing a side" at this time because only the previously wealthy—with the privileges of economic security as well as access to elite health care and child-rearing assistance—come out on top. Money, power, privilege, and the role they play in maternal decision-making have never been clearer to a wider audience of parents and nonparents alike. It is a key reminder that we need to revisit the idea of who had agency in maternal choice to begin with.

Kenya Adjekum Bradshaw from Wakanda
@KenyaBradshaw

In the last 2 weeks I have talked to 5 women who are pausing or leaving their careers to support their children virtually. The weight of this pandemic on the shoulders of women is something we should monitor.

9:16 AM · Sep 15, 2020 · Twitter for Android

1.7K Retweets   **186** Quote Tweets   **7.8K** Likes

Bookmasterp @bookmasterp2019 · Sep 18
Replying to @KenyaBradshaw
Left my dream job this week to support three kiddos doing a mix of hybrid and in person and virtual school. I'm taking a huge step back career wise because we have no other choice. Glad I spent all that time fighting to have it all...so now I have to give a big part back....

♡ 1   ⟲   ♡   ⬆

TammyLee Marlene @TammyLeeMarlene · Sep 16
Replying to @KenyaBradshaw
I was scheduled to start back to school last week and I had to withdraw. There was no way I could manage my kids virtually and start classes and homework. I was sad but I will hopefully try again sometime next year.

♡ 1   ⟲ 1   ♡ 16   ⬆

Biologicalmother @wisecomplainer · Sep 16
Replying to @KenyaBradshaw
Absolutely. I've reduced my hours at work to facilitate online kindergarten while my husband continues to work full time. If I leave my profession now (in my 40s) I stand almost no chance of reentering the work force at the same level.

♡ 1   ⟲ 2   ♡ 23   ⬆

Figure 7.1
Series of tweets illustrating consequences for moms choosing childcare over careers during COVID.
Source: K. Bradshaw (2020).

PRIVILEGE, MOTHERING, AND CHOICE IN THE CORONAVIRUS PANDEMIC

Much of our book has targeted discourse produced on social media platforms populated by white, middle-class mothers from the United States. In analyzing this discourse, we have identified patterns accounting for a modern phenomenon known as Optimal Motherhood, which we define as comprising three tenets:

1. Shifts the Victorian insistence that women be exclusively responsible for nation-saving by raising strong, morally upright families as wives *and* mothers to mothers *only*
2. Valorizes private, personal improvement and necessarily *rejects communal support*, even while it contributes to a sense of nation-state moral superiority—in the true spirit of neoliberal individualism
3. Doubles down on an increased and intense demand for perfection

As we stated in the introduction, the Optimal Mother must perfect her family, and she must do so in a vacuum, because perfect women shouldn't need help.

We have argued that Optimal Motherhood is further defined by a perpetual insistence on the binary nature of parenting choices; yet there is a more complex continuum of experiences existing in contemporary motherhood that deserves to be accounted for. These disparate narratives are often rendered invisible because our discourse practices amplify the voices that fit neatly into those problematic binaries. These discourse practices tend to leave those who would benefit most from a digitally supportive community feeling, themselves, invisible; in a digitally mediated world, it is sometimes easy to forget that a body, a mind, and a heart are attached to the words on the screen—as well as a significant number of vulnerable bodies attached to voices *not* circulating in our online support communities. Access to these discourse communities and the choices they present—even if they are fraught choices—*is a privilege*.

Jenna Vinson and Clare Daniel write about this privilege in light of the reproductive justice framework. This framework was developed by BIPOC activists in the mid-1990s in response to reproductive *in*justices (e.g., forced sterilization, high maternal mortality rates, limited access to abortion and family leave, involuntary family separation), injustices ignored by the white-centered reproductive rights movement of the 1960s (which largely focused on women's right to contraception and sex education). Vinson and Daniel (via Ross and Solinger) adeptly remind us of the many nodes of influence in the network of motherly discourse and decision-making that render some women (women of color) *without choice*:

> The rhetoric of "choice" that characterizes that movement presents various reproductive behaviors and technologies as rightfully existing in a marketplace of options from which women can freely choose. This formulation constructs "women" as a category of interchangeable individuals with equal ability to make any given choice, thus "[disguising] the ways that laws, policies, and public officials differently punish and reward the childbearing of different groups of women as well as the varied access women have to healthcare and other resources to manage sex, fertility, and maternity." (Ross and Solinger 47, quoted in Vinson and Daniel 2020)

Because "women" are so often considered collectively rather than inter-sectionally, women of color are forced to participate in a construction of Optimal Motherhood that is not adequately captured in this book. For that reason, we encourage future research, which takes painstaking time. But we also encourage our online motherhood communities to start doing the work of diversity, equity, and inclusion in maternal decision-making *now*. There is no better time than a pandemic to begin the very *real* work of authentic community building, of welcoming disparate voices into the online network of motherly discourse. This is no better illustrated than in figure 7.2, a "White privilege in motherhood looks like" infographic, crafted and captioned by Leaky Boob (2020), a Facebook resource centered around baby and toddler feeding: "The inequities in pregnancy, birth, and lactation support for Black families is well documented. We know it is an issue. But what does that look like in real life? This graphic takes a look at the very real challenges. White privilege does not mean that white people do not have struggles or that they don't experience these difficulties. It means that their struggles and their experiences with these difficulties are *not* because of the color of their skin."

Figure 7.2

"White privilege" infographic.

Source: Leaky Boob (2020).

THE HAZY DAZE OF MOTHERHOOD ≈ PANDEMIC DISILLUSIONMENT: WHAT'S EVEN "REAL" ANYMORE?

The Substance Abuse and Mental Health Services Administration (SAMHSA 2020) relates that six months into a major disaster marks the "disillusionment phase," in which "optimism turns to discouragement and stress continues to take a toll. Negative reactions, such as physical exhaustion or substance use, may begin to surface." The administration further describes how the lack of need fulfillment can increase feelings of abandonment: "Especially as the larger community returns to business as usual, there may be an increased demand for services, as individuals and communities become ready to accept support." The United States entered the disillusionment phase of the coronavirus pandemic around mid-September 2020. The SAMHSA suggests the disillusionment phase can last months and even years. Need we reiterate that *now* is the time to support your fellow mothers?

One problem in actualizing support, perhaps, is a nostalgic longing for the maternal support communities of the past. Consider the "washing machine anecdote" that is popular on social media: "I think it was Brene Brown who told a story about a village where all the women washed clothes together down by the river. When they all got washing machines, there was a sudden outbreak of depression and no one could figure out why. It wasn't the washing machines in and of themselves. . . . It was the absence of time spent doing things together. It was the absence of community" (Sister, I am with you 2020). Commenters flock to such posts, replying with similar stories—lamenting how nobody drinks tea in the backyard with their female neighbors, aunts, and cousins anymore. What is ironic is that they don't acknowledge that their support-seeking commiseration is with a digital *community*. What is troubling is that the surface-level rhetoric consistently negates the value of that support and that community.

The washing machine anecdote inherently encourages women to pine for a "normalized" image of motherhood attached to warm and fuzzy feelings emoted by embodied persons around material machines. Jordan Frith (2020), however, reminds us of the very "real" work always already being done online, that "offline" does not exclusively equate to "in real life."

"In real life" or IRL is popular rhetoric used to semantically separate offline from online, the body from the digital. More specifically, aligning the term "IRL" with offline or physical face-to-face experiences is meant to privilege those embodied encounters as more direct and, therefore, more "real." The problem with this logic, as Frith (2020) points out, is that "there is no pure communication even if face-to-face is often viewed as the gold standard." *All* communication is mediated—whether through bodies and verbal language or delivery of text and image through social media—and the "divide" between immaterial and material is much smaller than it used to be, in part because of the rise of the smartphone. Consider the following examples: "A breakup through *Facebook Messenger* hurts a physical body. An external tenure letter I compose digitally and send through e-mail may determine where someone physically lives. *It's all real life*" (Frith 2020; emphasis added). In short, online interaction has significant, real-life consequences, and pretending that it doesn't paves the way for the performance of anonymity and troubling communication such as trolling—or even much more sinister consequences. Yet we believe the metaphors we use to describe our online interactions, and, therefore, those online interactions in and of themselves, *can be an empowering experience for contemporary mothers facing the impossibly binary decisions of contemporary motherhood.*

Whether it is the hazy days of motherhood that leave us feeling confused and disoriented or larger pandemic fatigue that leaves us grasping for a sense of the "real" and the "normal," social media can be that life-giving village by the river. But how? We're the first to admit that we do not have the definitive answer (or believe that a *singular* solution somehow exists), so we provide the following food for thought in the hopes that scholars will continue to assemble solutions in a positive path forward.

ACTION ITEM #1: KEEP IT REAL

We can learn something from the vulnerability of Chrissy Teigen's digital storytelling. Teigen is a well-known American model, television personality, author, and entrepreneur. She is also known for speaking her piece on Twitter. On September 30, 2020, she posted an intimate selfie: hunched over in a hospital bed, hands folded near her face, and tears streaming down her cheeks. The accompanying text revealed she and husband John Legend had suffered a stillbirth, losing their third child, Jack, at around twenty to twenty-four weeks. While some followers taunted Teigen for indulging in "look at me culture" and for exhibiting attention-seeking behavior during what should have been a "private family affair" of mourning, others praised her use of the platform to give voice to the voiceless (figure 7.3).

The experts agree with Teigen's follower Marquita Bradshaw. While pregnancy loss is unfortunately common, so is the stigma that surrounds it: "'Chrissy's openness helps to shed this stigma and advance conversations

Figure 7.3
Bradshaw tweets support for Teigen's courage in sharing her miscarriage story on social media.
Source: M. Bradshaw (2020).

about the topic, and help people realize that in the vast majority of cases, there is nothing that anybody did or didn't do that could prevent this devastating event,' Dr. Lilli Dash Zimmerman, a fertility specialist at Columbia University Fertility Center," stated (quoted in Miller 2020). Not only does Teigen's communicative act contribute to the larger assemblage of maternal knowledge, but it also affords hope, through targeted language and visual expression, to other grieving mothers.

As we discussed in chapter 2, "Take Back the Delivery Room," the lack of narrative precedent for discoursing on such a difficult topic can turn mothers away from sharing their stories of loss—or, as we discussed in chapter 3, "We Have Never Been Normal," from sharing their unknowingly common but also dark and often deemed disturbing feelings of things like "mom rage": It is not a topic that gets talked about because "'You know, mom shame'" (anonymous mom quoted in Dubin 2020). But if we do not confront the hard stuff, we cannot learn from it, and if we do not share the hard stuff, we will perpetuate mothers internalizing shame for such rageful postpartum loneliness.[1] Not everyone is ready to wade so vulnerably deep into the river of social media motherhood. And that's OK. What we're suggesting is that you combat the culture of toxic positivity and the performance of perfect motherhood online by *making room for* a motherhood collective that includes the real of raw motherhood.

ACTION ITEM #2: COMMIT TO COLLECTIVE CARE

There is no "being real" on the already always real platform of social media without commitment to collective care within a social media mothering group. Being community directed or otherwise committed to collective care means, at its core, when a need is identified, the community gathers to meet it. Maybe you've heard this story: "Anthropologist Margaret Mead . . . said [to a student that] the first sign of civilization in an ancient culture was a femur (thighbone) that had been broken and then healed. . . . A broken femur that has healed is evidence that someone has taken the time to stay with the one who fell. . . . Helping someone else through difficulty is where civilization starts" (Byock quoted in Hedlund). Helping someone else through difficulty is where civilization *starts*. Collective care in the context of social media motherhood, we argue, should be an extension above and beyond meeting basic needs.

In fact, we reject neoliberal insistence on self-care in favor of such collective care (see figure 7.4). Maybe this means reading between the lines to identify the new mother's needs. Maybe this means encouraging the new mother's vulnerability and rewarding that vulnerability. Maybe this means purposefully creating space for disparate voices and promoting language that serves a healing function. We see that kind of collective care in chapter 6, "Can I Get a Tweak?," which details a grassroots online group of pregnancy test Tweakers, a community that is created by and for women, a community

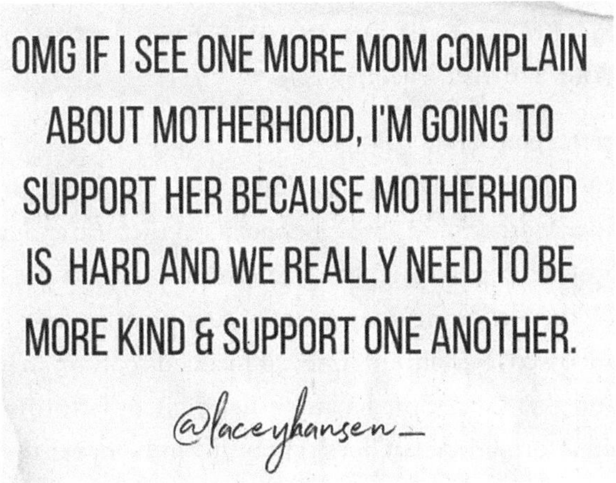

Figure 7.4
A Facebook meme championing collective care.
Source: Spokane Mama (2020).

that is uplifting and hopeful in the face of infertility and otherwise "failure to procreate" cultural messages—a community that goes one step further and *gets things done* for women's health care in productive and meaningful ways.

It's important to recognize that such collective care is not all kittens and kindness; such an (admittedly warm and fuzzy) echo chamber would only continue to reinforce the problematic binaries fueling Optimal Motherhood, which we have spent this entire book trying to dismantle. Collective care, rendered most productively, might be accomplished through mentorship. And, whether that mentorship is championed collectively or one-to-one, as discussed with infant formula feeding group initiatives in chapter 4, "Breast/Fed Is Best," we need to remember that mentorship is about growth and change. Simply shouting our DIFFERENT OPINIONS (ALL CAPS) at strangers in social media mothering groups won't engender growth and change. Call it religious, rhetorical, or being an empathetic human being, productive mentorship means building a relationship *before* criticizing your discourse partner. A community whose members are committed to collective care and that sponsors purposeful mentorship in one form or another stands half a chance at challenging the disabling binaries that plague modern motherhood.

ACTION ITEM #3: FLIP THE DOUBLE-SIDED COIN (A BINARY TO BELIEVE IN)

Personal Responsibility

We also have to take personal responsibility for our part in keeping the narrative of Optimal Motherhood alive. As scholars of rhetoric and literature, we think about these things through the frameworks of digital and information literacy. We acknowledge the importance of cognitive dissonance, confirmation bias, and selective attention in social media discourse. In other words, we understand that "social media and other digital platforms . . . make it easier to avoid information that doesn't fit neatly into our existing narratives" (Sano 2018)—and believe there is value in making sure others understand this too. As humans, we tend to inherently reject stories that don't necessarily fit neatly into our preexisting narratives, and social media interfaces make it exceedingly easy to simply scroll past unpleasant stimuli. As humans, we need help in seeing past our own experiences *and in slowing down*—things that are particularly difficult to negotiate amid the daily tasks of mothering. So, as much as we need informed guidance from an online village of mothers committed to collective care, we also need to be *open* to that collective care, open to growing in relationship with that internet village, and open to changing our opinions through comprehensive education. "Safe" relationships breed brave conversations.

Personal Forgiveness

It would be easier to engage in this critical personal responsibility mode of parenting if we hadn't all internalized the neoliberal ideals of capitalism: "feeling guilty for resting . . . placing productivity before health . . . feeling lazy, even when you're experiencing pain, trauma, or adversity" (@therapy-withlee quoted in Robinson 2020). It would be easier to engage in this critical personal responsibility if we hadn't all internalized the stories of Optimal Motherhood birthed of this neoliberal nightmare. And it would be easier to engage in this critical personal responsibility if we weren't dealing with a pandemic, a surreally fraught political election, and a world that is quite literally on fire. But if there's anything approximating a silver lining to this pandemic, it has perhaps imprinted on our DNA the *necessity* of grace and letting go. Mamas, give grace to yourself, for without personal forgiveness, there is no reason for engaging in personal responsibility and committing to growth (figure 7.5).

ACTION ITEM #4: CALL FOR CORPORATE RESPONSIBILITY

In chapter 1, "It Was Never about the Coffee," we call out CDC recommendations and their role in exacerbating fetal alcohol fears. In chapter 5, we call out the National Institute of Child Health and their rigid insistence on the inverse correlation of back-sleeping and SIDS. Though this concluding chapter largely focuses on civilian-led action items, we cannot close without emphasizing the need for change at the corporate level—in essence, for the corporate bodies currently governing and otherwise intervening in women's health care to

when a mother
somewhere
forgives herself
for being human,

earth exhales
A little

– breeze

Figure 7.5
A Facebook meme suggesting the collective value of personal forgiveness.
Source: breeze (2020).

take responsibility for and engender positive change in maternal health-care discourse and practices. Personal forgiveness is, in fact, recognizing that you are not *personally* responsible for fixing the massive (and messy) assemblage that is contemporary maternal decision-making (it is only the neoliberal voice on your shoulder insisting you need to fight this war on your own). One "battle" we are willing to fight, for example, is encouraging productive interventions in the rhetorical education of health-care practitioners.

There is no better time than now to follow the lead of an eastern Washington state hospital that uses humanities training to ground its patient-care practices. Doctors at this hospital regularly engage in literature not only for literature's sake but also to engender empathy; after reading *East of Eden*, for instance, a third-year resident proclaimed, "That has always stayed with me—that I shouldn't lose touch with my emotions" (quoted in Iannelli 2020). For those who may find this a trite proclamation, we beg you to remember the anecdotes included in this book, such as the nurse who told us to "just quit being uptight" to ensure breastfeeding success or being released from the hospital with little hands-on education despite our protests of "Oh, no. You can't just hand me a baby without teaching me how to hold one first!" Words have power.

Such empathy is *critical* for impressing on our health-care practitioners the need for "empowering parents with comprehensive education" (Ghosh 2020). All parenting choices can be rendered unsafe, and Ghosh (2020), much as we do, champions risk mitigation in light of *dynamic* (not binary) circumstances. The dynamics of those circumstances are easy for health-care practitioners to forget when electronic medical record (EMR) software "has sterilized the emotional connection between medical professionals and their patients. . . . EMR software also has the potential to reduce living, breathing, hurting patients to cold, hard data. Or quantifiable units that have to be checked off like a to-do list" (Iannelli 2020), yet another example of a technological actant impressing on contemporary maternal decision-making.

However, as health-care practitioner education makes leaps and bounds in "creating common ground between physician and patient" and "foster[ing] better relationships between the physicians-in-training and their more seasoned counterparts" (Iannelli 2020) we have the potential for long-term productive impact on women's maternal health. The research these empathetically informed health-care practitioners perform has a direct influence on the health-care policies circulated by governing agencies such as the CDC or NIH. Public health policy creation and circulation is much more complex than the neat and tidy circle we have presented here, but the larger point is that bringing practicing physicians into the conversation we have started in this book is a much-needed extension of the research on Optimal Motherhood and its problematic construction in contemporary parenting discourse.

OH THE PLACES WE'LL GO

We set out writing this book to put into plain language the problem of binary-bound decision-making in contemporary motherhood. This problem—fueled by an oppressive context we call Optimal Motherhood—excludes disparate parenting experiences in reducing very real and very complex parenting decisions. This problem is exacerbated by neoliberal postpartum

American traditions in which the mother is supposed to heal quickly, go back to work, and pump breast milk for her baby. This problem is exacerbated further under pandemic circumstances in which women, historically situated as the primary caretakers, are forced to, very literally, choose between their jobs and child-rearing.

We do not have all the answers, but we do see a way out—and how we talk about motherhood (especially in our social media villages) has as much to do with that way out as our behavioral choices, our mothering in action. We need mothering group discourse that empathizes, recognizes diversity, and centers on the mother's experience. We need to stop indulging in very white, middle-class ideals and to recognize that Optimal Motherhood is not the only way. We need researchers to continue the conversation, delving into venues above and beyond social media discourse in which women do the hard work of gathering and contending with contemporary maternity advice.

To all the mamas we look forward to learning from, remember:

> There's no way to be a perfect mother and a million ways to be a good one.—Jill Churchill

Notes

INTRODUCTION

1. For additional discussion of the Cult of True Womanhood, see Welter (1996).

2. See also Roberts (2002) for an extension of Welter's arguments.

3. For academics, it will by now be clear that our study is birthed at the intersection of science and technology studies (STS) and critical health studies. As related by Deborah Lupton, critical digital health studies have pursued a variety of approaches: (1) "a focus on digital social inequalities, medical dominance and medicalisation, globalisation, the role played by commercial entities such as Big Pharma, the biotech industry and digital developers, and the implications for *social justice*"; (2) "Foucauldian perspective on the *discursive construction of knowledge* and matters relating to biopolitics and biopower, disciplinary power, governmentality and surveillance"; (3) "the sociomaterial approach that directs attention at the intersection of human and non-human actors in creating *digital assemblages*"; and (4) "the digital cultures or cybercultures literature, focusing on the *production and experience of selfhood and embodiment* via digital technologies" (2014, 1348; emphasis added). Our study involves cross-category concerns: how the discursive construction of maternal decision-making knowledge by digital assemblages (social media mothering groups and the techno-actants circulated within) produces the bodily and psychosocial identities of contemporary mothers as a matter of social justice.

4. Henwood and Marent (2019, 5–6) productively expand Lupton's list of critical digital health study approaches to address a new wave of concerns at the cusp of sociology, health, and STS: (1) "the configuration of discourses that enact contradictory virtues and imaginaries by which digital technologies and practices gain momentum within the provision of health"; (2) "how ambivalence is experienced when digital information and data is generated, negotiated, and shared within practices of care"; (3) "new digital networks and their often contradictory implications for relationships and collaboration between different actors in healthcare"; and (4) "algorithms . . . and new forms of authority within decision-making, diagnosis and treatment." "Contradictory," "ambivalence," "actors," and "algorithms" are all key terms in our study. That is, we explore and analyze the discourse in social media mothering groups

(digital assemblages that include algorithms and other techno-agents as actors who influence maternal decision-making), a public health context that, more so than many others, is dominated by uncertain and ambivalent approaches to contradictory "evidence" but otherwise fiercely trenchant binaristic thinking at the ready for "risk-averse" decisions regarding the mother's un/born child. We are not explicitly concerned with assessing the pros and cons of digital health interfaces as technologies per se; rather, we seek to "draw attention to the role played by digital technologies in configuring and enacting concepts and experiences of embodiment, selfhood, and social relations in the context of medicine and public health" (Lupton 2014, 1349).

5. An important note about our methodology: we established our methods in accordance with the Association of Internet Researchers' IRE 3.0 (franzke et al. 2019). Internet research has long been noted as a complex ethical gray area in academic inquiry. IRE 3.0 asks internet researchers to more specifically pay attention to two elements: (1) differentiating the ethical concerns of each *stage* of research and (2) contemplating the complexities of "informed consent" in big data research approaches; moreover, IRE 3.0 emphasizes the need for researchers to consult with IRBs and other stakeholders in individual research contexts because internet research is ultimately about judgment calls. IRE 3.0 provides guidelines rather than recipes.

CHAPTER 1

1. It is also worth noting that the CDC's party line on "Alcohol Use in Pregnancy" was last updated on December 14, 2021 but remains the same: "There is no known safe amount of alcohol use during pregnancy or while trying to get pregnant. There is also no safe time during pregnancy to drink. All types of alcohol are equally harmful, including all wines and beer. FASDs (Fetal Alcohol Spectrum Disorders) are preventable if a woman does not drink alcohol during pregnancy" (CDC 2018).

2. See chapter 2, "Take Back the Delivery Room: Narrative Control, Traumatic Discourse, and the #MeToo Labor Movement," for a brief discussion of the rhetorical impact of emojis in such discourse.

3. The defensive nature of binary-bound infant feeding discourse is further discussed in chapter 4, "Breast/Fed Is Best: Whose Algorithm Is Feeding My Baby?"

4. See, as one example, Clements 2013.

CHAPTER 2

1. List items taken from Emerald Doulas (2017); Martinelli (2019); and Hamilton (n.d.), respectively.

2. Interestingly, the Association of American Medical Colleges (2008) suggests that, in 2007, 57 percent of doctors practicing in obstetrics and gynecology were male and 43 percent were female, while in 2017, 43 percent were male and 57 percent were female. We wonder if this literal reversal speaks to a productively changing dynamic in the *ethos* of contemporary maternity advice from within the medical community itself.

3. As Kaufman (2007, 48) writes, "Doctors and nurses are human beings with their own opinions and experiences, which may not always match expectant parents' desires. Physicians and hospital staff may function on experiential evidence and find it hard to break their routines."

4. Anderson et al. (2017, 309) helpfully point out that medical practitioners are likely to believe that all of the recommendations they make are "medically necessary."

5. Some practitioners have standardized an "extended educational visit," scheduled at thirty-four to thirty-six weeks, with the specific goal of discussing realistic, available, and medically advised choices in concert with the pregnant woman's values and preferences for her unique birthing experience (DeBaets 2016, 32).

6. See Full Frontal with Samantha Bee (2019a, 2019b).

CHAPTER 3

1. Think Luvs NightLock Plus TV commercial. See Luvs (2013).

2. We use *ethos* here and throughout in a rhetorical sense—concerning persuasive contexts based in ethics, credibility, and authority—as explicated in our introduction.

3. Dr. Cohen is director of the Ammon-Pinizzotto Center and professor of psychiatry at Harvard Medical School.

4. Dr. Stewart is a university professor and inaugural chair of women's health at University Health Network and University of Toronto.

5. Note here the conflation of "postpartum" as a metonym for "postpartum depression." The interviewee subconsciously supports our sense that the postpartum period itself is nonnormative and not easily mapped onto already fraught normative binaries of ab/normality.

6. In the words of a health-care practitioner: literal word choice juxtaposition—"postpartum" and "blues," a mix of "postpartum depression" and "baby blues"—that rhetorically conflates the two real-world clinical conditions.

CHAPTER 4

1. See, as one example, Foss 2017.

2. "Breastfed children perform better on intelligence tests, are less likely to be overweight or obese and less prone to diabetes later in life. Women who breastfeed also have a reduced risk of breast and ovarian cancers" (World Health Organization, n.d.).

3. See also Safiya Umoja Noble's (2018) *Algorithms of Oppression*, in which she explicates data discrimination as a social problem and more specifically illustrates how search engines like Google do not offer an equal playing field for all forms of ideas, identities, and activities.

4. We want to remind readers that it is both human actors and technological actants that are responsible for composing and circulating discourse that qualifies the benefits of breastfeeding as unequivocal in the face of inconclusive scientific data. This harks back to our discussion

of the tyranny of evidence-based medicine and how it, ironically, holds maternal decision-makers in limbo as they try to ascertain which approach is more effectively evidence based. See chapter 1 or chapter 5.

5. See also Reneau 2019.

CHAPTER 5

1. We say this with great reverence for Black, Indigenous, and people of color (BIPOC) communities who—without the privileges of white, middle-class America—*do* create and sustain productive social networks that support expectant and new mothers through their complex maternal experiences. We acknowledge here and throughout that there is much to learn from these communities that is not directly addressed within the scope of this book.

2. For more about the problematic nature of predetermining how one will feel after a fundamentally transformative act like becoming a parent, see Carel, Kidd, and Pettigrew (2016).

3. Consider the confounders mentioned in chapter 1: How do we define "healthy"? Healthy for the mind? For the body? There are also measurement difficulties. How do we track overall health of the body (cortisol levels? weight gain? percentage of time spent smiling?), and how do we ensure that such correlational data is in fact related to sleep rather than a host of other factors?

4. "Collective Culture is a digital platform that inspires audiences through content created with data and technology. Our mission is to inspire audiences to raise awareness, invite action, and spark emotions through quality content" (Cultura Colectiva, n.d.).

5. For a refresher on how and why infant and pregnancy safety data is often so unclear, please see the discussion of fetal alcohol syndrome in chapter 1.

6. This can be seen, for instance, in the Interactive Safe Sleep Room, in which a recliner is marked as unsafe, and in McKenna (2012).

7. Other notable ones include AM Smiles Sleep Training, Blissful Baby Sleep Coaching, Family Sleep Institute, Dream Baby Sleep, and the Cradle Coach Academy.

CHAPTER 6

1. It should be noted that while some women in these communities were trying to conceive a second or third child, the focus within these spaces (as will be elaborated on in this chapter) was solely on new conception and on the desire for *new* motherhood. We felt that the space of pre-motherhood psychologically applied, therefore, even to second- or third-time moms, as their focus in this space was not on their extant motherhood roles but on future ones.

2. For additional discussion of Pregnancy Pro and its impact on TTC community groups, see Healey 2016.

CHAPTER 7

1. Consider the growing scholarship on mothering and motherhood, especially "Section 3: Bringing It to Light: Giving Voice to Motherhood's Challenges," in Young (2015).

References

Allers, Kimberly Seals. 2019. "Six Things I've Learned about Making Breastfeeding Accessible for All." *Washington Post*, August 2, 2019. https://www.washingtonpost.com/lifestyle/2019/08/02/six -things-ive-learned-about-making-breastfeeding-accessible-all/.

Alternative Mama. n.d. "A Letter from a Sleep-Training Baby." Accessed March 13, 2020. alternative-mama.com/a-letter-from-a-sleep-training-baby/.

American Academy of Pediatrics. n.d. "Benefits of Breastfeeding." Accessed March 20, 2020. https://www.aap.org/en-us/advocacy-and-policy/aap-health-initiatives/Breastfeeding/Pages /Benefits-of-Breastfeeding.aspx.

Anderson, Clare-Marie, Rosie Monardo, Reni Soon, Jennifer Lum, March Tschann, and Bliss Kaneshiro. 2017. "Patient Communication, Satisfaction, and Trust before and after Use of a Standardized Birth Plan." *Hawaii Journal of Medicine & Public Health* 76 (11): 305–309. https://www .ncbi.nlm.nih.gov/pmc/articles/PMC5694973/.

Anxiety and Depression Association of America. 2018. "Postpartum Disorders." Accessed March 13, 2020. https://adaa.org/find-help-for/women/postpartum-disorders#Types%20of%20Post partum%20Disorders.

Arao, Brian, and Kristi Clemens. 2013. "From Safe Spaces to Brave Spaces: A New Way to Frame Dialogue around Diversity and Social Justice." In *The Art of Effective Facilitation: Reflections from Social Justice Educators*, edited by Lisa M. Landreman, 135–150. Sterling, VA: Stylus. https://www .gvsu.edu/cms4/asset/843249C9-B1E5-BD47-A25EDBC68363B726/from-safe-spaces-to-brave -spaces.pdf.

Aristotle. 2007. *On Rhetoric: A Theory of Civic Discourse*. 2nd ed. Translated by George A. Kennedy. New York: Oxford University Press.

Association of American Medical Colleges. 2008. *2008 Physician Specialty Data*. https://www.aamc .org/system/files/2019-08/2008-physician-specialty-data.pdf.

Association of American Medical Colleges. 2018. "Active Physicians by Sex and Specialty, 2017." *2018 Physician Specialty Data Report*. https://www.aamc.org/data-reports/workforce/interactive -data/active-physicians-sex-and-specialty-2017.

BabyCenter. 2020. "Test Tweakers! –All Members Can Tweak!-" Babycenter.com, February 24, 2020. https://community.babycenter.com/groups/a6715291/test_tweakers_-all_members_can _tweak-?.

Bacon, Amanda. 2016. "Motherhood uncensored." Facebook, July 6, 2016. https://www.facebook .com/photo.php?fbid=10101599736906616&set=a.811525739156&type=3&theater.

Bartick, Melissa. 2015. "Opinion: 'Lactivism' Has Trump-Like Appeal for Breastfeeding Back-lash, but Science Is Off." Boston Public Radio, December 25, 2015. https://www.wbur.org /commonhealth/2015/12/25/breastfeeding-backlash.

Bash, Dana, Bridget Nolan, Nelli Black, and Patricia DiCarlo. 2020. "Andrew Yang's Wife Reveals She Was Sexually Assaulted by Her OB-GYN While Pregnant." CNN, January 17, 2020. https:// www.cnn.com/2020/01/16/politics/evelyn-yang-interview-assault/index.html.

Bass, Joel, Tina Gartley, and Ronald Kleinman. 2016. "Unintended Consequences of Current Breastfeeding Initiatives." *JAMA: Pediatrics* 170 (10): 923–924.

Bass, Joel, Tina Gartley, and Ronald Kleinman. 2020. "Outcomes from the Centers for Disease Control and Prevention 2018 Breastfeeding Report Card: Public Policy Implications." *Journal of Pediatrics* 218:16–21.

Beck, Cheryl Tatano. 2006. "Pentadic Cartography: Mapping Birth Trauma Narratives." *Qualitative Health Research* 16 (4): 453–466. https://doi.org/10.1177/1049732305285968.

Berger, Paige K., Jasmine F. Plows, Roshonda B. Jones, Tanya L. Alderete, Chloe Yonemitsu, Marie Poulsen, Ji Hoon Ryoo, Bradley S. Peterson, Lars Bode, and Michael I. Goran. 2020. "Human Milk Oligosaccharide 2'-Fucosyllactose Links Feedings at 1 Month to Cognitive Development at 24 Months in Infants of Normal and Overweight Mothers." *PLOS ONE* 15 (2): e0228323.

Berlant, Lauren. 2011. *Cruel Optimism*. Durham, NC: Duke University Press.

Bradshaw, Kenya (@KenyaBradshaw). 2020. "In the last 2 weeks, I have talked to 5 women." Twitter, September 15, 2020. https://twitter.com/KenyaBradshaw/status/1305903432692387840 ?fbclid=IwAR1SjW1NhoUE45jPakqzREbe7XZbpvh8GSY27vXRK1qP2PZRODxW97_wIz4.

Bradshaw, Marquita (@Bradshaw2020). 2020. "Sending you and your family so much love and peace." Twitter, October 1, 2020. https://twitter.com/Bradshaw2020/status/1311 734563727724544.

Braff, Danielle. 2019. "The Failure of 'Baby Friendly' Initiatives." Romper, November 22, 2019. https://www.romper.com/p/the-failure-of-baby-friendly-initiatives-19374870.

Braman, D., D. M. Kahan, E. Peters, M. Wittlin, P. Slovic, L. Larrimore Ouellette, and G. N. Mandel. 2012. "The Polarizing Impact of Science Literacy and Numeracy on Perceived Climate Change Risks." *Scholarly Commons, Nature Climate Change* 2:732–735. http://scholarship.law.gwu .edu/faculty_publications/265.

breeze. 2020. "When a mother somewhere forgives herself for being human." Facebook, September 3, 2020. https://www.facebook.com/photo/?fbid=10157765613338337&set=gm .3467221929965400.

Brodsky, Phyllis L. 2008. *The Control of Childbirth: Women versus Medicine through the Ages*. Jefferson, NC: McFarland.

The Bump. n.d. "Birth Plan." The Knot. Accessed February 29, 2020. https://images.thebump.com/tools/pdfs/birth_plan.pdf.

Burbidge, Anna. 2019. "Alcohol and Breastfeeding." La Leche League GB. https://www.laleche.org.uk/alcohol-and-breastfeeding/.

Burke, Tarana. 2018. "The Inception." Me Too. Accessed March 17, 2020. https://web.archive.org/web/20200709010844/https://metoomvmt.org/the-inception/.

Butler, Judith. 2011. *Bodies That Matter*. New York: Routledge.

Bynum, W. F. 1994. *Science and the Practice of Medicine in the Nineteenth Century*. Cambridge: Cambridge University Press.

Cara (@caraandthecubs). 2019. "I wasn't going to post this picture." Instagram, September 17, 2019. https://www.instagram.com/p/B2hcO_BBZEE/?hl=en.

Carel, Havi, Ian James Kidd, and Richard Pettigrew. 2016. "Illness as a Transformative Experience." *Lancet* 388 (10050): 1152–1153.

Carter, Ashleigh. 2020. "Here's the 'Graphic' Commercial You Didn't See during the Oscars." Now This News, February 11, 2020. https://nowthisnews.com/news/heres-the-graphic-commercial-you-didnt-see-during-the-oscars.

CDC (Centers for Disease Control and Prevention). 2016a. "Alcohol and Pregnancy: Why Take the Risk?" Vital Signs. Reviewed February 2, 2016. https://www.cdc.gov/vitalsigns/fasd/infographic.html.

CDC (Centers for Disease Control and Prevention). 2016b. "Drinking Too Much Can Have Many Risks for Women" (graphic), in "The CDC's Incredibly Condescending Warning to Young Women," Washington Post, February 3, 2016, https://www.washingtonpost.com/blogs/compost/wp/2016/02/03/the-cdcs-incredibly-condescending-warning-to-young-women

CDC (Centers for Disease Control and Prevention). 2018. "Alcohol Use in Pregnancy." Fetal Alcohol Spectrum Disorders (FASDs). Reviewed March 27, 2018. https://www.cdc.gov/ncbddd/fasd/alcohol-use.html.

CDC (Centers for Disease Control and Prevention). 2020. "CDC Organization." About CDC 24–7. Reviewed January 30, 2020. https://www.cdc.gov/about/organization/cio.htm?CDC_AA_refVal=https%3A%2F%2Fwww.cdc.gov%2Fabout%2Forganization%2Findex.html.

CDC (Centers for Disease Control and Prevention). 2021. "Trends in Sudden Unexpected Infant Death by Cause, 1990–2019." Sudden Unexpected Infant Death and Sudden Infant Death Syndrome. Reviewed April 28, 2021. https://www.cdc.gov/sids/data.htm.

Chen, Jen. 2020. "Social Media Demographics to Inform Your Brand's Strategy in 2020." Sprout Social, January 15, 2020. https://web.archive.org/web/20200220084929/https://sproutsocial.com/insights/new-social-media-demographics/.

Clements, Jessica. 2013. "The New Face of Ethos: Assembling Students' Ethical Competencies." PhD diss., Purdue University.

Cleveland Clinic. 2018. "Depression after the Birth of a Child or Pregnancy Loss." Reviewed January 1, 2018. https://my.clevelandclinic.org/health/diseases/9312-depression-after-the-birth-of-a-child-or-pregnancy-loss.

Colleen (@Colleen1704785). n.d. "MOTHERHOOD. Powered by love." Someecards, accessed January 19, 2022. https://www.someecards.com/usercards/viewcard/motherhood-powered-by-love-fueled-by-coffee-sustained-by-wine-2309e/amp

Cook Children's Health Care System. n.d. "Safe Infant Sleep." Accessed March 13, 2020. https://cookchildrens.org/health-resources/safety/Pages/safe-infant-sleep.aspx.

COPE (@COPEorg). 2019. "If you cried this week because the exhaustion was so physical your limbs felt like lead." Facebook, October 19, 2019. https://www.facebook.com/COPEorg/posts/2423805857733855.

Cultura Colectiva. n.d. "About Us." Accessed March 17, 2020. https://culturacolectiva.com/about.

Cultura Colectiva (@culturecolectivaplus). 2018. "It all dates back to when they were babies . . . #Infoccplus." Facebook, March 1, 2018. https://www.facebook.com/culturacolectivaplus/posts/2113381452012640.

DeBaets, Amy Michelle. 2016. "From Birth Plan to Birth Partnership: Enhancing Communication in Childbirth." *American Journal of Obstetrics and Gynecology* 216 (1): 31.e1–31.e4. https://doi.org/10.1016/j.ajog.2016.09.087.

Derrida, Jacques. 1982. *Margins of Philosophy*. Translated by Alan Bass. Chicago: University of Chicago Press.

Dickson, E. J. 2020. "Coronavirus Is Killing the Working Mother." *Rolling Stone*, July 3, 2020. https://www.rollingstone.com/culture/culture-features/working-motherhood-covid-19-coronavirus-1023609/?fbclid=IwAR05HoTUEkhEje_n6Fy6fCvTMmEZtw2fra_xBGKMMxIyNju-RYIggOTMcBE.

D'Ignazio, Catherine, and Lauren F. Klein. 2020. *Data Feminism*. Cambridge, MA: MIT Press.

Disney, Melissa. 2016. "Similac Commercial. The Mother 'Hood." YouTube video, 2:38. October 4, 2016. https://www.youtube.com/watch?v=JUbGHeZCxe4.

Drucker, Sally Ann. 2018. "Betty Friedan: The Three Waves of Feminism." Ohio Humanities, April 27, 2018. https://web.archive.org/web/20210630170648/http://www.ohiohumanities.org/betty-friedan-the-three-waves-of-feminism/././.

Dubin, Minna. 2020. "'I Am Going to Physically Explode': Mom Rage in a Pandemic." *New York Times*, July 6, 2020. https://www.nytimes.com/2020/07/06/parenting/mom-rage-pandemic.html?action=click&module=Well&pgtype=Homepage&section=Parenting)&fbclid=IwAR1S3eWDMQjHlvQ-vradNbyXfpMy4_QXqP0TnrmResQdZ39DSkrVUyrG3jI.

East, Andrew (@andrewdeast). 2019. "9 months no drinking = lightweight." Instagram, November 14, 2019. https://www.instagram.com/andrewdeast/?hl=en.

emccaskey. 2018. "Baby Blues vs. PPD." What to Expect, June 13, 2018. https://community .whattoexpect.com/forums/may-2018-babies/topic/baby-blues-vs-ppd-67945178.html.

Emerald Doulas. 2017. "Five Ways That Transform a Hospital Room into a Birth Cave." December 5, 2017. https://www.emeralddoulas.com/blog/createabirthcave.

Evans, Jon. 2019. "Facebook Isn't Free Speech, It's Algorithmic Amplification Optimized for Outrage." *Tech Crunch*, October 20, 2019. https://techcrunch.com/2019/10/20/facebook-isnt -free-speech-its-algorithmic-amplification-optimized-for-outrage/.

Fed is Best. 2018. "Nurses Are Speaking Out about the Dangers of the Baby-Friendly Health Initiative." October 21, 2018. https://fedisbest.org/2018/10/nurses-are-speaking-out-about-the -dangers-of-the-baby-friendly-health-initiative/.

Feldman-Winter, Lori, and Jay Goldsmith. 2016. "Safe Sleep and Skin-to-Skin Care in the Neo- natal Period for Healthy Term Newborns." *Pediatrics: Official Journal of the American Academy of Pediatrics* 38 (3).

Filloon, Whitney. 2016. "CDC's New Infographic Blames Women's STDs on Their Drinking Hab- its." Eater, February 3, 2016. https://www.eater.com/2016/2/3/10907480/cdc-women-drinking -poster-wtf.

First Response. n.d. "First Response Pregnancy Pro." Accessed March 20, 2020. https://www .firstresponse.com/en-ca/products/pregnancy/pregnancy-pro.

Foss, Katherine. 2017. *Breastfeeding and Media: Exploring Conflicting Discourses That Threaten Public Health*. London: Palgrave.

Foucault, Michel.1984. "What Is an Author?" In *The Foucault Reader*, edited by Paul Rabinow, 101–120. New York: Pantheon.

Freeman, Andrea. 2019. *Skimmed: Breastfeeding, Race, and Injustice*. Stanford, CA: Stanford Uni- versity Press.

Freidenfelds, Lara. 2020. *The Myth of the Perfect Pregnancy: A History of Miscarriage in America*. Oxford: Oxford University Press.

Friedman, Jaclyn. 2020. "Deadly Silence: What Happens When We Don't Believe Women." *The Guardian*, January 21, 2020. https://www.theguardian.com/lifeandstyle/2020/jan/21/what -happens-when-we-dont-believe-women?CMP=share_btn_fb&fbclid=IwAR1DGUddqvV9iZd cMlyQVYaD-OxayxayELeyXONg7A7tUNK9EFt_AAhK-gg.

franzke, aline shakti, Anja Bechmann, Michael Zimmer, Charles M. Ess, and the Association of Internet Researchers. 2019. *Internet Research: Ethical Guidelines 3.0*. https://aoir.org/reports /ethics3.pdf.

Frith, Jordan. 2020. "Pushing Back on the Rhetoric of 'Real' Life." *Present Tense* 8 (2). http://www .presenttensejournal.org/volume-8/pushing-back-on-the-rhetoric-of-real-life/.

Full Frontal with Samantha Bee. 2019a. "After #MeToo Pt 1: Sam Bee and Tarana Burke Talk Past, Present, & Future of #MeToo TBS." November 26, 2019. YouTube video, 11:56. https://www .youtube.com/watch?reload=9&v=rD9Cxvh1ZpY.

Full Frontal with Samantha Bee. 2019b. "After #MeToo Pt 2: Sam Bee & Tarana Burke Talk #MeToo: Misconceptions, What Redemption Can Look Like." November 27, 2019. YouTube video, 9:08. https://www.youtube.com/watch?v=9Hbsa9Zz4yk.

Garbes, Angela. 2018. *Like a Mother: A Feminist Journey through the Science and Culture of Pregnancy*. New York: Harper Collins.

Ghosh, Ranjini. 2020. "Safe Infant Feeding: Parents Aren't Getting the Information They Need." SciMoms, August 6, 2020. https://scimoms.com/safe-infant-feeding-are-parents-getting-the -information-they-need/?fbclid=IwAR0K9qRXJKrQxN-KH1fA9_t9xHYz0zpDpF8ICQgy0 -t0barHQTHlC_4xJEA.

Giganti, Chris. 2016. "Drinking Too Much Can Have Many Risks for Men" (graphic), in Time Donnelly, "The CDC's New Alcohol Guidelines for WOmen, Updated for Men," Brokelyn, February 8, 2016, https://brokelyn.com/cdc-alcohol-guidelines-for-a-violent-man.

Gilbert, Sandra, and Susan Gubar. 1979. *Madwoman in the Attic*. New Haven, CT: Yale University Press.

Goldberg, Michelle. 2015. "Breast-Feeding Extremists Are Even Worse Than You Thought." Slate, December 4, 2015. https://slate.com/human-interest/2015/12/the-breast-feeding-extremists-who -put-lactivism-ahead-of-protecting-babies-from-hiv.html.

Gorter, Courtney. 2018. "A Short History of the Wine-Mom Meme." Romper, July 17, 2018. https://www.romper.com/p/a-short-history-of-the-wine-mom-meme-9709313.

Gunter, Jen. 2019. "Drinking While Pregnant: An Inconvenient Truth." *New York Times*, February 5, 2019. https://www.nytimes.com/2019/02/05/style/drinking-while-pregnant.html.

HaCohen, Nehama, Dana Amir, and Hadas Wiseman. 2018. "Women's Narratives of Crisis and Change: Transitioning from Infertility to Pregnancy." *Journal of Health Psychology* 23: 5720–5730.

Hamilton, Hayley. n.d. "This Has Been Voted the Best Song to Give Birth To." *Baby Magazine*. Accessed February 29, 2020. https://www.baby-magazine.co.uk/best-songs-to-give-birth-to/.

Haraway, Donna. 1990. "Situated Knowledges: The Science Question in Feminism and the Privilege of Partial Perspective." In *Simians, Cyborgs, and Women*, 183–201. New York: Routledge.

Hausman, Bernice L. 2005. "Risky Business: Framing Childbirth in Hospital Settings." *Journal of Medical Humanities* 26 (1): 23–38. https://doi.org/10.1007/s10912-005-1050-3.

Hays, Sharon. 1996. *The Cultural Contradictions of Motherhood*. New Haven, CT: Yale University Press.

Healey, Jenna. 2016. "Bluetooth Babies: Reproductive Technology in the Information Age." *Technology's Stories* 5 (1). http://www.technologystories.org/bluetooth-babies-reproductive-technology -in-the-information-age/.

Hedlund, Siiri. 2020. "Years ago, anthropologist Margaret Mead." Facebook, August 9, 2020. https://www.facebook.com/photo/?fbid=10157400345227283&set=a.10152163059632283.

Hendry, Chris. 1999. "Fetal Alcohol Syndrome: How Much Alcohol Is Too Much?" *Journal of Addiction and Mental Health* 2 (3).

Henwood, Flis, and Benjamin Marent. 2019. "Understanding Digital Health: Productive Tensions at the Intersection of Sociology of Health and Science and Technology Studies." *Sociology of Health and Illness* 41 (S1): 1–15. https://doi.org/10.1111/1467-9566.12898.

Home of Hope. 2014. "Say No to Alcohol While Pregnant" (graphic), in "Child Protection NPO Warns of Alcohol Dangers in Pregnancy." Gateway News, September 3, 2014, https://gatewaynews .co.za/child-protection-npo-warns-of-alcohol-dangers-in-pregnancy.

Hookway, Nicholas, Shandell Elmer, and Mai Frandsen. 2017. "Risk, Morality and Emotion: Social Media Responses to Pregnant Women Who Smoke." *Health, Risk, and Society* 19 (5–6): 246–259. https://doi.org/10.1080/13698575.2017.1385731.

Howard, Jacqueline. 2017. "Is Light Drinking While Pregnant OK?" CNN, September 11, 2017. https://www.cnn.com/2017/09/11/health/drinking-alcohol-pregnant-study/index.html.

Humphriss, Rachel, Amanda Hall, Margaret May, Luisa Zuccolo, and John Macleod. 2013. "Prenatal Alcohol Exposure and Childhood Balance Ability: Findings from a UK Birth Cohort Study." *British Medical Journal Open* 3 (6).

Iannelli, E. J. 2020. "Using the Humanities to Help Heal." Humanities Washington, August 13, 2020. https://www.humanities.org/blog/humanities-medicine/?fbclid=IwAR1S3eWDMQjHlvQ -vradNbyXfpMy4_QXqP0TnrmResQdZ39DSkrVUyrG3jI.

IMDb. 2018. "Tully." Accessed March 13, 2020. https://www.imdb.com/title/tt5610554/.

Jones, Kenneth Lyons, and Ann Streissguth. 2010. "Fetal Alcohol Syndrome and Fetal Alcohol Spectrum Disorders: A Brief History." *Journal of Psychiatry and Law* 38 (Winter): 373–382.

Justin (@Justin3344188). n.d. "It's strange how 8 glasses of water." Someecards, Accessed January 19, 2022. https://www.someecards.com/usercards/viewcard/its-strange-how-8-glasses-of-water-a-day -seems-impossible-but-8-glasses-of-wine-can-be-done-in-one-meal--4c1a2/?tagSlug=drinking/amp

Kaiser Family Foundation. 2019. "Professionally Active Physicians by Gender." Timeframe: March 2019. https://www.kff.org/other/state-indicator/physicians-by-gender/.

Kaufman, Tamara. 2007. "Evolution of the Birth Plan." *Journal of Perinatal Education* 16 (3): 47–52. https://doi.org/10.1624/105812407X217985.

Kelly, Y. J., A. Sacker, R. Gray, J. Kelly, D. Wolke, J. Head, and M. A. Quigley. 2012. "Light Drinking during Pregnancy: Still No Increased Risk for Socioemotional Difficulties or Cognitive Deficits at 5 Years of Age?" *Journal of Epidemiology and Community Health* 66 (1): 41–48.

Komninou, Sophia, and Victoria Fallon. 2016. "Mothers Are Made to Feel Guilty Whether They Breastfeed or Formula Feed Their Baby." The Conversation, November 21, 2016. https://www -2018.swansea.ac.uk/press-office/news-archive/2016/mothersaremadetofeelguiltywhethertheybr eastfeedorformulafeedtheirbaby.php.

Kuhn, Thomas. 1996. *The Structure of Scientific Revolutions.* 3rd ed. Chicago: Chicago University Press.

Kulik, Taylor (@taylorkulikpostpartum). 2019. "Use guilt to fuel growth." Facebook, June 30, 2019. https://www.facebook.com/taylorkulikpostpartum/photos/a.1732738696806893 /2346139418800148/?type=3.

LaFrance, Adrienne. 2016. "Understanding Sudden Infant Death Syndrome: Figuring Out How Many SIDS Cases Are Misclassified May Be the Key to Preventing It." *The Atlantic*, June 2, 2016. https://www.theatlantic.com/health/archive/2016/06/understanding-sids/485147/.

Latour, Bruno. 2005. *Reassembling the Social: An Introduction to Actor-Network-Theory*. Oxford: Oxford University Press.

Layne, Linda. 2009. "The Home Pregnancy Test: A Feminist Technology?" *Women's Studies Quarterly* 37 (1–2): 61–79.

Leaky Boob (@_HAPPYASAMOTHER). 2020. "White Privilege in Motherhood Looks Like." Facebook, June 5, 2020. https://www.facebook.com/TheLeakyBoob/photos/a.562959473742024 /2973029372735010/.

Leavitt, Judith Walzer. 1986. *Brought to Bed: Childbearing in America, 1750 to 1950*. New York: Oxford University Press.

Leavitt, Judith Walzer. 1996. *Typhoid Mary: Captive to the Public's Health*. Boston: Beacon.

Levine, David. 2017. "Is There a Better Way to Screen for Postpartum Depression?" *U.S. News & World Report*, December 22, 2017. https://health.usnews.com/health-care/patient-advice/articles /2017-12-22/is-there-a-better-way-to-screen-for-postpartum-depression.

Li, Li, and Yue Yang. 2018. "Pragmatic Functions of Emoji in Internet-Based Communication—a Corpus-Based Study." *Asian-Pacific Journal of Second and Foreign Language Education* 3 (16): 1–12.

Librizzi, Ronald, Sherokee Ilse, and Ann Coyle. 2016. "What to Say and Do Right When Things Go Terribly Wrong in Obstetrics," *Contemporary OB/GYN* 61 (11).

Lorde, Audre. 1983. In Cherrie Moraga and Gloria Anzaldua (eds). *This Bridge Called My Back: Writings by Radical Women of Color*. Saline: Third Woman Press, 2002.

Lupton, Debora. 2014. "Critical Perspectives on Digital Health Technologies." *Sociology Compass* 8 (12): 1344–1359. https://doi.org/10.1111/soc4.12226.

Lupton, Debora. 2016. "Digital Companion Species and Eating Data: Implications for Theorising Digital Data–Human Assemblages." *Big Data and Society*, January–June 2016, 1–5. https://doi .org/10.1177/2053951715619947.

Luvs. 2013. "Luvs NightLock Plus TV Commercial, 'Going to the Park.'" iSpot.tv. Accessed March 13, 2020. https://www.ispot.tv/ad/AFyG/luvs-nightlock-plus-going-to-the-park.

Mamluk, Loubaba, Hanna Edwards, Jelena Savovic, Verity Leach, Timothy Jones, Theresa Moore, Sarah Lewis, Jenny Donovan, Deborah Lawlor, George Smith, Abigail Fraser, and Luisa Zuccolo. 2016. "Effects of Low Alcohol Consumption on Pregnancy and Childhood Outcomes: A Systematic Review and Meta-Analysis." *Lancet* 388 (S14). https://doi.org/10.1016/S0140 -6736(16)32250-4.

Martin, Emily. 1987. *The Woman in the Body: A Cultural Analysis of Reproduction*. Boston: Beacon.

Martinelli, Katherine. 2019. "The Best Essential Oils for Labor." The Bump. Updated November 2019. https://www.thebump.com/a/essential-oils-for-labor-and-delivery.

May, Philip, Kari Hamrick, Karen Corbin, Julie Hasken, Anna-Susan Marais, Lesley Brooke, Jason Blankenship, H. Eugene Hoyme, and J. Phillip Gossage. 2014. "Dietary Intake, Nutrition, and Fetal Alcohol Spectrum Disorders in the Western Cape Province of South Africa." *Reproductive Toxicology* 46: 31–39.

McFly, Marty. 2016. "Insider Series: A Day in the Life of a Pilot—Preparing for Takeoff." The Points Guy, May 27, 2016. https://thepointsguy.com/2016/05/day-in-the-life-of-a-pilot-part-1/.

McKenna, James J. 2012. "Safe Co-sleeping Guidelines." Mother-Baby Behavioral Sleep Laboratory. Accessed March 17, 2020. https://cosleeping.nd.edu/safe-co-sleeping-guidelines/.

Meredith, George. 1879. *The Egoist*. London: Kegan Paul & Co.

Milkie, Melissa A., Joanna R. Pepin, and Kathleen E. Denny. 2016. "What Kind of War? 'Mommy Wars' Discourse in US and Canadian News, 1983–2013." *Sociological Inquiry* 86 (1): 51–78. https://doi.org/10.1111/soin.12100.

Miller, Anna Medaris. 2020. "Chrissy Teigen and John Legend Are in 'Deep Pain' after Their Pregnancy Loss. Here's What You Should Know about Miscarriage and Stillbirth." Insider, October 1, 2020. https://www.insider.com/chrissy-teigen-what-to-know-about-miscarriage-and-stillbirth-2020-10.

MOMentous Moms. 2015. "Similac's Viral Video: Helping or Hurting the Mommy Wars." Momentous Motherhood, February 8, 2015. https://web.archive.org/web/20201014075201/http://momentousmoms.com/2015/02/similacs-viral-video-helping-hurting-mommy-wars/. /.

Moore, Julia, and Jenna Abetz. 2016. "'Uh Oh. Cue the [New] Mommy Wars': The Ideology of Combative Mothering in Popular U.S. Newspaper Articles about Attachment Parenting." *Southern Communication Journal* 81 (1): 49–62.

Moskin, Julia. 2006. "The Weighty Responsibility of Drinking for Two." *New York Times*, November 29, 2006.

Moyers, Stephen. 2017. "The F Pattern: Understanding How Users Scan Content." *UX Magazine* July 24, 2017. https://uxmag.com/articles/the-f-pattern-understanding-how-users-scan-content.

Multivu. 2016. "First Response Unveils Bluetooth-Enabled Pregnancy Test." YouTube video, 1:00. January 6, 2016. https://www.youtube.com/watch?v=YLL5sl8Y3u8.

National Institute of Child Health and Human Development. n.d. "Safe to Sleep." Accessed March 20, 2020. https://safetosleep.nichd.nih.gov/.

Nixon, Kari. 2014. Pregnancy Test. Personal Photograph edited using Pregnancy Test Checker App. October 15, 2014.

Nixon, Kari. 2017. "'A Speculative Idea': The Parallel Trajectories of Financial Speculation, Obstetrical Science, and Fiscal Management of Female Bodies in Henry James's Washington Square." *Journal for Medical Humanities* 38 (3): 231–247.

Nixon, Kari. 2020 *Kept from All Contagion: Germ Theory, Disease, and the Dilemma of Human Contact in Late Nineteenth-Century Literature*. Albany: State University of New York Press.

Noble, Safiya Umoja. 2018. *Algorithms of Oppression*. New York: New York University Press.

Norris, Roger. 2015. "Similac—The Mother'hood." Vimeo. https://vimeo.com/123131961.

Oster, Emily. 2013. *Expecting Better*. New York: Penguin.

Pappas, Stephanie. 2017. "Questioning Taboos: A Pregnant Economist Walks into a Bar." Parent Co., February 22, 2017. https://www.parent.com/questioning-taboos-a-pregnant-economist -walks-into-a-bar/.

Peck, Emily. 2020. "COVID-19 Is a Rolling Disaster for Working Mothers." *HuffPost*, August 19, 2020. https://www.huffpost.com/entry/coronavirus-working-mothers-census-child-care _n_5f3d1376c5b6835236047b8b?fbclid=IwAR2f8C4MrL5NkhdUxM8ennweCTiongCX4M6d pCCUh94z48YdF2ptKqMaftI.

Perelman, Deb. 2020. "In the Covid-19 Economy, You Can Have a Kid or a Job. You Can't Have Both." *New York Times*. July 2, 2020. https://www.nytimes.com/2020/07/02/business/covid -economy-parents-kids-career-homeschooling.html?fbclid=IwAR0rse1L7rqeCMCxhD12Q6BU oQCPcl1arcpurVJeEdO6NwhpCVs6hcTdnJA.

Petri, Alexandra. "The CDC's Incredibly Condescending Warning to Young Women." *Washington Post*. February 3, 2016. https://www.washingtonpost.com/blogs/compost/wp/2016/02/03/the -cdcs-incredibly-condescending-warning-to-young-women/.

Pierri, Francesco, Alessandro Artoni, and Stefano Ceri. 2020. "Investigating Italian Disinformation Spreading on Twitter in the Context of 2019 European Elections." *PLOS ONE* 15 1: e0227821.

Powell, Chadd. 2021. "Target Competitors on Facebook Using Interest Based Audiences." Hero Blog. February 1, 2021. https://www.ppchero.com/target-competitors-on-facebook-using-interest -based-audiences.

Prushinskaya, Anna. 2015. "The Quantified Baby." *The Atlantic*, April 10, 2015. https://www .theatlantic.com/health/archive/2015/04/the-quantified-baby/389009/.

Psychology Tools. n.d. "Edinburgh Postnatal Depression Scale." Accessed March 13, 2020. https:// psychology-tools.com/test/epds.

Puget Sound Birth Center (@PugetSoundBirthCenter). 2018. "Although the popularly desired outcome is 'healthy baby.'" Facebook, December 6, 2018. https://www.facebook.com /PugetSoundBirthCenter/posts/2184952151555869.

Puget Sound Birth Center (@PugetSoundBirthCenter). 2019. "Mothers Need Attention." Facebook, December 9, 2019. https://www.facebook.com/PugetSoundBirthCenter/posts /2235203273197423.

Remedy Health Media. 2018. "Postpartum Depression Test." Psycom. Updated December 19, 2018. https://www.psycom.net/postpartum-depression-test/.

Reneau, Annie. 2019. "It's Black Breastfeeding Week. Wondering Why? One Gut-Punching Poem Says It All." Upworthy, August 8, 2019. https://www.upworthy.com/its-black-breastfeeding-week -if-you-wonder-why-this-gut-punching-poem-offers-one-reason.

Roberts, Mary Louise. 2002. "True Womanhood Revisited." *Journal of Women's History* 14 (1): 150–155. DOI: 10.1353/jowh.2002.0025.

Robinson, Gina. 2020. "Internalized capitalism looks like." Facebook, September 29, 2020. https://www.facebook.com/photo/?fbid=10157717497405878&set=gm.1219537688417427.

SAMHSA (Substance Abuse and Mental Health Services Administration). 2020. "Phases of Disaster." Updated June 17, 2020. https://www.samhsa.gov/dtac/recovering-disasters/phases-disaster.

Sano, Michael. 2018. "Fake News, Confirmation Bias, and Selective Attention: Teaching Digital Literacy #DLNChat." EdSurge, September 13, 2018. https://www.edsurge.com/news/2018-09-13-fake-news-confirmation-bias-and-selective-attention-teaching-digital-literacy-dlnchat.

Schmidt, Fabian. 2016. "Study Finds Many Pilots Have Depression but Don't Talk about It." *Deutsche Welle*, December 16, 2016. https://p.dw.com/p/2UHLd.

Senior, Jennifer. 2014. *All Joy and No Fun: The Paradox of Modern Parenthood*. New York: Harper Collins.

Sister, I am with you (@sisteriamwithyou). 2020. "I think it was Brene Brown." Facebook, September 20, 2020. https://www.facebook.com/sisteriamwithyou/photos/a.452010615361649/756478318248209.

Sobe, Brian (@sobebrian). n.d. "And you're why mommy drinks wine." Someecards, Accessed January 19, 2022. https://www.someecards.com/usercards/viewcard/MjAxMy1mNGUwOD k3ODBhMTE3NTk2amp/.

Spokane Mama (@laceyhansen). 2020. "OMG. If I see one more mom complain about motherhood." Facebook, August 16, 2020. https://www.facebook.com/spokanemama/posts/1008655292890153.

Stacey, Kiran, and Hannah Kuchler. 2020. "US Health Body's Reputation Takes a Knock over Coronavirus." *Financial Times*, March 11, 2020. https://www.ft.com/content/928219ca-63c6-11ea-b3f3-fe4680ea68b5.

Stark, Luke, and Kate Crawford. 2015. "The Conservativism of Emoji: Work, Affect, and Communication." *Social Media + Society*, July–December 2015, 1–11.

Strauss, Elissa. 2016. "Baby-Friendly Hospitals Can, Paradoxically, Be Unsafe for Newborns." *Slate*, August 23, 2016. https://slate.com/human-interest/2016/08/baby-friendly-hospital-initiative-criticized-as-unsafe-in-new-jama-paper.html.

Szabo, Liz. 2016. "CDC: Young Women Should Avoid Alcohol Unless Using Birth Control." *USA Today*, February 3, 2016. https://www.usatoday.com/story/news/2016/02/02/cdc-urges-young-women-avoid-all-alcohol-unless-theyre-using-contraception/79701890/.

Tamtris Web Services (@fertilityfriend). n.d. "Chart Variations." Fertility Friend. Accessed March 20, 2020. https://www.fertilityfriend.com/courses/lessons/1/Chart-Variations-_-Illustrations.html.

Teigen, Chrissy (@chrissyteigen). 2020. "We are shocked and in the kind of deep pain you only hear about." Twitter, September 30, 2020. https://twitter.com/chrissyteigen/status/1311517048858574848/photo/2.

Theo, Lois, and Emily Drake. 2017. "Rooming-In: Creating a Better Experience." *Journal of Perinatal Education: Advancing Normal Birth* 26 (2): 79–84.

Turkle, Sherry. *Alone Together: Why We Expect More from Technology and Less from Each Other.* New York: Basic Books, 2012.

UNICEF. 2005. "The Baby-Friendly Hospital." Updated January 2005. https://web.archive.org/web/20190910040751/https://www.unicef.org/nutrition/index_24806.html.

Vinson, Jenna, and Clare Daniel. 2020. "'Power to Decide' Who Should Get Pregnant: A Feminist Rhetorical Analysis of Neoliberal Visions of Reproductive Justice." *Present Tense* 8 (2). http://www.presenttensejournal.org/volume-8/power-to-decide-who-should-get-pregnant-a-feminist-rhetorical-analysis-of-neoliberal-visions-of-reproductive-justice/.

Wallace, Samantha. 2020. "The #MeToo Effect: Testimony and Contemporary Narratives of Sexual and Gender-Based Violence." Presentation, Modern Language Association Conference, Seattle, WA, January 11, 2020.

Welter, Barbara. 1996. "The Cult of True Womanhood: 1820–1860." *American Quarterly* 18 (2): 151–174. https://www.jstor.org/stable/2711179.

Wertz, Richard W., and Dorothy C. Wertz. 1989. *Lying-In: A History of Childbirth in America.* Expanded ed. New Haven, CT: Yale University Press.

What to Expect Editors. 2019. "Tips on Writing a Birth Plan." Reviewed May 3, 2019. https://www.whattoexpect.com/pregnancy/labor-and-delivery/birth-plan/.

World Health Organization. n.d. "Breastfeeding." Accessed March 20, 2020. https://www.who.int/health-topics/breastfeeding#tab=tab_1.

Xenia Tsolaki Metaxa Private Institute (@XTMPI). 2019. "How to Be a Parent in 2019 vs. in 1982." Facebook, July 16, 2019. https://www.facebook.com/XTMPI/posts/10156080910666783.

Young, Anna M., ed. 2015. *Teacher, Scholar, Mother: Re-envisioning Motherhood in the Academy.* Lanham, MD: Lexington Books.

Zadrozny, Brandy. 2017. "Non-pregnant Women Now Guilted for Fetal Alcohol Syndrome." *The Daily Beast*, April 13, 2017. https://www.thedailybeast.com/non-pregnant-women-now-guilted-for-fetal-alcohol-syndrome.

Zero to Three. n.d. "Crying It Out." Accessed March 10, 2020. zerotothree.org/espanol/crying-it-out.

Zielinski, Alex. 2016. "The CDC Has Some Insulting Advice for Women Who Drink." Think Progress, February 3, 2016. https://thinkprogress.org/the-cdc-has-some-insulting-advice-for-women-who-drink-cfe25c1bdc8a/.

Index